PRAISE FOR
TOO FAST TO THINK

'Chris Lewis's book underscores that 30 minutes of peaceful, personal reflection a day keeps the world in perspective, our heads straight and the priorities which really matter to the forefront of our minds.' **Lord Chadlington, serial entrepreneur in the communications and PR industries**

'*Too Fast to Think* perfectly captures the zeitgeist of our exhausted world. It resonated profoundly with me both as an entrepreneur and as a parent.' **Alison Cork, entrepreneur, writer and broadcaster**

'We neglect holism at our peril. In our complex world only a life lived in the round can give us the connections and space for reflection that nurture creativity and compassion. Chris Lewis has seen the danger of being overwhelmed by the particular and the need to restore the balanced life necessary for human flourishing and for meeting the global challenges before us.' **The Rt Revd and Rt Hon Richard Chartres, Bishop of London**

'This book is an important reminder that the time has passed when we got our best ideas in the work environment. The proximity gained from the internet and social media has come at the price of continual disruption and the risk that we shut out what we don't agree with. The insights that Chris Lewis provides, from both the theory and the people trying to take a different path, underscore the importance of not neglecting that which makes us creative.' **Charlotte Lindsey-Curtet, International Committee of the Red Cross (ICRC)**

'*Too Fast to Think* crackles with good ideas and advice for creative thinkers. It's a must-read for the media, politicians and business people alike.' **Baroness Jenkin of Kennington**

'Chris gives us permission to Stop, Think, Dream, Be and shows us how to replace Hurry Sickness with creative success. His examples are universal, relevant to all people and professions.' **Dr Pippa Malmgren, former US presidential adviser and author of** *Signals: How Everyday Signs Can Help Us Navigate the World's Turbulent Economy*

'Time is a luxury that's available to everyone if they have the discipline to use it properly. In the digital age, our decisions are pressurized by the speed of events. Making the time to really think is the key to success. Chris Lewis is a living testament to this philosophy.' **Lord Bell, Executive Chairman of Bell Pottinger**

'Chris Lewis's book is an aide-mémoire to the importance and enriching power of creativity in business. Lewis has identified a growing trend that industry is finding it hard to adapt to new communications challenges and is having difficulties developing creative ideas, strategies and the necessary infrastructure to meet those challenges. I recommend his bold ambition to renew our confidence in creativity.' **Mark Borkowski, publicist, author and entrepreneur**

'This fascinating book bubbles with the effervescence of a creative mind. Chris would want you to explore his ideas, extract your own, expand on them and share them. Chris Lewis provides a timely and apposite reminder for all leaders of the need to confront conventional practices. He does so through an infectious curiosity and shares bold insights, both pragmatic and paradoxical, to challenge us all to take time to think.' **Squadron Leader John Peters**

'This is a business book of real credibility because it was written by someone who has actually built a successful global enterprise. The original thinking here should inspire entrepreneurs, but it will also fascinate anyone who is interested in maximizing their potential.' **Luke Johnson, Chairman of Risk Capital Partners, entrepreneur and author**

'Having led several hundred people into one of this country's most unpopular wars and brought them all home again, this book never leaves my side.' **Air Commodore David Prowse OBE**

Too Fast to Think

How to reclaim your creativity in a
hyper-connected work culture

Chris Lewis

Kogan Page

First published in Great Britain and the United States in 2016 by Kogan Page Limited

2nd Floor, 45 Gee Street	122 W 27th St	4737/23 Ansari Road
London	10th Floor	Daryaganj
EC1V 3RS	New York NY 10001	New Delhi 110002
United Kingdom	USA	India

www.koganpage.com

© Chris Lewis, 2016

The right of Chris Lewis to be identified as the author of this work has been asserted by him in accordance with the Copyright, Designs and Patents Act 1988

ISBN   978 0 7494 7886 5
E-ISBN 978 0 7494 7887 2

British Library Cataloguing-in-Publication Data

A CIP record for this book is available from the British Library.

Library of Congress Cataloging-in-Publication Data

Names: Lewis, Chris, 1961– author.
Title: Too fast to think : how to reclaim your creativity in a
    hyper-connected work culture / Chris Lewis.
Description: 1st Edition. | New York, NY : Kogan Page, 2016.
Identifiers: LCCN 2016031317 (print) | LCCN 2016039458 (ebook) | ISBN
    9780749478865 (paperback) | ISBN 9780749478872 (E-ISBN) | ISBN
    9780749478872 (ebook)
Subjects: LCSH: Creative ability. | Psychology, Industrial. | BISAC: BUSINESS
    & ECONOMICS / Workplace Culture. | PSYCHOLOGY / Creative Ability. |
    PSYCHOLOGY / Industrial & Organizational Psychology.
Classification: LCC BF408 .L623 2016 (print) | LCC BF408 (ebook) | DDC
    153.3/5–dc23
LC record available at https://lccn.loc.gov/2016031317

Typeset by SPi Global
Print production managed by Jellyfish
Printed and bound by CPI Group (UK) Ltd, Croydon CR0 4YY

To my daughters, Georgia and Pip.
With love, may you find your own potential
in this world boundless.

There are shadows in my head
From all the words I left unsaid
And rainfall in my heart
For the distance we're apart

Our lives no longer our own
Since that damned iPhone
Then, one day, I just let it drop
And found ideas start, only when I stop

CONTENTS

Foreword x
Preface xii
Acknowledgements xvi

Introduction 1

01 The information overload and the way it's changing us 9
The scale of the overload 12
Disproportionate effect of overload on millennial adults 14
How overload is changing the media 19
How news is changing 22
How the world is actually getting better 26
No information is correlated with 'nothing happening' 27
Disproportionate effect of overload on women 29
Conclusion 36

02 How did we allow ourselves to become so overloaded? 37
Competition and confidence 41
What are the problems in the system? 43
What should education be trying to do? 46
Two worlds, still too far apart 47
How it can be different 52
Art used in science 56
Conclusion 62

03 The 'always on' environment and its effect 63
Understanding the Type A 74
The meeting 77

The greeting 78
Office layouts 79
Conclusion 82

04   Your brain and how to use it 83
What you are capable of 90
The impact of overload on the structures 90
The left-brain process 93
The right-brain process 93
The left and right in history and culture 97
So is the left brain, right brain a dead end? 98
The awkward interview 98
The boring presentation 101
When things go wrong: the link between creativity,
    mental illness and depression 102
Flow and pulse: the way to sustainable creativity 104
Conclusion 107

05   Sleep matters 109
The link between technology and sleep 120
The role of light 122
The link between technology and general well-being 123
Conclusion 125

06   Where great ideas come from 127
The 'to-do list' versus the 'to-be list' 131
The sense of flow 132
The big inhibitors 134
Fear 136
Mastery and failure 139
The power of art 141
Truth, beauty and aesthetics 144
Conclusion 145

07   Generating better ideas 147
Generating better ideas: it's all about you 147
The Eight Creative Traits (QED3RPT) 152

Generating better ideas: it's all about others 158
Training principles 163
So, what else do you need to know? 165
Taking others into the zone 168
The Rise Academy at LEWIS 171
The Rise Four I's Creative Cycle 175
Conclusion 178

08   How leaders apply creativity 179
A business success that doesn't understand business 180
Fighter 181
The outsider's insider 182
An unlikely CEO 184
'You can't polish a turd' 188
Expelled for reading too much 190
Just your average cat-breeding, stargazing,
    portrait-painting, military reservist politician 193
Complete focus 194
The power of logic and emotion in leading the Royal
    Navy 197
Conclusion 200

Confession 201

Index 205

FOREWORD

Creativity is at the heart of being human. In the end, there isn't much that sets us apart from the rest of life on earth. Like all living creatures, we're mortal; our lives are relatively short and we depend entirely on what the earth supplies to live at all. But in one respect, at least, we are radically different from other species: we have powerful imaginations and seemingly boundless powers of creativity. These powers are the wellspring of all that's distinctive in human culture, from theories to artifacts, from languages to technologies, from the sciences to the arts.

Ironically, our natural ingenuity is now generating circumstances that may be inhibiting our creative powers exactly when we need them most. How and why this is – and what we need to do about it – is what this book is about.

For many years, my own work has been driven by a passionate commitment to transform the culture of education and organizations with a richer conception of human creativity and intelligence. This mission, which many others share, is becoming increasingly urgent as the world is transformed by technology, population growth and all the searing strains on the natural environment. *Too Fast to Think* is focused on the same mission and for the same reasons.

Chris Lewis himself illustrates the power – and his own practical grasp – of the ideas he presents. He started his working life in a range of jobs from barman to grouse beater (look it up). He went on to found and lead one of the world's most successful communications companies, where success depends a constant culture of creativity. His book draws from all of these experiences. It's part memoir, part meditation on why creativity matters in life and work and why it's at risk, and part manual on what leaders in every sort of organization can do to help it flourish.

It covers a wonderful range of ideas, people and projects, including the wisdom of clergy, artists, business people, politicians, academics, scientists, philanthropists and military strategists. In doing so, it shows that creativity is not exclusive to any particular walk of life, discipline, culture or social group. It's part of the warp and weft of human consciousness in all its tremendous diversity.

Too Fast to Think draws together important insights from many disciplines on the nature of creativity. It also highlights the threats in 'information overload' to personal creativity, and to the quality of our work, relationships, physical health and states of mind. (I especially appreciate his recommendation that we all get more sleep. I'm not a morning person.) Chris argues rightly that understanding and managing these pressures are essential to fostering creativity and to solving the many challenges we now face. If we don't look after our own mental and physical health, he asks, how can we look after each other and our planet?

Our capacity for creativity is one of the hallmarks of human intelligence. It's the source of our greatest achievements and now of some of our deepest problems. Whether we're focused on ending poverty or hunger, ensuring gender equality, improving health or the environment, or making the world safer and fairer, we depend on our unique abilities to generate and implement good ideas. Solving them means investing more deeply in these powers, in education, in business, in politics and in our communities. Whether or not we do that will prove just how intelligent we humans really are. And that's what this book is really about.

Sir Ken Robinson

PREFACE

If you're interested in creativity, I wrote this book for you.

On the merest mention of creativity, some reach for their gun. Creativity has often been used as an excuse for people who are ill-mannered or unable to keep to a clock, a budget or the correct side of the road. As if, somehow, you couldn't be creative and credible. You can, but you have to recognize the world has changed.

Time has now become so much more important to all of us. If we can pack more into less time, then we will. The Fear Of Missing Out has become greater. The more we pack in, the less time there is to think. That is the central premise of this book. That we are moving too fast to think and creating the illusion of speed rather than the actuality of it. We're now moving so fast that it's stopping us really thinking about the problems that face us. We tend to go for temporary fixes rather than addressing the causes.

The need to do things to time and with predictable results has meant the imposition of tighter rules onto creative people. Of course, you don't have to follow the rules. After all, since when was sticking to the rules a recipe for success? But as anyone with experience knows, the rules were made for the obedience of fools and the guidance of wise people. You really don't have to follow all the rules, all of the time, but it helps. Does that sound confusing? A lot of this is.

So this is a book about creativity, as well as about business. It's also about philosophy, fun and more fun. And about keeping things simple (there I go complicating things again).

I like things to be simple. Intelligence is not mandatory for business or creative success. It helps, but determination and enthusiasm are more important.

The Harvard Business School once defined business as: 'The management of social relationships for profit, where profit may be financial.' In short, business is about people, whether they are customers, colleagues or shareholders. If you're good socially, you'll probably be good at business. In any case, passion for people and for creativity doesn't emanate from profit or numbers – it comes from you. Money is just a by-product of successful cultures.

I like the Harvard definition because it's simple and it's true. Remember, the best ideas involve simplification. As Harry Beck said in *Selling the Invisible*: 'The more you say, the less people hear.' That's why I've written 71,000 words here. Sorry Harry.

I hope this book will allow you to discover more truths about yourself and what you are capable of. After all, you are something special. We'll find out just how special later.

Why should you listen to me? Well, you shouldn't. I've been a waiter, a barman, a window-cleaner, a factory labourer, a bed stapler, a painter, a car washer, a motorcycle and car mechanic, a door-to-door jam salesman, an IT consultant and trainer, a financial analyst, an author, a speech writer, a journalist, a political coach and consultant and, for the last 20 years, a chief executive officer and philanthropist.

I also founded one of the world's most successful communications companies and created a foundation for the Arts. I also started a global training academy, Rise, which trains people in global leadership.

I can honestly say I'm not an expert. Not because I don't know what I'm doing but because I always think there's more to learn. Success is very different from mastery.

Really though, this is just another book on creativity. And I'm just another boring author. You knew it all along.

There are some differences to the other books though.

Firstly, I didn't write this book to make money, or do a TED talk, or win an award, although of course, I'm happy to receive donations, invitations and gongs. I just thought it might help.

Secondly, all I've done is to build a global business. You're probably brighter than me; all I've been is determined and enthusiastic.

Thirdly, what I've written here is work in progress. I never considered this book finished. On the back page you will find a large smear from where the publisher tore it from my panicking hands.

I've spent the last 20 years trying to find ways of doing things better. It's brought me into close contact with a huge variety of people: journalists, artists, the military, celebrities, royalty, politicians, scientists, philanthropists, clergy and, of course, financiers, business people and a few drunks, nutters and bigots. I've learnt from all of them. I'm grateful to them all for allowing me to listen.

Many of them are profiled in this book because I've been impressed by their ideas, where they came from and what they do with them (obviously, not the drunks, nutters and bigots).

Personally, I've applied new ideas, new technologies, new management methodologies, launched new products and all the time sought to do things in a less conventional way. You'll find out who I learned that from soon.

There have been lots of failures on the way – I continue to fail, but I've been fortunate to find brilliant colleagues and clients that always allowed my company to thrive.

Although I've always been in a creative environment, surrounded by designers, copywriters and campaign strategists, over the years I had a sense of something missing at the heart of the creative process.

Every year, I worked harder and got more productive. I used every hour of every day, often at the weekends, early mornings and late nights, as entrepreneurs frequently do. Sometimes it got close to *Days of Wine and Roses*, but anything that blunts your senses is bad. We'll hear about that later.

Not only was creativity elusive, but it seemed to become more difficult the faster and more 'efficient' my working methods became. Some of the ways we found creativity – the brainstorm, for instance – seemed completely counter-intuitive to where I knew my best ideas came from. These came (and still do come) in the quiet moments on my own, when I wasn't trying, like during long flights, cycling or the shower.

I also found that ideas flowed when I tried to explain something. I would reach for metaphors and similes when required spontaneously.

For instance, it struck me that there were always two ways to give a speech – write it then give it, or vice versa. People can often speak more movingly when they don't over-intellectualize the message.

When I asked other people about where they got their ideas, they told me the same thing. I began to wonder if what I'd been told about creativity was wrong. I thought it would be worth asking some other high achievers if they'd had the same experience. This journey led me away from journalism, media and business to religion, art, medicine, education, politics and philosophy. I discovered that education hadn't worked for quite a few successful people. This was reassuring, because it didn't work for me, either.

I found in my career that the more I stepped away from what I called leadership – hands-on, client-facing leadership – the better the company did. I figured this was down to better delegation and, frankly, removing someone as stupid as myself from the process.

It just seemed like the less I did, the faster the company could move. If that sounds paradoxical to you, it did to me as well. I just seemed to get better ideas, the less I tried to do. The more time I spent out of the office, the more ideas I seemed to get.

This book is also an attempt to explain why this happens. This is the essence of the philosophy in *Too Fast to Think*. By taking the time to think through the direction and process, less energy and time is expended and goals are achieved faster. Life can be more fun, more productive, more sustainable and way more creative.

Everything that's around you had to be imagined. There must have been an idea at its root. It's fundamental to the human condition to invent, create, design and build. It's at the centre of our being.

I hope that by the end of this book you will feel liberated and inspired. Understanding your potential is not only essential for you. It's also essential for all of us.

Our future depends on it.

ACKNOWLEDGEMENTS

Thanks to:

Sarah Aitchison, Sarah Aitchison, Sarah Aitchison and Sarah Aitchison, and also Brian Alberti, Lucy Allen, Angela Ao, Jheni Arboine, Eloi Asseline, Fernando Batista, Bill Beatty, Eric Beaudette, Sinclair Beecham, Lord Tim Bell, Dror Benshetrit, Joanna Berger, George Blacklock, Daniel Blank, Sascha Blasczyk, Vanessa Brady, Mark Burr, John Caudwell, Lord Chadlington, Michael Chaney, Elaine Chao, Krzysztof Chodkowski, Alasdair Coles, Geraldine Collard, Fred Cook, Professor Sir Cary Cooper, Jackie Cooper, Stephen Corsi, Eric Davies, Kerry Davis, Kristine de Guzman, Peter De Haan, Delphine de Pauw, Jurriaan de Reu, Jacqueline de Rojas, Jutta Deuschl, Umang Dokey, Keith Elliott, Fanny Feng, Jason File, Kate Finigan, Professor Russell Foster, Steve Frampton, Miek Gielkens, Robyn Graham, Lauren Grassetti, Chris Green, Martina Guckeisen, Michael Hay, Rogier Heemskerk, Florian Heinrichs, Paul Holmes, Freek Janssen, Ruth Jones, Gemma Kavanagh, Lewis Keyte, Catherine Koo, Vera Kops, Ray Kurzweil, Debbie Laird, David LaVine, MD, Sir Geoffrey Leigh, Georgia Lewis, Jo Lewis, Pip Lewis, Johannes Liebl, Abi Lloyd, Gijs Moonen, Penny Mordaunt MP, Anna Moss, Andy Murphy, Nilufer Nasir, James Oehlcke, Sally O'Neill, Tony Palmer, Giles Peddy, John Peters, Scott Pettet, Katie Pierini, Pedro Ramos, Kelly Redding, Karim Rhalimi, Matt Robbins, Peter Robinson, Sarah Robinson, Alba Roig, Gugs Sarna, Jen Scheer, Ken Schild, MD, Sir Martin Sorrell, Sarah Spaziano, Dietmar Spehr, Helayne Spivak, Chris Ulbrich, Claire Unwin, Ruvina Uppal, Yvonne van Bokhoven, Sander van Buuren, Cathelijne van den Bosch, Renate van der Wal, Richard Verbeek, Sebastian Vonderau, Jade Wilkinson, Andres Wittermann, Jennifer Wu, Joshua Y'Barbo, Albert Yung, Admiral Sir George Zambellas and Katrin Zwingmann.

Introduction

It's the early 21st century. In the first few years of the new millennium, we've experienced an explosion in both the speed and the volume of information we're required to consume. We've moved from technologies that automated mail, thus saving days' worth of time, to new media that can update and change in as little as the 45 seconds it takes for Twitter to update its servers. We're moving faster than ever before.

Could it be though that the disruptive, 24/7, multi-channel communications we value so much are actually eroding our ability to think clearly, creatively and expansively? The rush has forced us to process yesterday as if it were trash, and left us no time to recall, review and learn. We're beginning to see profound changes in the way we react to this environment.

Two types of people have emerged. One that sees themselves as liberators and the other type that sees them as invaders. The first are those who, like all internet evangelists, are excited by the future and its opportunities and can't wait for it to emerge. For them, it will be global, multicultural, creative, fast, anarchic, amnesiac, visual, indirect, ambitious and massively interconnected. The other type, technophobes and traditionalists, feel like they've taken the wrong exit from the freeway. They look back to a utopian time when everything was safer, slower, more truthful, more predictable, clearer and *more sensible*. They believe the world is falling apart in chaos and getting worse, almost by the day. They're convinced of this by the pace of change and the volume and the apocalyptic nature of the news.

No longer do the people argue about capitalism or communism. They argue about the need for change. Politicians weaponize the word for their campaigns: 'Change we can believe in.' Or: 'Vote for change.' The technologists are in charge of change and they are difficult to stop. Legislators sometimes try but, eventually, they fail.

The last 20 years has paralleled the rise of the internet age. The early millennial years were when many feared being left behind. Others embraced the technology and used every opportunity they could to communicate and exploit the change. I was in the latter group. All around, I saw my life getting faster and I saw my own family, colleagues and friends become engulfed in distraction – email, then the web, then search, then social media, then social search, then instant messaging, Skype and ever-increasing hardware sophistication. We have invented so many new ways to interrupt ourselves. We find out more about this in Chapter 1.

Of course, I'm not alone in noticing this. There have been many books written about the role of quiet in creativity. Susan Cain's *Quiet: The Power of Introverts in a World That Can't Stop Talking* is perhaps the best of these. In this book, I will be looking at both scientists and artists and the shared methods of creative thinking they use. It's fitting that Einstein theorized about time because he used so much of it to formulate his ideas. He described creativity as 'the residue of time wasted' but, in our packed modern world, nobody wastes time. Everyone feels busier now than they've ever been, but they're not necessarily more productive.

Was Einstein right? Could it be that for real creativity we actually need to 'waste time'? Some might argue that no one will miss a few ideas, but I have also uncovered evidence to suggest that the overload of information is affecting our health and our relationships.

Why is creative provenance important? Well, it's at every level. It's the lifeblood of my firm, my industry and my life. It's also becoming fundamental to Western culture. The countries of the world have a choice to either compete with those that work harder and longer for less, or try to differentiate themselves in another way.

I see a world moving faster, but somehow making less progress. There is more communication, but less conversation. There is more information, but not more learning. These paradoxes are the manifestation of having gone as far we can on the linear progression of what Tony Schwartz calls 'more, bigger, faster' in his book *The Way We're Working Isn't Working*.

At a wider level still, we're told that we must maximize the resources of the planet. We're also told to make the best of ourselves. These must go hand-in-hand. How could we ever make better use of our scarce resources if we know nothing about our own potential? Even worse – what if the very things that were supposed to make us more efficient were actually eroding our innate creative abilities?

Creativity is not confined to the creative industries such as advertising, public relations, design and marketing. There's enormous creativity in professions such as law, architecture, accountancy and management consultancy. But it has been subject to the same problem. Every profession has suffered from a decreasing amount of time to really think deeply about problems. Sometimes recessions can be exactly the times when people are receptive to new ideas. When a rising tide lifts all economic boats, the need for innovation gets overlooked. There is room for better creativity in all industries. Indeed, it could be argued that there's never been a better time for it.

To do this, we have to move away from some of the sacred cow thinking about how the brain works. We've historically defined this as left-brain and right-brain thinking. The former is analytical while the latter is more conceptual. This thinking has changed over the years and it will continue to change. In short, the thinking remains in flux and is likely to remain so. For clarity, it's wrong to say left-brain and right-brain *activities* because both sides contribute. However, we can call them *processes* (which is how I will refer to them throughout this book) because they are distinct and identifiable, but definitely not located in just one side of the brain.

It may also be unpopular with creatives, but so-called 'left-brain' accountants and finance people can be highly creative, too. Creativity is not just provenance of the 'right brain' creative industries. Some of the innovations that caused so much trouble in the 2009 recession were a direct result of left-brained people being too right-brain creative! If anything, a new wave of creativity is needed now to reassure markets and investors that it is safe for innovation to return (the issue of trust – a right-brain process, if ever there was one).

There's a misconception here because creativity draws upon both sides of the physical brain, but for different tasks. We'll find out more about that in Chapter 4. It's clear though that right-brain process 'beliefs' like trust cannot be validated by left-brain process logic and vice versa.

The problem of overload

There is evidence that information overload changes behavioural patterns. This is especially reported in university education where students feel under greater pressure than ever before. The brain responds in different ways to pressure. A little is helpful, a lot can be harmful.

Evidence shows that the brain itself physically develops when required to perform specific tasks – for instance, with taxi drivers having an enlarged hippocampus. Some processes are developed, others are diminished, and this affects both actual behaviour and expected behaviour.

This obsession with busy-ness is changing our national life. Our working hours are longer. More of our work is measured. Our leaders now need to be seen to be doing more, if not actually doing more. Yet when we're asked about our role models, we always describe who they *are*, not what they *do*. We find this out in Chapter 6.

The sheer speed and noise seem to have undermined the fact that creativity is a quiet process. And it matters greatly that we appear to be losing it. We're losing it because we're trying to move too fast and deluding ourselves with the illusion rather than the actuality of speed. That's why I wrote this book. I wrote it as a confession.

Creativity is how businesses and individuals can stay ahead. It's how they can sustain rapid growth with rapid renewal. It's how they can keep sane. It's not only at the commercial level that creativity matters – it's philosophical as well.

Not only do creative societies thrive, but they can also sustain much higher output levels because they understand how potential and learning are an essential part of renewal.

Creativity around the world

Creativity is all about the future. It brings insights, novelty and change. During the last 20 years I made repeated trips to Asia, the United States and many other parts of the world – I found wildly differing attitudes towards creativity. In the United States, for instance, there was invariably so little history that when the future knocked at the door, it was welcomed warmly and invited in. In Europe, by contrast, the future was viewed with more suspicion. In Asia, everything was changing so fast, they just got used to the pace of change.

I found Europe a better place for creative standards because there's a greater resistance to change. Ideas have got to be really good to be adopted because they're challenged by the whole weight of history. This makes Europe a place that is open to ideas, but only when they have been properly justified, overcome all objections and tried elsewhere. US culture sees lots of new ideas being tried. It creates many more failures, but many more successes, too. This is possibly due to a difference in intellectual capital. According to the *Times Higher Education* World University Rankings 2015, only three of the top ten universities are located in Europe (and all of these are in the UK). The California Institute of Technology, Berkeley and Stanford are at the top of this list.

Wherever there is more competition, there's a higher standard of creativity. In Asia, everything is growing so fast, and in many instances just simply scaling existing processes. There are examples of breathtaking creativity, for instance, in architecture. Take the Marina Bay Sands Hotel in Singapore, for example – it's one of the most extraordinary buildings in the world. It was developed by the Las Vegas Sands Corporation with a budget of $8 billion. It was designed by Moshe Safdie who said it was initially inspired by card decks. In addition to the casino, other components of the plan are three hotel towers with 2,500 rooms. On top of this was placed a connecting deck and Skypark with the world's longest elevated swimming pool. The resort's architecture was also approved along the way by its feng shui consultants, the late Chong Swan Lek and Louisa Ong-Lee. Architecture is the 'show not tell' of how creative a city is. We'll examine later in the book how architecture and interior design changes the way people think.

I found the best balance of applied creativity though in the United States. Creatively, the country is unrecognizable to where it was 30 years ago. Then, shows like *Family Guy* would have been unthinkable. The United States has single market social media mass and this has provided the channels for a cultural revolution. Ironically, it may have been the United States that gave the world the social media channels, but it is European liberal standards that have populated it. These days you can hear social media opinion in Europe that complains that Europe is culturally becoming like the United States. In the United States you can hear the opposite. The truth is that the rise of social media and online commerce has made everywhere feel a lot like everywhere else.

The Eight Creative Traits

Everywhere may be more familiar, but everywhere is moving faster than ever. How can we cope with this accelerating pace? It requires a system of creative thinking that includes the Eight Creative Traits of Quiet, Engage, Dream, Relax, Release, Repeat, Play and Teach (QED3RPT). Each of these is a vital component in a new way of thinking that should be mastered by those looking to be liberated by the new environment, rather than vice versa. Otherwise, we will end up moving too fast to think. We will explore these throughout the book.

As the book continues you'll encounter interviews with academics, artists, business people, clergy, military leaders, designers, politicians, psychologists, lawyers and educators. Hearing from them in their own words is invaluable. What's clear is that everyone employs some of the Creative Traits in some way. They also combine left-brain and right-brain processes, but in different ways. There are no 'one-club' golfers – that is, people that only use one process. All these people consider themselves to be creative. All problem-solvers should. All team members should develop their creative abilities, because they are vital for health as well as productivity.

You may not find everything in this book wholly original. I'm not an academic, but you'll find further thoughts about this in Chapter 2. My career has all been about releasing potential – both individually and corporately. Well, really, how can you possibly separate them?

The information overload and the way it's changing us

01

In this chapter, we'll look at why people are so much busier than they were a few years ago. This will help us understand the new pressures that people are under to keep up with the news. We'll look at growth of the interrupting technologies and how they change behaviour. The media itself is being changed by the information overload. This can be quite subtle and difficult to spot because it's changed over time. We'll look at what makes news and how that's changing. This is creating a more pessimistic (and inaccurate) view of the world because young people are reading less. The rise in social media has particular gender effects with opportunities being created, especially for women. At the end of this chapter, you should understand the causes of the acceleration and how, if you're feeling burned out, that's to be expected!

Do you find yourself being interrupted a lot more these days? It's not easy to concentrate when you feel constantly interrupted. Worse, it contributes to a feeling of stress. It can make us feel like everything is slightly out of control.

Our working lives have changed dramatically in 20 years. They are very different to those of our parents because communications have become:

- fast;
- pervasive;
- disruptive;
- personal;
- portable;
- demanding;
- unpredictable.

Our social life is interrupted by our work life and our work life is interrupted by our social life. In fact, even our social life is interrupted by other aspects of our social life: we can't even watch TV without a second screen to read the social media about the show we are watching.

But apart from being interrupted and not being able to concentrate, have you also noticed how much busier you are these days? Are you more productive or just busier? The problem here is simple: because we *can* fill every minute of every day, we do. In February 2013, a *USA Today* national survey of 2,020 US adults aged 18 and over, by Harris Interactive for the American Psychological Association, reported that the vast majority of Americans felt busier that year than the year before. Also, they were busier last year than the year before that. People often talk of a productive day being where every minute of the day was used.

CASE STUDY

Carol is a 42-year-old international executive high achiever that came to me complaining about her boss. She said she felt underappreciated and badly managed. Every minute of Carol's day from getting up to going to sleep was managed. She had every day organized by 30-minute sessions, sometimes even 15-minute sessions. She had a great track record and was a popular and energetic leader. Yet she still reported feeling guilt and even shame when she had an idle moment. She felt that, because she was a woman, she had to prove that she was good enough – not just from time to time, but all the time.

This is the extraordinary situation that some high achievers find themselves in. This is not necessarily a system which is forced upon the unwilling. It is a method which is also actively perpetuated by the recipient. The very 'busy-ness' of the person seems to legitimize the nature of their work. As such, any criticism has to be carefully handled. I spoke to Carol's boss and she said Carol was a very hard worker but often failed to see the big picture or add ideas. Worse, she said that working with Carol was joyless. Everything was taken seriously, as a matter of life and death. I asked Carol how she felt about some of the feedback that she'd been given. The response was stark. 'Why can't they see that I'm flogging my guts out for them? Every hour of the day, even weekends, I'm working flat out. I can't work any harder. I never get any praise. It's so unfair.'

This illustrates the problem well. Carol had learned (or perhaps taught herself) that hard work and 'presenteeism' was the only way to progress. Allied perhaps to her own insecurities of having to prove herself. My advice to Carol was to do less, not more. Carol was able to make this change because she controlled her diary so completely. I advised her to clear out an hour every day to do, well, absolutely nothing. This was not easy for her and she came back two days later complaining that the time doing nothing was unproductive. It took two weeks before she saw any benefit. The result was that, although she was already well organized, she started to feel more organized. Mentally she became calmer and she was able to start looking at other aspects of her life in context, in 360 degrees. She started to cut down on her caffeine intake. She used an hour every other day to walk. She even started having walking meetings.

Carol remains an inspiration to me because she was actually prepared to abandon some of her own certainties – that was how much she wanted to improve. Sounds paradoxical, doesn't it? Most people wouldn't even attempt to try doing less as a method for achieving more.

Perhaps the most interesting response in Carol's case was not what happened to her personally, but the change experienced by her team. Not only did it change the way they saw her, but newcomers to her team – not knowing her previous modus operandi – attributed this to the 'culture' of the company.

This stood as a stark warning. The culture of your direct reports is not the culture of your company. The culture of your company can be as diverse and as fragmented as the different personalities of the managers in the business.

If you want cultural change, focus on the whole company, not just those around you.

After this exercise I also asked Carol's team to describe her. These are the adjectives they used:

- energetic (previously frenetic);

- full-on (previously domineering);

- driven (previously ruthless);

- enthusiastic (previously manic);

- supportive (previously micro-manager);

- fun (previously frightening!).

This was good progress, but I wanted to know more about how Carol had learned her behaviour. I asked Carol to describe someone she felt was a leadership role model. She said her father. This is how she described him:

- constant;

- loving;

- generous;

- funny;

- sympathetic;

- successful.

Of course, you could be struck by the similarity of these adjectives. They're not close enough to suggest that Carol had learned her style from her father, but it was in a quiet moment when the link between the two sets of adjectives struck me.

You can't 'do' any of these words. You can only 'be' them.

Carol could have told me all the things her father did for her. But all that mattered was what he was. It's the same with leadership. Carol worked very hard doing things, but over and above a certain level of direction, all her team cared about were her values.

You can't project values clearly when you're too busy to see the overall picture. How did this happen to so many people?

The scale of the overload

According to The Radicati Group, Inc, a market research firm in Palo Alto, California, the average business user in the United States sent and received on average 121 emails a day in 2014, and this is expected to grow to 140 emails a day by 2018. If we assume a 10-hour day at work, even at today's levels, that's 12 an hour or 1 every 6 minutes.

Their survey said the number of worldwide email accounts is expected to grow from over 4.1 billion in 2014 to over 5.2 billion by the end of 2018. The total number of worldwide email users, including both business and consumer users, will increase from over 2.5 billion in 2014 to over 2.8 billion in 2018.

Interestingly, email is still not the most frequently used communication. WhatsApp has recently eclipsed SMS messaging with the company handling a whopping 30 billion messages every day from 800 million users. SMS (texting) is around half this number and declining.

Email still remains the most pervasive form of communication in the business world. Depending on which research house you believe, Facebook users have between 130 and 300 friends on average. A recent study of advertising exposure by Media Dynamics, Inc, revealed that while a typical adult's daily media consumption has grown from 5.2 hours in 1945 to 9.8 hours currently, this has not been reflected in a huge spike in advertising exposure. The study summarizes that 'the number of ads that adults are now exposed to across all five media (TV, radio, internet, newspapers and magazines) is about 360 per day; of these, only 150 to 155 are even noted, and far fewer make a strong enough impact to be recalled, make an impression, and, ultimately, make a sale.'

Again, if we assume a 10-hour day then that's 36 ads, 12 emails and countless Facebook updates per hour. And that's just the basics. We haven't included instant messaging, mobile calls, Skypes, FaceTime, Instagram, Twitter, WeChat and WhatsApp. You can see it's a wonder anyone has any time to concentrate on any real thinking at all.

The problem with this media is that it's highly compelling and often arrives with an alert noise and demands attention. So, it's not just the scale of the communication, it's also the pervasiveness.

Our quiet thinking space, by contrast, has nowhere near the same level of alert, or attention-getting compulsion for us. So it's therefore no surprise it gets ignored. This is a message you won't hear unless you're prepared to listen.

Let's add another factor into this. In the last 20 years, according to the International Coffee Organization (ICO) coffee consumption has increased by 40 per cent. Since 1975, it's doubled. We'll come on to the health implications of this later.

The pressure to keep up with emails and other communications is changing human behaviour not always in expected ways. A survey by Adobe in 2015 asked more than 400 US-based white collar workers, 18 and older, about their use of email and other social media. The company found that Americans are practically addicted to email, checking it around the clock. More than half of Millennials check email from the bathroom. Nine of ten respondents say they check personal email at work and work email from home. More than one third report having multiple personal accounts.

Disproportionate effect of overload on millennial adults

Apart from the bathroom, people most commonly check their email while watching TV (70 per cent), from bed (52 per cent), on vacation (50 per cent), while on the phone (43 per cent), and even while driving (18 per cent). Millennials, though, are apparently more mobile and more frequent users of email than any other age group. They're more likely to check work email outside of normal work hours. One third is comfortable using emojis to communicate with a direct manager or senior executive. Eighty-eight per cent use a smart phone to check email. Millennials are also more likely than any other age group to check email while in bed (70 per cent), or while driving (27 per cent).

The proliferation of bathroom phone usage was reflected in my interview with Kevin. He's the sort of colleague you can build a company with. He's loyal, resourceful, hard-working and, frankly, long-suffering. He's been in charge of IT for over 10 years. He really knows his stuff. I asked what the most common type of iPhone repair was, he puts his fingers in the air to describe quotation marks: 'Water damage' he says pulling a face. I asked how could this be. He explained that women, in particular, took their iPhones into the toilets to check email and often ended up dropping them into the bowl. To describe this, it sounds like a neurosis but Kevin says it's common practice at many companies he's worked in. He smiles thinly. He places their phone into a bag of rice and leaves it overnight.

Sometimes it works. Sometimes it doesn't. One rule is constant, however – he never eats the rice.

According to Pew Research Center (2015), a good third of smartphone owners are using WhatsApp, Kik or iMessage and around half of these (17 per cent of the total) use apps that automatically delete sent messages such as Snapchat or Wickr.

Both of these kinds of apps are particularly popular among young adults. Half (49 per cent) of smartphone owners aged 18 to 29 use messaging apps, while 41 per cent use apps that automatically delete sent messages. These apps are free and, when connected to Wi-Fi, they do not use up SMS (Short Messaging Service) or other data allowances. Furthermore, they offer a more private kind of social interaction than traditional social media platforms such as Facebook or Twitter.

This reflects the growing concern and suspicion among the younger users about mainstream social media applications such as Facebook which, at a penetration of 72 per cent of online adults, is no longer growing. While 77 per cent of online females are on Facebook, only 66 per cent of men are.

Newer competitors such as Instagram (24 per cent of online men and 31 per cent of online women) and Pinterest (16 per cent of online men and 44 per cent of online women) have more than doubled their number of users from 2012 to 2015.

How to document creativity

Tony Palmer is a film director and author whose work includes over 100 films, ranging from early works with The Beatles, Cream, Jimi Hendrix and Frank Zappa to classical portraits of Maria Callas, Margot Fonteyn, John Osborne, Igor Stravinsky, Richard Wagner, Yehudi Menuhin, Carl Orff, Benjamin Britten and Ralph Vaughan Williams.

Among over 40 international prizes for his work are 12 Gold Medals from the New York Film Festival, as well as numerous BAFTAs and Emmy Awards. He is a fellow of the Royal Geographical Society and an honorary citizen of both New Orleans and Athens.

In addition to films, Palmer has also directed in the theatre and in the opera house and published several books. He has written for *The New York Times*, *The Times*, *Punch*, *Life* magazine, *The Observer* and *The Spectator*.

'Social media has been a catastrophe for the young', he says. 'No one reads enough anymore. They don't listen to classical music. It's stopped them thinking deeply.' He says that he correlates peace with creativity. 'The two have a linear relationship. With the decline of peaceful spaces has come a decline in deep levels of creativity.' Palmer's home in Cornwall is on a remote clifftop above a remote bay. It's the most westerly house in England.

Palmer knows a thing or two about creativity, because he's worked with many of the film greats – Kubrick, Spielberg, Ingmar Bergman and Orson Welles. The latter told him that creativity was 'all about the edit'. Get that right he says and the film is also right.

In his career, he's studied many of the great composers, like Shostakovich, who he says was demonized and lionized by the Soviet establishment in equal quantities: 'But he just had to continue with his creativity. He would say anything, sign any confession in order to continue with his passion. I don't think anyone would want to be like any of these great artists if they really knew the price they had to pay. The greater the artist, the greater the torture', he says. 'We're not all of us prepared to pay the price for greatness, creatively because it comes with great loneliness.'

The best definition of the creative for Palmer, is really an act that illuminates the human condition and makes us understand more about ourselves: 'They must bear witness.'

Reflecting Carol's experience, he says that great creatives 'are' something, they don't 'do' something: 'That's why they're great.'

He says when you are something, then things happen because people are motivated by someone who stands for something. It takes great discipline to be something.

Palmer has specialized in studying creativity in film and music close up, and making documentaries about several great musicians and composers. He looks for evidence that they are great and then lays it out. 'You can't attempt to explain their creativity. It's for you to make up your mind. They're dealing in metaphor. It doesn't need explanation. That's the beauty of it.'

Palmer considers himself a complete outsider. His friend Lord Bragg is a Labour Peer, and often said to be an insider, but he voted against every piece of Labour legislation in the field. He said the same of Steven Spielberg: 'Even he wouldn't say he is an insider. You have to be an outsider to be creative. You have to shake things up. The BBC used to be very good at this. It's more led by focus groups now.'

He says there's no shortage of creativity among young film-makers. The only problem is that people aren't getting to see it because it's not deemed commercial.

'Orson Welles was a genius, but no one trusted him. Kubrick only took on a project when he was inspired.' He admires Kubrick more than any other director: 'He was brilliant creatively and he made money. He only made 15 films in 50 years. Between *Eyes Wide Shut* and *Full Metal Jacket* there were 12 years and during that time was he lazy? No. He was busy thinking. He just didn't do anything unless he knew it was going to be brilliant. Genius takes time to distil.'

Palmer gets his best ideas in the bath, but says that isn't really the difficult bit. He says that one of the barriers to driving further creativity is finding the finance. 'The film industry is run by accountants – there's a real lack of courage', he adds. Palmer sees a direct comparison between creative and political courage: 'All art is politics. You can't lead people creatively or politically by researching their views and playing them back.' He says that some of the very best creatives have just got a vision which is impossible to ignore and everyone has to fall in behind it.

'I'm not sure creativity can be taught. Film Schools are great. They can teach you which lens to use and the basic cinematography. But it has nothing to do with where the idea comes from', he says. 'Cambridge really taught me nothing. I can honestly say I gained nothing from it. I learned more from Ken Russell at the BBC, shooting *Isadora*, than I did from university. I discovered Joseph Conrad later and quite by accident. He is one of the very greatest creatives.'

Is creativity enhanced by hardship? 'Peter Maxwell Davies was like that. He moved himself to the Orkneys to boost his creativity and he rarely came back. William Walton moved to the Italian island of Ischia. The further away you get, the better a creative you can be.'

His favourite film: '*Master and Commander*.' His favourite director: 'Kubrick.' His favourite poet: 'Eliot.'

He is particularly scathing about social media: 'Being barraged by this endless flow of input is creating a real problem, especially at the creative end, because they can get no peace. You don't need external input to provoke your imagination. You already have it within you.'

Books have become 'daunting'

In a piece by Matthew Reisz in the *Times Education Supplement* in early 2016, he asked universities about the reading habits of students: 'Our undergraduates – and postgraduate students as well – seem mainly not to be avid readers', said Jo Brewis, Professor of Organization and Consumption at the University of Leicester. As a result, she accepts that 'recommending whole books would be rather daunting' for students.

Reisz said that student aversion to the traditional contents of university libraries was commonplace among academics, with the internet identified as the reason: 'Incoming undergraduates have had their attention habits fashioned in a totally different world than that of those who are teaching them', said Tamson Pietsch, fellow in history at the University of Sydney. The piece observed that students are less used to concentrating for long periods of time and working through the nuances of an argument developed over the course of many pages.

It seems this problem is not confined to the students because even academics are reading fewer whole books than they used to. Stephen Curry, Professor of Structural Biology at Imperial College London, was sufficiently keen to remind himself that 'not everything can be argued in 800 to 1,000 words', so he made 'a recent New Year's resolution to read less on the internet and more [in] books.'

Curry said that books permit a deep and sophisticated development of ideas: 'Students often come from school feeling they understand the concept of "energy" or "the atom"', he explained. But 'these were struggled over fiercely before they gained wider acceptance. Even concepts that seem grounded can be undermined and superseded. It is tempting to think that the 20th century was such a great age of science that we are now just fiddling at the edges. A historical approach can help students realize that there is still room for them to make a contribution.'

Brewis herself would like to see students reading more because 'it would enable them to make more considered arguments in their coursework or examinations, and to demonstrate to us, as assessors, that they have considered the debates and controversies in the literature and arrived at reasoned conclusions on that basis.'

This shows how the overload is affecting people, but it's also changing the way they receive their information.

How overload is changing the media

The overload is also creating strange effects on people's perception of their environment.

Veteran journalist and taxidermy enthusiast Keith Elliott describes the way news has changed: 'Once upon a time, news was pretty simple: Man Bites Dog and a few variations thereof. But the rise of both the celebrity cult and the pervasiveness of the internet have made traditional news values almost obsolete. When the major story of the day is that a celebrity has been found drunk, or taking drugs, or switching sponsors, then it challenges news-gatherers to re-evaluate their approaches and priorities.'

He describes something that many of those interviewed in this book have observed: 'Young people aren't reading enough. If they do, it's short takes. Before long, we'll be reading news, whatever that is, on wristwatches. How many words can you use to deliver important information in such a format? Reading just isn't cool.'

Elliott describes a story about an English Premier League football player. His teammates looked suspiciously on him because he was reading a book. He also knows a teacher at a tough school who gave one of the kids a book to take home. It came back with all the pages torn out because the child, who had no books at home, had no idea that you didn't throw the pages away once you'd read them.

So the issue of news and the perception of the world is changing. It is inextricably bound with reading habits changing. Something that has grown and grown is the power of pictures. Elliott agrees: 'Pictures are easy. All research shows that it's the pictures that draw the eye. So pictures replace what were once vast columns of newsprint: the *Hello!* syndrome. The smarter outlets are conveying a sort of news by using pictures: once static, now moving, thanks to the advances of technology. Many websites like the *Daily Mail* (now the largest online news site in the world) work on the shotgun principle: fire as many pellets as possible, and some will probably hit your target. BuzzFeed has a different approach: we'll get one thing absolutely right, rather than putting out 20 stories. The latter must be more intrinsically satisfying for the creator, while the former is ultimately self-defeating: the more you feed the online monster, the more it demands.'

He says that only 10 years ago, journalists would maybe write three or four stories a week. Now, it's three or four a day. This has caused real problems for newsdesks. Writing in *The Guardian* in April 2016, in a piece entitled 'How newsroom pressure is letting fake stories on to the web', Kevin Rawlinson wrote: '*The Guardian* has heard numerous accounts from journalists about the pressures in UK newsrooms that lead to dodgy stories being reported uncritically, but none would go on record. One person working for a UK news publication claims the industry is now "like the wild west".'

This has led to a chase for numbers rather than quality: 'This trend has caused real problems for the traditional news outlets because the creators of news, the journalists, have to write news for an online audience as well as a print readership. Writers had to create more stories (web+print) with sharply limited resources. Some magazines in particular tried creating separate teams, with one working totally online, others on a print version. Surprise, surprise, it didn't work.'

As the volume of stories has gone up and so has the amount of clickbait designed to attract readers. We're left with a cacophony of shouts, in many cases for our attention to be diverted to entertaining trivia which may or may not be true. One thing is for sure – it sucks up our time so we don't want to waste it on talking to people.

Elliott says this also led to something he calls telephonobia: 'Many journalists don't get out of the office. They don't even pick up the phone, relying on email. There's fear of the phone. It got to the stage where sometimes people would disconnect the internet to force them to use the telephone and find out information. But one of the biggest problems in employing young people today is they lack core communication skills.'

Is this because they've developed different skills? 'Yes possibly. One of the most favourable things that has happened over the past decade particularly has been the rise of infographics. Pictures attract, but it doesn't have to be a photograph. Any sort of illustration will draw the eye to that spot, and infographics are a wonderful way of communicating a great deal of information quickly: what I call at-a-glance information. Try to write the changes in a company's annual pre-tax profits over the past five years and it's very dull: produce a pie chart, bar chart and best of all, an infographic which conveys that data quickly and simply, especially now that colour is taken as standard, rather than a luxury.'

This clears the way for information deliverers to do what they should be doing with their words, and using them to analyse what those figures mean. Increasingly, print titles are realizing that they can't compete with the speed of online information. Even daily newspapers can't do that. But what they can and should be doing is using their experts to assess what those figures mean for readers. This is information that people will pay for: the stuff they can't get elsewhere.

Which brings me round to paywalls and money. Elliot again: 'Ultimately, most deliverers of news have to make money – unless they are the BBC. The problem is that the BBC's coverage is so vast, its resources so huge, that you can't compete with it. It also gives information away for free, so readers have come to expect everything for nothing. It's been a huge battle to make readers pay. It's sort of working in a few cases, where you have very specialist information, but many have given up the struggle. A lot more newspapers and magazines might still be around today were it not for the BBC, though ultimately, the future of newspapers, especially local ones, is not favourable.'

Local papers lost their classified market – once a great cash cow. To make up the shortfall, they cut areas that weren't making money (the journalists, who are a cost rather than a profit stream). So the quality of the newspaper and its pagination went down, at the same time as a new young generation, who didn't really want to read, came through.

Elliott says news will survive: 'It's gone through vast changes and it will be different in the next few years. Investigative journalism will become rarer than it already is, the reliance on PR to provide a great deal of content will continue; young people (becoming older people) will not read much news, and they'll read it in short bursts through tweets and who knows what will soon come.' He says though in times of strife, as the Malaysian Airlines disaster and Paris attacks showed, we still demand news from an institutional source.

How news is changing

Elliott says there have always been basic stories that make news; for example, the psychology of the unexpected – policeman robs bank – but even these are giving way to celebrity gossip.

Does he feel that the omnipresence of news is creating more understanding of the world or less? 'Sadly, I think it's less, because people's knowledge is now on a far more superficial level. The days when *The Times* had its own correspondents in New York, Paris and other major seats of presence are gone. Ask 20-year-olds what Kim Kardashian is up to and they can tell you. Ask them who else competed in the US elections besides Trump and Clinton, or why Switzerland turned down EU membership, and you get a blank look.'

So what can we pull out from this about how the world will be filtered in the future?

The drive to the local

Information has increased in quantity but it has very much decreased in terms of quality. This is partly due to the economics of news production, but it's also become a lifestyle choice. You would think that the ever-increasing availability of news would mean that people would be better informed than ever. That's true to an extent. People are better informed about what's of interest to *them*. Because there is so much information, they only want what is directly relevant to them. This level of constant interruption has led people to tailor their news. Worse, they shut out news which they don't agree with. We'll return to this 'echo chamber' effect later.

Improved chances for radicals (good and bad)

When you connect up far-flung groups of minority interests, suddenly they can feel like a small majority. Radicals and extremists can find wider groups when they use the internet to join up. This is leading to a rise in extremism and intolerance because a message only supported by a few can now easily reach those few and create a critical mass. What was an isolated minority can quickly gather a following.

This can be used positively by creative people to create their own insurgent movements. Many of the ideas promulgated in this book first coalesced around blogs, websites and authors. Indeed, many now-mainstream ideas were often considered insurgent or radical when they first appeared; notable examples being consumer protection, veganism and environmentalism.

Less willingness to offend

The opposite dynamic to the overload is the strong desire not to offend. No one wants to listen to an opposite opinion, because the overload forces a simplification. No one has time for 'grey'. Binary is so much faster to process. People can't keep up with news which is local to them about their friends, family and personal interests, let alone find time to consider opinions opposite to their own. Now that every minority hears every story, the response at the broadcast end is to make the messaging even more inoffensive and bland. The net result is that people who are offensive and hold controversial views are hailed for freshness and for 'telling it how it is'. The radical in all walks of life is often a direct result of the 'race to vanilla' in communications.

This only applies to legitimate and accountable sources of news. In complete counterpoint, the world of the anonymous commentators has become increasingly unpleasant and in some cases illegal, as we'll find in Chapter 3.

More unreliability

There's also another problem here and it's in the relationship between speed and truth. It has a tendency to the inverse (see Figure 1.1). The faster the story, the less truth is associated with it. This is especially the case on breaking stories. Invariably, the death toll in every plane crash rises as more information comes in. When stories are breaking, that's often the time when rumour can gain purchase. Possibly the best example of this is weapons of mass destruction.

Figure 1.1 Speed kills truth

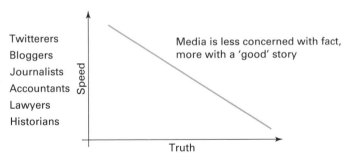

Twitterers
Bloggers
Journalists
Accountants
Lawyers
Historians

Speed

Truth

Media is less concerned with fact, more with a 'good' story

SOURCE LEWIS Rise Academy.

People tend to believe the first thing they're told about a breaking story because it has a news angle – a programmed channel or form within which it is presented. If a story is presented as a 'threat to the community', it's difficult to subsequently reposition it. First impressions, as ever, count more. The story though can quite frequently be either untrue or incomplete.

In the diagram above, historians can tell you what happened, but it can take decades. Lawyers can tell you the truth after a few years. Accountants after about 18 months or so. Journalists can tell you in a matter of weeks or days. Twitter can tell you a news story every 45 seconds. At each stage, the facts become less reliable and verifiable.

Picture stories

As the volume of information increases, there's a natural tendency to move towards picture-based news. Video and pictorial stories move much faster because they are easier to digest, cross borders without being as encumbered by translation, and reach all age groups. As we'll see later in Chapter 6, this has profound implications for what people believe to be true.

Funny stories

As we'll see later, there's a widespread perception that the world is getting worse in every respect. The way the brain works is to make a judgement then look for evidence to back up the initial conclusion. So broadcast news in particular is frequently a litany of bad news.

If we take the BBC News bulletins of February 2016, the following packages aired:

- European break-up;
- child meningitis;
- Zika virus;
- hospitals bombed in Syria;
- destruction of the polar ice cap;
- report on Russian state murdering a British citizen in London.

It's difficult to share these types of stories on social media because our friends are not necessarily going to be interested in this. What's more, not everyone likes to receive depressing news on social media.

Instead we share 'Ten Cats That Look Like Hitler'. Is this frivolity or just a reaction to the relentlessly depressing qualities of global broadcast bad news? The reason is that, because the story is visual, it's instant and provides immediate relief to the overload. It also travels internationally because it's not language-based. It doesn't take long to digest and it's easily sharable. It passes as creativity because it's fresh, but it's not actually deep. We'll hear more about this later.

Bad news focus

When the overload is relentless and frequently of a consistently negative narrative, it has real implications for creativity. No new ideas can withstand a relentless cynicism about the future. We therefore have to engage our creativity within the context of the *Weltanschauung* (world view). The world is becoming a terrible place. That must be true because that's all I hear. This is not a time for idealistic ideas, in fact any idea must be prepared to fight for its life.

This is one of the great inhibitors of new ideas. The fear of rejection may be so great that people may not put forward an idea because if the world really is so bad, then what chance have we got with our individual idea? This is where the institutions can help. There's a definite role for government and universities to help in providing ideas with greater legitimacy.

How the world is actually getting better

By any historical standards, the world is becoming a safer, less diseased and war-torn place. According to the US Department of Agriculture Economic Research Service, real global GDP more than trebled between 1970 and 2010. Real global GDP per capita nearly doubled. In April 2015, *The Economist* quoted the United Nations Millennium Development Goals Report from 2012. The proportion of the world's population living in 'abject poverty' fell from 36 per cent in 1990 to 18 per cent in 2010. This means around 900 million people escaped poverty. According to the United Nations, moreover, the mortality rate for children under five fell from 90 per thousand births to 46 during that same period. The proportion of the world's population that is 'clinically malnourished' dropped more than seven points.

The world is healthier and wealthier, but is it less violent?

'Violence exists', says Harvard psychologist Steven Pinker. 'It hasn't gone down to zero. But past decades were far more violent.'

Pinker's book *The Better Angels of Our Nature: Why Violence Has Declined* shows that during World War II, the human population lost 300 of every 100,000 people each year. During the Korean War it was in the 20s, before dropping into the teens during the Vietnam era. In the 1980s and 1990s, it fell into single digits. For most of the 21st century it's been below one war death per 100,000 people per year.

Of course, there has been an increase as a result of the civil war in Syria, doubling from 0.5 per 100,000 to 1. But Pinker says 'you can't compare 1 with 15 or 25 or 300.' Everywhere else in the world, the stats are still trending downward. The same is true for homicides. 'If you get your view of the world from the news, you're always going to think that we're living in violent times', Pinker says. 'Because if anything blows up, if there's any shooting anywhere in the world, it instantly gets beamed across the globe. News is about stuff that happens. It's not about stuff that doesn't happen. And as long as violence hasn't gone down to zero, there will always be enough incidents to fill the news.'

Pinker points out that we should look at all the places that aren't blowing up. That's not going to be on the news. 'You never see a reporter standing on the streets in Mozambique or Colombia saying there's no war this year.' He says, 'We forget about old wars because they're not news.'

Pinker suggests two explanations as to why people believe the world is falling apart. Cognitive psychologists speak about the 'availability bias' – a term invented by Daniel Kahneman and Amos Tversky – according to which we judge risk by how easy it is to remember examples.

Pinker also says that psychologically there can also be a moralistic bias. 'If you have some sort of cause, if you're trying to rally supporters behind a movement, people think the most effective way to do it is to give people an impression that things are getting worse, and that they have to act now, otherwise things will get worse still.'

No information is correlated with 'nothing happening'

Again within the context of the overload, unless an organization is heard from regularly, it's deemed not to be active. 'I haven't heard from them in a while' is the phrase most commonly used. This accounts for the growth in professional communications – to keep the pot boiling. The equation here for all retention is:

$$\text{Retention} = \text{Frequency} \times \text{Duration}$$

It's therefore not enough for any message to be a one-off. It must be part of a narrative. Only by doing this consistently can trust be built. Perhaps the best example of this is the US stock market. It requires companies to report every 90 days. Unsurprisingly, they live by a quarterly cycle. It's got to the stage where unless a company is pumping out information every week, it's perceived not to be busy enough.

This all adds up to an information environment that is relentless by volume, by unreliability and by negativity.

The overload is thus created not only through the additional channels, but by the expectation that organizations (and their leaders) should be communicating perpetually. Incidentally, this knocks on to economic volatility. Everyone notices the warnings, but nobody remembers whether they turn out to be true. The anonymous quotation

'The stock market has forecast 17 of the last 6 recessions' comes to mind.

This torrent of short-term information is replacing the long-term information contained in books. The result is that the long-term perspective gets easily lost in the short-term 'crisis'.

Does the lack of reading also damage creativity?

Many of those interviewed in the research for this book – film director Tony Palmer, businessman Lord Chadlington and creative director Helayne Spivak – believe it definitely does.

In a report in *The Boston Globe* entitled 'Young people reading a lot less' in 2007, David Mehegan said that we can all see what young people are doing more of: watching television, surfing the web, listening to their iPods, talking on mobile phones, and instant-messaging their friends.

He cites a report by the National Endowment for the Arts (NEA). This makes clear what they're doing a lot less of: reading.

The report was a compendium of more than 40 studies by universities, foundations, business groups, and government agencies since 2004 and it painted a dire picture of plummeting levels of reading among young people over the past two decades.

Among the findings:

- Only 30 per cent of 13-year-olds read almost every day.
- The number of 17-year-olds who never read for pleasure increased from 9 per cent in 1984 to 19 per cent in 2004.
- Almost half of Americans between ages 18 and 24 never read books for pleasure.

NEA chairman Dana Gioia, said: 'We are losing the majority of the new generation. They will not achieve anything close to their potential because of poor reading.'

It's not just the quantity of the reading either. According to the report, reading ability has fallen as well. Only about a third of high school seniors read at a required level, a 13 per cent decline since 1992. 'And proficiency is not a high standard', Gioia said. 'We're not asking them to be able to read Proust in the original. We're talking about reading the daily newspaper.'

The report incorporated national studies carried out since the NEA's 2004 report, 'Reading at Risk', found that literary reading – fiction, poetry, and plays – had crashed over 20 years among adult Americans.

If the lack of reading is damaging the young, it seems to be indirect, at least according to a paper by Jim Rubin entitled 'Technology's impact on the creative potential of youth' in *Creativity Research Journal* (June 2012). In Howard Gardner's (2001) study of seven creative profiles (Einstein, Freud, Picasso, Stravinsky, Eliot, Graham, and Gandhi), one common trait emerged. Each grew up in a household that promoted a strong work ethic, a trait that Robert W Weisberg (1993) also mentioned as a necessary component in the creative process in his book *Creativity: Beyond the Myth of Genius*.

Researchers have warned about growing up with digital habits (TV, mobile phones, video games, etc), and the resultant changes in the physiology of the brain. Some have said these are detrimental to the kind of focus that previous generations had from reading traditional text. Some researchers, however, have argued the prefrontal cortex of the brain is more active in subjects that were internet savvy. However, Gary Small and Gigi Vorgan (*iBrain: Surviving the Technological Alteration of the Modern Mind*, 2008) warned of overexposure to digital resources, whereby brain regions that control mood can be altered. Other research showed, however, that the brain was elastic enough to bounce back quickly from techno-burnout. Sara Mednick and Mark Ehrman (*Take a Nap! Change Your Life*, 2002) held that by manipulating the way information was presented on screen and allowing intermittent naps, participants were able to recover from overexposure. This held promise for the potential to shape and optimize the digital environment to allow the human brain to more fully absorb knowledge.

It would seem therefore that some of the danger of burnout can be mitigated or avoided. The dangers, though, are not evenly spread.

Disproportionate effect of overload on women

A peculiarity of social media is that women dominate. According to statistics compiled in 2014 by financesonline.com, women dominate all social media save for LinkedIn where they are in equal numbers to men. The data appears to show that women are more likely to stay in touch with friends on social media than men and particularly more likely to do so using mobile devices. Women post more than men on Facebook by almost one third. Women also dominate Twitter, Instagram and Tumblr and it seems the more visual the medium becomes, the more likely it is to be female dominated, Pinterest being a particularly strong example of this.

The upshot seems to be that women use social media more often than men and in many more ways. They are more likely to interact with brands to show support, stay current, comment and access offers. Importantly, they also use social media to consume more news.

The research clearly shows that women are more engaged on social media than men.

Corporate America is taking advantage of this. A survey conducted by Women's Marketing, Inc, and SheSpeaks by Pew Research Center in January 2014 published three main conclusions:

1 Women are more likely to purchase brands they follow

This is not a difficult conclusion considering the above. In the United States, women head 40 per cent of all households according to a Pew Research Center analysis of census and polling data released in 2013. This share, the highest on record, has quadrupled since 1960.

2 Women use social media to connect aspects of their lives

For 40 per cent of women, the primary benefit of social media is to connect with family and friends. According to the survey almost as many think the primary benefit is being alerted to coupons, promotions and deals by connecting with brands. This appears to show that women are engaged with social media to make connections with their personal circles, but a similar set is also willing to interact with brands. This has led to many companies humanizing or personalizing brands to create a social media presence that women are willing to connect with – and share with friends. According to the Pew survey, the majority of women use social media to connect various parts of their lives. 'Women use social media to integrate disparate roles – family, work and personal – online', says Bonnie Kintzer, CEO of Women's Marketing, Inc. 'They use it to connect with family, friends and brands.'

3 Different women have different outreach

Not all women use social media in the same way. Age and background change social media behaviour in various ways according to Pew.

The data shows some other interesting trends. In general, 46 per cent of women turn to their smartphones first thing in the morning; 31 per cent access their computers. This again shows the importance of mobile. Women under 40, however, are more likely to check their smartphones first thing, whereas women over 40 are more likely to check their computers and/or watch TV. Furthermore, full-time employed women more often turn to smartphones, but homemakers rely on computers for their first doses of information.

'All the channels feed off each other. If a potential customer hears or sees your message in more than one context or venue, she will remember it, and it is far more effective', says Kintzer.

Overall, 30 per cent of women report they have become more social offline since participating in social media. That doesn't mean they're spending less time on social media. The more women interact with a brand online, the more likely they are to carry that experience into their everyday lives.

In short, marketers are making the most of the disruption to supplant or be additive to the noise. Women are more creative than men in the way they interact with brands online, and marketers are aware of this (see the Dove campaign below). Consequently, female creativity online is used as a platform for brand marketers.

What damage is the overload doing to women?

There is a cost for this online engagement as it is getting to the point of absorbing all free time. By any research and measure, women are more susceptible to online social engagement.

According to Pew Research Center findings, sometimes a social media user's awareness of others' lives includes hearing the news about a friend or family member getting fired or losing someone close to them. Learning of these events can result in higher levels of stress. In sum, it seems social media users are likely to feel more stress, but gender differences are a part of this story. Women and men have different levels of stress; their use of digital technologies varies; and the impact of their technology use is different. The broad patterns are:

- Women tend to report more stress than men, but, those who use a number of digital technologies report less stress than those who don't.

- Women are more aware of stress in the lives of friends and family.

- Awareness of stress in others' lives is a contributor to their own stress. The number of undesirable events associated with stress is greater for women than for men.

In a piece by Danica Lo in *Glamour* magazine in 2015, she cites a survey by the soap brand Dove which seemed to indicate that social media sets unrealistic beauty standards.

Dove's survey combined their findings with Twitter data to reach these conclusions:

- Women wrote more than 5 million negative tweets in 2014.

- Four out of every five negative beauty tweets from women were about themselves.

- Women are 50 per cent more likely to say something negative (rather than positive) about themselves on social media.

Furthermore, 82 per cent of women felt the beauty standards set by social media are unrealistic according to the Dove study and 'almost three quarters of women believe social media comments critiquing women's beauty are destructive to their self-esteem.'

Dove's response to this was to launch a campaign called #SpeakBeautiful, which encourages women to 'realize the role our online words play in impacting our confidence and self-esteem.' The company also has partnered with women including self-esteem ambassadors to create responses to negative tweets on Oscar night. This positive approach recognizes the damage that online critique does disproportionately to women and helps to reduce it and build confidence. This, in turn, encourages more ideas to come forward about the brand.

It seems that while women are more creative with the ways they interact online, this can be used in a dystopian as well as utopian manner. In Dove's case, its campaign has been quick to recognize the dystopian problem and turn it into a positive. What was a mixture of noise and news has become a social platform.

'It's not enough just to be creative'

Vanessa Brady doesn't really walk, she sort of glides. I don't think I know anyone who appears quite so much in another world. She's listening intently but is always looking at things as if she's coming up with ways to improve them. The look can be deceptive. She's a creative, yes, but she's also a business leader.

Brady is an international multi-award winning interior designer and founder of the Society of British and International Design. She's worked with: Hard Rock Cafe, the Design Council, Kabaret Club, British Luxury Club, Unilever, high security government offices, His Majesty The Sultan of Brunei, King of Saudi Arabia, the private residences of numerous diplomats and VIPs. In 2014, she began a collaboration with Sunseeker International on the new Predator II yacht. In 2015, she received an honorary degree titled *Doctor of Design* from Southampton Solent University (for services to education), in recognition of her outstanding contribution to the interior design industry.

Brady says British people are inventors and engineers at heart, so always want to know how things work but, just as importantly, we want to understand why things don't work: 'By discovering the inner workings of a product or design, you can come up with a solution to make it both practical and beautiful. One part without the other won't work and good design does both well.'

Standards are getting higher in creativity and this is being driven by Millennials, she says. They've been brought up to expect it. If you don't address design, especially online, you won't keep up the pace. It's the most design-minded, globally and creatively ambitious generation ever: 'Too many older creatives see the internet as a threat. It's not. It's a huge opportunity.' But the Millennial mindset can be a problem.

She says that social media really is a misnomer: 'It prevents people from talking to each other. It's anti-social. People don't talk. You can see people together in restaurants looking at their iPhones. They're not talking to each other.' She says this has important implications when Millennials come for a job: 'They're not good at talking, making eye contact and shaking someone's hand. Social media seems to create people who are a lot more insular.' But she's also a huge fan of social media even though she finds it addictive.

Brady feels it's important for people to find time to talk and to eat together. She says so many problems come from an email culture, where minor misunderstandings in a creative brief can escalate rapidly. She has a straightforward rule after two emails have failed to solve a problem. 'It's called "Ping – Pong – Ring". It's a quick way of clearing up misunderstandings because it's much harder to do this on email.'

She says she comes up with her best ideas first thing in the morning, when she's on her own and when her mind is allowed to wander. She says that engineers don't think in that way because they work in straight lines: 'I have more ideas than I can possibly develop', she says. Perhaps it's for this reason that she feels that finance and business is much more important. She says this is what separates out creatives. 'They're unable to convert a good idea into a business. They don't know finance, law or how to secure investment', she adds.

She specifically needs to separate her time out, between the creative and the commercial sides, and says that creatives should also be taught to have this discipline. She does all commercial work on Mondays and Fridays, and only checks email in the morning and evenings. She says she's always happy to take a phone call, but points out that Millennials struggle with this.

The discipline extends into meetings. They all last one hour: 'At first my team struggled with this, then they got faster and faster that meetings never even lasted an hour. A creative person wants to give. You might ask them for 40 hours and they will freely give 60 hours. So you have to measure how productive they are.' This possibly accounts for one of the words used to describe her by her staff: 'Scary'. Fortunately, they also use words like 'amazing, lively and bubbly' as well.

The resulting time saved, she uses for exercise. She hates going to the gym or working on exercise machines, so she learnt to tango: 'It's all about balance and weight – just like life.' She always walks to her classes which can be way across town. She uses the time to clear her head and think.

Sleep is essential to her. She needs at least eight hours, but can sleep for ten quite easily: 'The only time I wake up in the middle of the night is, when

I'm not active enough.' She's normally to be found up a ladder or on scaffolding on her client sites.

Does she think that women are marginalized in the creative industries? 'Sometimes women truthfully are more restrictive to other women's development than men are. I think men do more to elevate women, than women do for other women. Women are often very negative about other women. Very often men don't even notice it.' A key to success is not responding to that negativity, she says. It's best just to ignore it.

She points out that some career problems for creative women come when they have a family, because they tend not to want to go to work and fight for their career: 'Their priorities often change. Men are more likely to keep fighting in their career. They fight to win and be taken seriously.'

She notes that women tend to dominate the creative industries, because it's easy for them to drop back in their work. The more compliant industries, she says, like law or accountancy need people to have updating exams to get current.

Did she have to force herself to understand the business side? 'Yes! Because I just couldn't make money from my ideas.' Interestingly she started out wanting a career in law. She liked the organized and structured side of the subject, but was told that law was 'not an appropriate subject for a girl.' It's clear that Brady – like a lot of other creative successes – has two distinct sides. In her case, dictated by different times of the week.

The problem with creativity is that it so often can't be quantified. She has therefore simplified and commoditized her time into a fixed price menu. The structure makes her creativity a success. But the problem with creative endeavour, is that it's still seen as a hobby: 'If you meet someone and you say you're an interior designer, they ask you what you think about their coffee table. If you're a solicitor, they don't pull out their will and ask you to review it.'

She makes the point that creativity is a bit like playing the guitar: 'Everyone can do it, but not many can do it well and get paid for it.' The payment, she says, makes it legitimate. 'Creativity is always questioned because it's so subjective. If we want to take it beyond question, we need to teach creatives to make it credible and commercial.'

Creative people can also help themselves by not being too quick to attack each other: 'It just makes us look unprofessional and all as bad as each other.'

Brady is from Bournemouth, which is a long way from London. She says this helped her a lot because she'd no preconceptions about life in the big city. Did she feel like an imposter? 'Yes! Especially when I was awarded the

OBE. I thought it was a joke!' It was the same when she was awarded her honorary doctorate: 'Both things were hugely validating and made me feel that what I was doing was being noticed.'

She says that creative thinkers should also try absolutely everything: 'It's doesn't matter whether you're any good at it. It will help you understand what you don't like.' She says that, if every child was taught how to be creative earlier, and for longer it would help them in all the other subjects because education would stay fun. She feels that a lot of education isn't fun.

Brady never went to university but she says that the business courses that she did at The Institute of Directors in London were excellent. She learned and absorbed the business skills because she was ready for it: 'Creative people can be better at problem-solving than business people, if we have the confidence and the training', she insists. It's another reason why being creative is just not enough: 'Creative people need to be harder on how they use their time.'

Conclusion

The rapid changes in social media have had a significant effect on communications, accelerating and widening it to being all-embracing. The resulting noise has created behavioural changes causing filters to be applied to what people consider to be fact. And this is just the media outside the world of work. Communicators then must overlay their own messages on top and then creatives overlay their own messaging on top of this. Noise upon noise, effectively. This is the environment that modern creativity needs to work within. Like creating a soufflé in a storm.

This tracks back directly to some of our characteristics of the Eight Creative Traits, especially those dealing with Quiet and Engagement. If we want to be more creative, we have to be careful how much noise we allow in our lives and how we allow ourselves to use or be used for engagement purposes.

How did we allow ourselves to become so overloaded?

02

To understand how we can reclaim creativity, we need to understand how we got into this overloaded state. We need to do this so we can identify areas to prioritize and take back control. Firstly, we need to look at education, particularly at the tertiary level, and ask some questions about why we've been taught to think in this pressurized way. We will look at the human effects of 'noise on noise' and what people are doing at the front line to cope. We'll look at what still needs to change and how some colleges are already making a difference by using their initiative. We look at examples of where education has challenged creative instincts and encouraged people to Dream and Relax (two more of the Creative Traits). At the end of this chapter, you should have an understanding of some of the limitations of the educational system and the role that extraordinary leadership can play in releasing creative potential.

It's a myth that education systems and their cultures are solely responsible for the mechanization and standardization of education. Controversial educationalist Sir Ken Robinson is an internationally recognized leader in the development of creativity, innovation and human resources in education and in business. In his work *Changing Paradigms of Education*, he makes the point that education systems were created in the image of the enlightenment and of industrialization.

He states that the majority of those educated were destined for the factories, but those that displayed intellectual potential could go to college, get a degree and get a good job. This idea has persisted to the present day but it's becoming harder to sustain.

Sure, graduate unemployment remains high in Greece and Spain, but it's also the *underemployment* we should be concerned with. Nearly half of college graduates are underemployed – they're not doing the sort of jobs their degrees prepared them for. It gets worse when you consider that these are the successful ones! Robinson makes the point that the education system only really works for the college graduates because only they proceed to tertiary level. 'It just seems like from the very beginning, all education is a protracted process of university entrance', he says.

If the end point is university entrance, then this explains the standardized testing and the 'teaching for the test' philosophy it drives. All that matters are marks and grades. The answers are either right or wrong and any non-adherence is tantamount to an admission of failure. If you're a late developer, or you have problems in adolescence such as parents divorcing, you can easily get left behind. I did.

Of course, with the decline of manufacturing jobs the outcomes become more terrifying. It's harder for poorly educated people to find a job with good money working in a factory. The pressure on children to perform intellectually at an early stage has become more intense.

Parents have therefore responded with pressure to protect and prepare their children for what they know is a competitive world. It's not just the school systems that exert the pressure – the parents are willing and complicit.

The result is an epidemic of mental health problems at the university level. The Reverend Dr Alasdair Coles is Rector of All Saints Episcopal Church and Chaplain for St Andrew's University in Scotland. He is calm personified. He listens a lot. He has to. He has no television and uses very little technology. As befits a clergyman, he is an expert at listening and, of course, playing table tennis (at which he is fiercely competitive, often invoking rules which permit a shot to be acceptable if it bounces off several unlikely objects before landing 'in'). Divine providence is clearly at work here.

He speaks in low, measured tones with a steady gaze. He moves slowly and gracefully and speaks slowly. He says the scale of overload and psychological pressure on students is overwhelming: 'The level of psychological problems that we're seeing is unprecedented. We're literally on our knees coping.' He says we need to remember the words of Desmond Tutu: 'There comes a point where we need to stop just pulling people out of the river. We need to go upstream and find out who's pushing them in.' He says it is a manifestation of a fragmented society and individualism that we can't have shared problems any more.

And these are the problems created before they graduate. Coles says we're teaching people lots of stuff, but not the important stuff. He says they arrive at university often unable to cope with relationships, because many of them have been online rather than face to face: 'Nobody seems to talk about the important things any more. It's a function of the digital age – there's a lot of communication, but not much conversation. There's a lot of quantity but not quality.' Coles says that the education system doesn't teach them how to behave towards each other: 'Sometimes people need to have their abusive attitudes towards themselves and others challenged.' Coles says this doesn't normally happen online. Cyberbullies and trolls largely go unpunished.

The lack of time for them to reflect is particularly a problem. It's rare for students to have had someone who takes time to listen to them.

George Blacklock, later in this chapter, talks about the relationship teachers have with students. He describes his teaching as like 'planting time bombs' with students: 'Sometimes students don't always understand in the class. Sometimes they understand a day later and sometimes years after.'

Coles is the other way around to Blacklock. He acts as a sort of delayed bomb disposal officer. The emotional bombs he's defusing have sometimes been there for many years before he sees them as a chaplain.

Quality thinking is not just about the presence of the positive. It's also about the absence of the negative. 'If you're looking for a deeper relationship, then you have to accept that status is unimportant in every respect', he says. 'To get the best out of people, you have to let them *be*. You have to accept that passivity is at least half of human existence. The state of waiting is important. It's part of the act of creative opportunism.'

Some of the way he ministers to these broken graduates is about picking the right physical place. How would he describe it? 'It's silent and respectful. It's full of power.' He says that places grow in power when you remove things – such as noise, interruptions and people.

Where are these powerful places now? 'Well, the churches are closed during the day, we've cut off the sporadic worshippers. Fortunately, we still have cathedrals and university chapels. There are real problems out there. I think we have to understand that normal people are the ones you just don't know very well.' Coles is very clear about where he gets his best ideas: 'When I'm listening. I have to listen very carefully then clarify what they're trying to say. It's very important to allow people to take up as much of your time as they feel they need.' If we follow Coles and his conclusions, it would be equally valid for us to build creative spaces which are empty and silent and built for listening rather than stimulating. A thousand years ago, the church was the orthodoxy. Now it's becoming very unorthodox to attend church. This is where Coles sees the opportunity: 'I feel strongly that a door is opening again, there are so many problems which can be solved by faith', he says. The implication here is clear, not only is the overload creating problems, it's done against the backdrop of ever-increasing competition and pressure to perform academically, even at the expense of spiritual and emotional health.

'It won't be about the services or the terminology, it will be about recognizing that the hole can't be stuffed with food, sex, money or possessions. It's a God-shaped hole.' Coles says that it's not necessarily about Christianity, it's about belief and faith. Coles sees the lack of faith as not only damaging for the individual but hints that it is actively encouraged because: 'Unhappy people spend more.' It's been said that the job of advertising is to create unhappiness. The problem that Coles is seeing is that while parents may think that achieving the grade or getting the grade point average is enough, it simply isn't. According to UNESCO, in the next 30 years more people will qualify as a graduate than ever before. Degrees are just not enough of an education. They're not rounded enough for the job market. They don't provide graduates with interpersonal skills.

There was a great political imperative in the 1990s to develop the tertiary level. A sort of fetish for graduate education became common. In the United States 'no child left behind', and in the UK, between the years 1997 and 2007, Tony Blair's government increased the number of first-time British students by 44,000 to 283,000. Having a degree was seen as enough. This, of course, is an admirable goal. Who wouldn't want a higher educational standard? The point Robinson makes, though, is that it's not enough just to expand the system by *quantity* and *quality*.

Robinson cites longitudinal studies of children – when asked at the age of five who can draw, everyone volunteers. Ten years later, having completed a large part of their education, nobody identifies themselves as an artist. They've learned by close comparison and grading that art is something for a talented few. Worse, they also learn that artistic pursuits have less value than other subjects. Take dance, for instance. Robinson makes the point that there is no school in the world that teaches dance as regularly and as consistently as they teach mathematics. He asks the question 'Why?'; 'Children dance all the time if they're allowed to.' As Robinson says though, the system 'educates progressively from the neck-up'. It concentrates just on the intellectual, reductive skills and not on the wider balance.

Robinson is not without his critics. Many see mathematics as simply more relevant to general education than dance. His point, though, is that if the system had flexibility it wouldn't have to be a 'one size fits all'.

Competition and confidence

When children start to be graded and compared, they can see how much better everyone else is. The received wisdom is that competition is good for excellence. For many people though, it just undermines confidence, especially in the gender that suffers more because of it.

From over 100 graduate interviews in the last two years at LEWIS, the most common characteristic of male and female applicants is that men tended to have fewer skills, but more confidence, and the women were the other way around. Unsurprisingly, we take commensurately more female graduates because, with this configuration, you can add confidence (provided the training is geared to do this). With low skill sets and high confidence, it's difficult to convince young men that they need to learn the skills to progress, so they tend to fail.

If we were ever looking to address any form of glass ceiling, the process needs to be addressed much earlier. The education system that our parents passed to us is not just a reflection of the enlightenment and industrialization, but also an overwhelming male point of view. Not only do we not teach creative provenance, but we also don't teach confidence. Why? Because it's less of a problem for men.

In 2013, I helped to found a political group trying to encourage more women to go into politics. I did this because I felt (and still feel strongly) that modernity, representation and aspiration are qualities that a political system should encourage. Political representation is a 'show' not 'tell'. It didn't surprise me that the male politicians were scathing of the venture, but even though the organization thrived, it was treated as a minority issue. Mainly only women attended the events. The few men who did, attended begrudgingly.

Can the reasons for this be found in the traditionalist lifestyle experienced by many MPs? Their work is usually six days a week and packed with meetings of 30 minutes or less. According to a report by the government's Social Mobility and Child Poverty Commission, in many of the UK's top professions there is a skewed proportion of the privately educated. Just 7 per cent of the UK public attended private school, which compares to 71 per cent of senior judges, 62 per cent of senior armed forces officers, 55 per cent of Whitehall permanent secretaries and 50 per cent of members of the House of Lords. A third of MPs went to private school and 25 per cent were educated at either Oxford or Cambridge.

The system doesn't change because it seems to work perfectly for the people who are now in charge of it. They apparently have been successful, yet politicians as a group also suffer high levels of depression, alienation and drink- and alcohol-related problems. And no politician will willingly talk about their own mental health and overload – for example, former business secretary Vince Cable and the late Liberal Democrat leader Charles Kennedy.

The political dysfunction knocks on to the way the creative industries are governed – lumped in with media and sport into the departmental hotchpotch of the Department for Culture, Media and Sport or DCMS for short.

What are the problems in the system?

So the model of education persists because there are very few academic leaders who have not benefited from the academic system as it is. They just don't perceive any requirement for change. That's because they aren't in a business which is trying to use the raw graduate output they provide. Let's talk to some who are.

Too siloed and institutionalized

Vanessa Brady, the award-winning interior designer, was asked to speak at a university recently to talk to students about her skills as a designer. 'Most creatives fail not because they can't come up with ideas, but because they don't know the business side.' She spoke to course leaders and said: 'Where is the finance side of the course? They told me that it wasn't their job to teach business. But you can't be a designer unless you understand this.' This was all the more frustrating given that the university had a strong business course, but it didn't have any overlap or input to the creative courses. It seems like academic snobbery – one course looking down on another.

She points out that this can have deadly consequences for the brilliantly talented, saying that it's not enough just to be skilled creatively and cites Alexander McQueen who, at the time of his suicide, was in significant debt. She also mentions that there are several big name celebrities who have no idea how the money side of the business works. If we want to get more people to universities who might not otherwise get there, we have to question what tertiary education is really there for. It is already beyond question that their output is not geared to what business needs. Ask any business leader, they will tell you that graduates sometime struggle to do the basics. If it's not what business needs, it's therefore not what students need, because all university success is measured on whether a student can gain employment.

Few would disagree that creativity is important to us personally and collectively. If this is the case, then why don't we teach it properly?

No response to the financial crisis generation

Much has been written about the recent financial collapse in 2009 and many explanations have been given. The economy and banking system didn't fall apart because people were too calm, too clear or too long-term in their thinking. It fell apart because the confidence in the system drained away. Many experts pointed to the underlying logic and rationalism of why the market shouldn't have failed, but that's the reason why markets ever fail. Fear and greed, as emotions, are irrational. It's ironic that the financial system, driven by logical, short-term, left-brained people collapsed because the right-brain process reasserted itself. Basically, everyone got scared.

Graduate employment was hit hardest by the collapse. According to the Economic Policy Institute, in its paper *The Class of 2015*, despite officially ending in June 2009, the recession left millions unemployed for prolonged spells. Recent workforce entrants such as young graduates were particularly vulnerable. Seven classes of students have now graduated into a weak labour market and have had to compete with more experienced workers for a limited number of job opportunities.

While recent improvements in economic conditions have begun to brighten graduates' job prospects, the labour market has not yet recovered from the 2009 recession. In addition, wages of young high school and college graduates have failed to reach their pre-recession levels, and have in fact stagnated or declined for almost every group since 2000. For young college graduates, the unemployment rate is currently 7.2 per cent (compared with 5.5 per cent in 2007), and the underemployment rate is 14.9 per cent (compared with 9.6 per cent in 2007).

Not working closely enough with employers

Although universities have worked closer to creative businesses, the culture remains different. Specifically, this affects the way employers work with universities. Vanessa Brady again: 'Why don't universities offer accreditation to those who get work experience? It means a lot to Millennials who are desperate to prove credentials more than just academic qualifications.' She also says that if universities worked more closely with employers, work experience would become something more than cheap labour: 'If employers and universities worked more closely together, then casual work experience could be given accreditation. Most of those getting "work experience" are doing little more than doing a Saturday job. Work experience is no good unless interns get the mentoring they need.'

The conclusions from the Economic Policy Institute's paper are interesting: 'Unemployment of young graduates is high today, but not because of something unique about the recession and its aftermath that has affected young people in particular. Rather, it is high because young workers always experience disproportionate increase in unemployment during periods of labour market weakness – and the Great Recession and its aftermath is the longest, most severe period of economic weakness in more than seven decades.'

In itself, this is logical enough but surely graduates should be emerging from education at their freshest, most creative and with most to offer? With any other product from any system, the tag 'new' would be an advantage. The high share of graduate unemployment in improving economic times must, at least in part, point to a problem in recognizing what employers need. Graduate education is increasing more rapidly than median family income, leaving students with little choice but to take out loans. From 1984 to 2014, the inflation-adjusted cost of a four-year education, including tuition, fees, and room and board, increased 125.7 per cent for private school and 129.0 per cent for US state schools (according to the College Board). Between 2004 and 2014, there was a 92 per cent increase in the number of student loan borrowers and a 74 per cent increase in average student loan balances (according to the Federal Reserve Bank of New York).

Graduating in a weak economy has long-lasting economic consequences. Economic research suggests that for the next 10 to 15 years, those in the Class of 2015 will likely earn less than if they had graduated when job opportunities were plentiful.

What should education be trying to do?

Let's start by asking some uncomfortable questions:

1 Is a university degree an aspiration pushed by politicians to create the impression, if not the actuality, of progress?

2 Does this result in graduates gaining an ill-suited qualification, that employers do not need and that the student cannot afford?

3 If education is really about potential, then why do we teach a subject rather than the meta-disciplines of creative provenance and alternative ways to think?

4 Why don't we teach creative thinking as early as possible in secondary education and teach its importance not just for ideas, but for health, working methods and sustainability. Should we teach the structures of the brain, how they work during the creative process and how to best use them? After all, it is our biggest asset.

5 How well can creativity be taught when the education system self-evidently does not value it? Or should we just go on producing ever more STEM graduates?

We must accept at least, that if students cannot find appropriate work, it's not the fault of the products in the system. Some might say it's a matter of attitude which can't be taught. If someone comes out of education, however ill-equipped for the world outside, the fault can hardly lie with them. Attitude might change the outcome later, but we should be able to prepare graduates better than this.

It highlights the need for closer cooperation between business and industry so they can tell universities what skills and attitude they want and at what level.

In Matthew Crawford's book *Shop Class as Soulcraft: An Inquiry into the Value of Work*, he points out many of the problems with education as he experienced it. He extols the virtues of the merits of skilled manual labour on both economic and psychological grounds. Crawford questions the 'educational imperative of turning everyone into a "knowledge worker", based on a misguided separation of thinking from doing.' He uses his own experience as an electrician and mechanic as a basis for the analysis.

Crawford points out that machine shop classes were dropped comprehensively by US schools in favour of teaching all kids to become knowledge workers. Consequently, there are loads of second-hand machine tools lying around that no one wants to use. He puts this down to a trend to hide all of the engineering. This was first started by Apple but has since been adopted by car and domestic appliance managers to stop people tinkering. Crawford received a doctorate in political philosophy from the University of Chicago, then took a job working in a Washington thinktank. He quit after five months to open a motorbike shop. He just found that work more engaging intellectually.

I'm right with him on this. I've always been a mechanic at heart. I want to know how things work. I don't just want to know what it is. I want to know how it works and what it needs to work better. It used to be the case that this was almost expected of young minds, especially boys, who were brought up on Meccano and Lego. There are some countries where this technical ethos still persists. Germany is one example. The apprentice system absorbs a large proportion of resources in their dual education system. Creativity, as Crawford points out, is about more than just ideas. It's also about technical problem-solving.

Two worlds, still too far apart

Despite the progress made in the university system, education culture remains different to the student's 'destination' culture in the following ways.

Universities have less formal hours of attendance, for instance, with much less daily imperative than do companies. They also tend to be run by academics rather than professional administrators. They remain in many instances physically separated from the business world, frequently on their own campus often in a 'cloistered' environment. Many US universities are privately run as businesses which provides a greater alignment to the ultimate destination of so many graduates. According to 2014/15 QS World University Rankings, of the top 20 US universities, only four are public.

In a *Forbes* guest post in March 2016 entitled 'What higher education can learn from the fall of the newspapers', Frederick Singer likened the challenges that newspapers have navigated to those now facing education. Singer was a founder of washingtonpost.com and an early employee at AOL. He is also the CEO and founder of educational tech company Echo360. He says that although the newspaper industry remains, it is a shadow of its former self and this is about to happen to universities because the value of the degree is being called into question. 'Students face a multiplicity of options to acquire knowledge outside of colleges and universities.' He says colleges and universities need to adapt and unbundle or 'go the way of the local newspaper'. He also says they need to re-engineer and protect the most profitable courses and make them more interactive. 'Passive consumption of classes and content doesn't square with the experience of screenagers who came of age in the internet era. Visionary professors are capitalizing on the explosion of mobile devices in the lecture hall to capture the attention and develop new modalities of teaching. Course scheduling is beginning to look more like Kayak [a travel search engine] than a traditional registrar, providing students with great choice and transparency into their path to completion. Creating a more interactive path for students is not just an esoteric problem for the classroom, but is also the foundation for schools improving outcomes and revenue.'

Singer remarks that what newspapers were slow to realize was the importance of leveraging real-time reader data to shape editorial decision-making. 'In 1994 and 1995, when our editors received their first "click through" reports, it was the first time that they could actually see in detail what was being read and where the engagement online was occurring. In the analogue world, our editors were flying blind, relying on customer polls to understand reader habits. Over time, they began to understand how news was consumed story-by-story to make daily adjustments that captivated readers, and culminated in new "paywall" strategies.'

He says that university leaders share a similar concern. 'They are awash in data from online courses that can be used to inform instructional design and improve outcomes, but the bricks-and-mortar classes that most of their students attend remain a black box. Without the ability to understand student behaviour, our professors are forced to teach without the most basic feedback mechanisms. At the same time, online courses and emerging modalities are designed from the ground up to track student behaviour, providing a competitive advantage and putting pressure on traditional higher education.'

He sees that there are many valuable lessons for leaders of universities and colleges to extract from the experience of the newspaper industry. By focusing on the key areas of threats, leveraging the power of interactive engagement to redefine the offering, and using real-time data to iterate, he says they can not only match the threat, but emerge with the opportunity to extend their mission and scope as hubs for lifelong learning. 'Incumbents can win wars of disruption if they move quickly and at scale.'

Universities, especially the public ones, need to recognize that the world of work is changing faster than they are. They can keep up, even in the public sector, if they adopt radical change.

Give a lot, then give some more

Peter De Haan is mischief personified. This 64-year-old workaholic swashbuckles around his office with a broad grin. He has a strong connection with the East End of London, where he was brought up. He is a businessman, philanthropist and as chairman of arts charity IdeasTap, invested £25 million in all aspects of creativity. He also founded his own Charitable Trust and was previously chief financial officer at Saga. He was awarded the Rothschild Medal in recognition of the outstanding contribution he has made to nature conservation since 2004.

What does he think about the wealthy? 'It's the extent of greed which is so disappointing. There are so many people in need of help. They need to understand that success and fulfilment are different things. It's a great privilege to be able to help people. A lot of these people just haven't matured.'

It's unusual to find someone trained as a Chartered Accountant who is so keen on creative people. Applicants do, though, have to stand the De Haan test. He says there are five broad categories of creatives he deals with:

1 Winners, who are very talented. He says all you can do here is connect them with quality organizations and/or mentors.

2 People who are influenced by the winners. He says you can help them with skills.

3 Shy people. This is all about getting them to join in with the hope they progress.

4 No-hopers who enjoyed their art form but would never make a living.

5 No-hopers who should try something else.

This sounds quite ruthless, but it's essentially a practical approach. He believes creativity is essential as a skill for young people to help them: 'Stand out from the crowd, think differently and to add to their presentation skills.' He says that it can also help them with communication skills which really is a key requirement.

Although De Haan spends most of his time out of the UK these days, he says creativity adds enormously to the British brand: 'London is a powerhouse and Britain has a wonderful range of creative endeavour with strength in depth in music, art, architecture, fashion and design.'

He believes this is very much despite the way it's taught in universities. His criticism is scathing: 'I feel they could do a lot better. They're really living on their reputation and they're under-invested and relying on foreign students for money.'

Like a few of the people profiled here, he didn't go to university. He said he matured later and he really became interested in philanthropy in his early thirties. He had five children very early on and most of his drive until then was looking after them.

So what could education do better? 'They need shorter courses which are better organized. Too much student time is left unfilled and they're not using it for reading as they should. There's no doubt that more investment would result in better trained students.' In particular, he echoes the comments of Vanessa Brady. 'They have to improve business, team work and research skills. And the support for students after they come out of education.'

In all the years he's been a philanthropist to the creative arts, never once has a college or university invited him to talk. I find this extraordinary: 'I've always been unimpressed by the university people I meet. They're also pseudo-intellectuals that know nothing about life, yet these are the people we put in charge of education.'

He's received the same reception from government as well: 'I went to them to talk about all the money we'd invested and they told me they weren't interested in that demographic! How can you not be interested in training young people? It was appalling. They were happy though to fund the Arts Council or the Royal Opera House. They don't plan. They don't know what's happening. These people live in a bubble. They're so far out of touch.'

He says there may have been two mistakes: 'Firstly, we were a big success. We ran like a private business and I think it embarrassed some of the government-run operations.'

He believes the mistake may also have been to approach government in a businesslike manner. He feels he might have done better with a sob story, or something which had some votes in it.

The difference in the approach epitomizes the difference between private and public money. The former wants to see a businesslike approach, the latter a political one: 'The government doesn't see any votes in young creatives – that's why the spending is channelled towards the high-brow stuff, because there's votes there for them. It's all political.'

De Haan also funded Kids Company for many years before it closed down. When it failed, no one from government approached him despite his knowledge of the operations.

He insists that it's really important for creatives that go looking for funding to understand about business, because philanthropists approach giving in a businesslike way: 'Of course, you're not running an operation to make money, but you do want to see it operate in a businesslike way. It needs a business plan, clear objectives and a reporting structure.'

The main mistakes creatives make are that they give up too easily: 'There's a lack of work ethic among many. They're not well-researched when they come looking for funding. In particular, they struggle to talk about their work in context and seldom work as a team.' In particular, he says: 'They don't know anything about business, almost as if they've been educated in a bubble.'

He's disarmingly straightforward about why he gets involved: 'I'm just a socialist! I am a rich guy who wants to try to help. I try to operate in a way that I can add value and that makes me feel good. Helping creatives was inspired by my family and their experiences.'

His own ideas come more easily since he's been spending more time in Switzerland and Spain: 'These days, I spend at least three hours a day exercising. I work for a while, then I go sit outside and stop – then the ideas come. It's all about balance. My performance improves, the more time I spend away from the office.'

I don't know anyone who has given so much, for so long to help the cause of creativity and had so little recognition. But then, that's not why he does it.

How it can be different

Frampton is a BFG (Big Friendly Giant). He's also the principal at Portsmouth College in the UK. He's unusual for an academic principal because he's not an academic. He's also not an intellectual (according to him). Furthermore, he's dyslexic and has experienced many educational challenges of his own as a youth. Nevertheless, he fought his way up and was successful in business before moving into teaching. The business environment taught him to be a risk-taker. That's exactly what he's done with this college. He's innovated in three key ways.

Firstly, he decided that, if the college wanted to prepare students for the next stage in their life, the technology they used needed to be excellent and universal. He therefore brought in a system where all 1,400 students and staff were based on Apple iPad minis. This system is fully interactive so staff can see students' work and share across classrooms. Students don't pay for these but they do pay for their insurance, in case they lose or damage the kit.

Secondly, he brought together a team of like-minded people. Like Kerry Jagger, who had previously been a chef before pursuing a Postgraduate Certificate in Learning and Teaching. This qualification prepares teaching staff to play a significant role in teaching and supporting student learning. Like Tom Lloyd, another non-graduate with hands-on entrepreneurial business skills. He hand-picked this team because he'd worked with them before. There is a deep level of trust. This is important because of what he did next.

Thirdly, Frampton decided to experiment with the whole academic timetable: 'No one knows where timetables came from', he says. 'They just seem to have been passed down year after year from someone that pulled the first together 40 years ago. They never seem to be challenged, so that's what we did.' The received wisdom is that adolescents are late chronotypes – they tend to be sluggish in the morning. Frampton agrees, but that's as far as he goes with the orthodoxy. 'People said that you couldn't engage adolescents for more than 45 minutes at a time. My experience is more nuanced. If you can engage them later in the day, you can engage them for longer.' So Frampton turned the timetable on its head. He started the day at 10 am and then only taught two lessons a day. If you're thinking this sounds like an easy day, each lesson is three hours long. Not only has this produced better results academically, as evidenced by three consecutive government inspections, but it brings radical change to other areas. For instance, many of his staff are primary carers. Morning is frequently the most difficult time to get children off to school on time and can leave them feeling rushed and tired first thing in the morning. For the staff, starting later, they are able to invest greater energy and enthusiasm into the lessons, hence the longer engagement times.

Did he walk into any objections about the shake-up? 'Yes, initially from the students, who, when I investigated, had been put up to it by academic staff, who didn't want their day changing. In actual fact, although the day now starts later for the staff, it doesn't finish later. The content is just rearranged.'

All this would be unusual enough for an academic culture – progressive, dynamic, flexible, etc. But there's something else. Frampton doesn't possess an iPhone or any other mobile device. Initially this was because of his dyslexia, but even though he is capable of using a device, he doesn't. 'It gets in the way of me doing my job', he says. 'I like to walk round and talk to people. If people send me an email they know it can be 24 hours before I reply. People have got to under-stand that just because you CAN do something, that doesn't mean you SHOULD.'

I probed further on this point and Frampton pointed out how much time he sees being wasted by using the devices. 'It's not that I'm against the technology. How could I be when we have invested so much in putting tech at the core of our proposition. It just seems to me to be a hindrance. I get my best ideas either when I'm driving or when I'm gardening. I'm also at my best when dealing with people face to face.' This dyslexia has been an enormous personal gift in the 21st century.

The culture in the college is noticeable for its warmth, spontaneity and democracy. Although I met the entire board, two of those were students who were allowed to talk freely. This is leadership out in the open. It's personal, it's accessible, it's warm but above all else, it works.

Nine months to live

Imagine you were given nine months to live. What would you do? Blair Sadler was a talented US squash player and a widely published writer, when a mole on his leg was diagnosed as a malignant melanoma. The character of the man is that this event is only mentioned in passing after we've been talking for an hour: 'Well, it was nearly 40 years ago, but it did have a profound impact on my life', he says with a quiet intensity.

He points at a framed poster on the wall from the original Rocky movie. It has the phrase: 'His whole life was a million-to-one shot.' He hung it up at the end of his bed as he began his recovery. 'It's been how I lived my life since then.'

His background as a squash player, a graduate of Amherst College and the University of Pennsylvania Law School would be impressive enough, but I'd actually come to talk to him about the role of creativity in healing. It turned out he was more interested in telling me about a charity that he's been involved in for the last 10 years called The Access Youth Academy. As one of San Diego's most innovative support programmes, it's based in a community with high poverty rates and youth that are often affected by gangs, alcohol, drugs and domestic violence. The programme is centred around what might be best described as a Squash 'Ladder' in every sense of the word. Sadler has put his passion for squash at the heart of a four-cornered process that includes Academic Achievement, Health and Wellness, Leadership and Social Responsibility. Kids graduate from the Academy and go on to university at some of the most prestigious schools in the United States. The next phase is to find $3 million to build nine new squash courts and class-rooms in the heart of the community to develop it.

This self-confessed, Type A, left-brain dominated, hard-driving, ambitious man was 36 years old when he received his diagnosis. It's clear that this life-changing pivotal experience did more than enrich his whole life, it changed the way he thought. He started to think *wider*.

It seemed almost ordained that he would spend 26 years of his life as chief executive officer of one of the US's best known children's hospitals, Rady in San Diego. His personal experience made him look at hospital environments from the patient's point of view. You can't get a more logical and scientific environment than a hospital, but Sadler's instinct was that more could be done to improve patient experiences and outcomes. He went on to pioneer the collaboration between medicine and art.

Of course, you can't do this with instinct alone – he had to convince sceptical colleagues: 'As a CEO, you can of course mandate change, but I always preferred to take my team with me.' He says that clinical staff don't always recognize how frightening and alien hospital environments can be: 'They just get used to them, but these experiences can really upset people, especially children.'

The power of Sadler is that he couches the right-brain process thinking in such strong left-brain process terms: 'When you're bringing artists, musicians, dancers and sculptors into a scientific environment you need a clear rubric.' He describes a 10-stage process:

1 Build a clear connection between the arts and the strategic goals of the organization.
2 Find a leader who can champion the programme.
3 Set up a specific pilot.
4 Work with a university third party for accreditation.
5 Develop a plan, programme and target date.
6 Find donors outside to help.
7 Seek support from all staff.
8 Keep everyone informed of progress.
9 Publish your results.
10 Expand and replicate the programme.

Sadler went on to show with clear evidence how the healing environment was impacted by the loss of privacy, unusual noises and institutional feel: 'When people feel in control and relaxed, they get better – it's as simple as that. Creating healing environments can improve medical outcomes because patients can use their energy to get well rather than cope with a new situation.' He went further to make Rady feel more like home with the use of healing gardens to create relaxed environments.

He knew that music before surgical procedures could reduce stress levels and even the level of morphine required: 'Music is inexpensive, simple and easy to put in place. It can reduce the perception of pain by patients and reduce the level of tranquillizers, requiring less sedation.' Now music therapists are used in many US hospitals for procedures such as echocardiograms and CAT scans.

Sadler's own experience changed everything. He knew that hospitals could be scary, especially for children. So he made Rady Children's less so. He insisted for instance that everything was designed to be child-size. He went on to write several journals about his experience, and his book *Transforming the Health Care Experience Through the Arts* is considered the seminal text.

Now, nearly 40 years on, Sadler considers every day after his misdiagnosis to be a bonus: 'It doesn't matter that the odds are against you, there's always hope.'

Art used in science

Another example of innovative thinking, this time in university education, comes from Lancaster University in the north of England (my alma mater). Lancaster's biomedicine students are being encouraged to experiment with ideas through drawing with bacteria as part of a lab competition. This was led by Jackie Parry and Rod Dillon from the Biomedical and Life Sciences team and was aimed at boosting creativity by visualizing how the bacteria interact and communicate. Their petri dish artwork explored themes like antibiotic resistance and Ebola infection, using images created by growing bacteria. Rod Dillon said: 'Employers want creative people who come up with new ideas based on concepts learnt on their degree and this is essential. It gives our students the edge when it comes to a job or PhD.'

The winner of a recent competition was a clock face entitled: 'Time is running out for antibiotics. Alternative treatments need to be developed fast before bacteria become completely resistant.' A red pigmented bacteria grew across the plate and the student placed different antibiotic discs around the clock. The clear zones around the first discs show that the antibiotics are working, but as the clock approaches midnight the antibiotics become weaker.

Dillon says art and biology has a long history, noting that Alexander Fleming was a lifelong member of the Chelsea Arts Club: 'It's about having an eye for patterns which helped him spot the way in which penicillin had wiped out the bacteria in the petri dish.'

'Why have you decided to do it in such a conventional manner?'

George Blacklock is the dean of Chelsea College of Arts. It is the closest school of art to the Parliament in Central London but, despite his invitations, politicians seldom visit.

George is a talented fine artist in his own right, but he has spent much of life teaching. This unselfishness defines him. This small, white-haired, mischievous man-dynamo is never far from an easy grin.

I'd sent him an email saying I was interested in Chelsea's work and wanted to bring the worlds of academia and business closer together. It was as dumb and as vague as that. Perhaps that's why he took a chance and invited me to his office. He immediately offered me a beer and said in a Geordie accent: 'So woss thus all abowt, man?' I liked him immediately. I thought I knew all about academics until I met him. George's main job in life is to open people's eyes. Oh, and he's also a black belt in ju-jitsu. So he knows how to close them, too.

The heading above is one of his many answers to a student that asks him for an opinion on their work. He doesn't bother to look at the detail, because that would invite an analytical response. He questions at a bigger level. His ambition is to challenge the student. He wants to find out what the inner relationship is and where the student will push themselves.

As an experienced and talented painter, it goes without question that George understands the principle of creative induction. He knows how to do it himself. The heart of his unselfishness is that he has spent most of his career inducing it in others.

George's question illustrates the fact that, in every case, our creative boundaries are self-imposed. The teacher's job is to challenge the student to release their own potential. It's where teaching meets learning. 'I never really understood my own creative process until I started teaching. I also didn't know how much I knew', he says.

In many respects, George's question is brilliant in its simplicity and its assumptions. Everybody's creativity is self-regulated. Remove the regulation and see what happens. It's easier than it sounds. When people are rebuffed, they blame the barrier.

In order to come up with new ideas about anything, we all have to ask George's question. We all have to reach our potential. When we've done that, we have to help others to achieve theirs.

One of the things that makes him such a good artist and teacher is his ability to remove creative barriers. The question we opened with: 'Why have you decided to do it in such a conventional manner?' is one of those interventions designed to remove a barrier. In this case it's the ego of the painter. 'The student is saying – look, this is me. And I'm trying to get them to go further – beyond what they think they can do. Being called conventional is the worst thing you can call an art student, so it forces them to go further.'

Blacklock says that the ego of the creative has to be dealt with carefully. One way of doing this is to get peers to correct and critique the art work rather than a teacher doing so. Sometimes, he says, it's just easier for people to accept a critique if there's either a consensus of critique or it's coming from someone they know, admire and trust. A friend is ideal for this.

Sometimes, he says, people just need to be dared to be creative. They need to be given permission. It's not enough to have a red wall or a bean bag. You must put people on the spot and ask them to perform.

Repetitiveness induces boredom and that causes people to be inventive, but these days, who's bored with anything?

Sustained creativity in the longer term is difficult. If you look at music, for all but the most talented, it fades after the first three albums.

Blacklock agrees with the idea of Flow. The studio is set up for Flow and people should set themselves up for it.

'There are forces both intellectual and emotional that must come together', he says. They are not predictable, not reliable, so how can you teach this?

'First of all, you have got to get rid of the barriers. In fine art these are simple. Have you sanded down between layers? Have you mixed enough paint? Are you using the right size brush? These are all minor problems that an artist can encounter which can interrupt their Flow.' Blacklock says this applies to all creative thinkers. He says that people often have great ideas when they're not at work and on their own because 'no one's there to stop them'.

He says barriers stop you getting into the zone: 'Anything that stops that Flow has got to be removed, because you never know whether you're going to lose that moment for all time.' He believes that learning to draw is an excellent discipline for all creatives because it teaches you how to think. Blacklock recently conducted a class of senior executives from LEWIS and all reported that it was an interesting exercise. 'You have to really concentrate to draw. Because you have to study the subject matter in detail. It makes you better at lots of other tasks.'

He also notes that sometimes the creative process can 'spiral in' to a conclusion. You have to find an aspect of the painting which is perfect then work around it: 'Sometimes, it's the other way around. You have to find something you really hate. Then you get into a cold sweat thinking that you've ruined a painting, then you work in a frenzy to turn it around. Usually when this happens, it ends up three times as good as it was before.'

'To come up with a really great idea, you sometimes have to have a good idea which you're prepared to completely risk to get a truly great one', he says. Is there a cycle to painting? Blacklock thinks there probably isn't but he's sure that he can 'over paint'. Type As in general are not good at knowing when to stop. Sometimes you bang away and it's not there. Some days it is. The days it isn't there, well, they contribute to the days when it is. This is like Reverend Coles's psychology for waiting and being passive.

The whole point of the creative process, is for you to be completely present. Blacklock says that he once watched Picasso paint. 'Every stroke was certain. Every addition to the painting looked like it was his last, but then he went back again with more certainty. In order to maximize the creativity potential, you have to maximize someone's presence – it's really as simply as that.

'One of the most important things for a student is to know what's required. But I try to do the opposite, the last thing I want students to give me is what I want. I want them to go beyond what they think I want. I'd encourage them to go way beyond what we expect from a traditional drawing.'

Blacklock believes that all creative thinkers need time to get their flow going and 'your job is to keep them in the game long enough, before they knock themselves out with an interruption or self-critique.'

The greater the inspiration, though, the more likely that they will vault the barriers. How does he know when he is seeing a great idea? 'When it addresses you. Great ideas address you and your place in the world.' This is an interesting idea because when we're doing the opposite of analysing things we're working conceptually – the bigger, the better.

Great art is really a metaphysical exchange. It's like meeting someone you really like.

One thing is for sure – creative people with something to say should not try to reinvent the wheel. There are all sorts of images and nuances that are passed on from one generation to another. Some of these are passed down from the classics.

Blacklock says that he actually learned creative leadership from ju-jitsu. Whenever you were trying to teach someone a hip throw and they did it wrong, the response was always positive – 'that's good, now try putting your feet slightly further apart and try it again' then they'd do it wrong again and the response would be 'great, now this time hold his arm much tighter and see if you can get it better'. The worst teachers, he says, are always the ones that just shout at the student and tell them that it's all wrong: 'No, no, no your feet are all in the wrong place. Try it again.' It has no sense of fun or wonder, and great teachers need to retain that. 'That approach just destroys confidence and that's the most fragile thing when you're trying to teach a new skill. You've got to get them to think that they can do it. You've got to find something good that you can build on. There is a process – you have to build trust – the student has to trust you to help them improve.'

All leaders can learn from this. If you really want people to improve, they have to trust you to help them improve. It's got to be fun, because learning needs to be fun because all competence follows preference. Besides, the consequence of not doing this is tragic and involves wasted times, skills and potential. None of us can afford to waste resources. He uses the example that most people stop drawing at the age of 10 or so usually because they've been criticized that 'it doesn't look like that'. They stop using metaphor and dreaming and start to become more rational, logical and figurative. He says it's better to build people's confidence: 'It's harder for people to get out of the dips than it is for them to come off the peaks.'

Type As are notoriously bad at this process. They're very hard on themselves. Consequently, they're very good at getting things done but maybe not the sort you want to get stuck in an elevator with. The ultimate purpose of Chelsea College of Arts is to give them the tools they need to keep learning and coach themselves.

Blacklock believes the world of business and the arts are too far apart: 'Aesthetics and ethics are closely linked and when the world of art is too far from business, it becomes easy to tolerate ugly behaviour.'

He says that metaphorical thinking leads to a higher truth: 'All ugly thinking has no metaphor. Whenever you talk to anyone about great events, they reach for simile. You can't do that with numbers.'

He categorizes for instance 'Surface learners' who are told to go and paint it red and they do. Other more competent learners paint it red then come back and say that they thought blue was a better metaphor for red.

He maintains that the metaphor is something very important to creativity: 'The gene pool that we get from Shakespeare has stuffed the British with metaphor. But we still struggle towards the unambiguous.'

Blacklock says that competence and correctness have been the English disease: 'Do it wrong and see what you learn! There are great inaccuracies in Michelangelo's work, but that's strategic art. You sometimes have to lose tactical correctness to win the bigger argument.'

He also believes that you have to pace creative endeavour by the age of the student: 'With younger people they're far more likely to let go of the side of the pool. The middle-aged find it harder. Fear is a big factor. Looking different, being different, standing outside the crowd. What they don't know, is that we're all outside the crowd! Everyone has an equal opportunity to hit the highest mark.'

How does he know when a creative idea is no good? 'There are no bad ideas! Nobody has to prove anything to anyone. You can never dismiss ideas because they might open doors to make progress in other ways at other times.'

How do you know when a painting is finished? 'It's not about when you're finished with it. It's about when it's finished with you.'

Blacklock says wherever you find certainty, mastery is never present: 'Picasso may look certain, but he's not. He's taking a risk just like you are. He's just doing it more confidently.'

This is a barrier to free thinking in all walks. In politics you can never be a true member of the party if you're uncertain: 'That's probably why politicians are suspicious of diversity. They prefer certainty. And art is always about doubt. Absolute certainty is the enemy of art.'

I've worked with George for many years and often asked him to comment on business with his artist's eye. He can spot when a business has lost its creativity: 'It's a sign of complacency. This is normally a stage that precedes failure. Destruction is not the opposite of creativity. Complacency is.'

One thing he is clear about, is the health benefits of a creative career when compared to his peers: 'It's certainly easier for me to talk to younger people. Undoubtedly, it's made me healthier because it allows a continuing sense of playfulness. That's what you get from metaphor. It allows you to maintain your wit.'

Why don't people use metaphor all the time? 'Possibly, because we're afraid that it will indicate a lack of articulacy. Personally, I don't use metaphor because I'm as thick as two short planks', he says, laughing.

So, why are we deciding to do this in such a conventional manner? Good question.

Conclusion

So we can see, although universities are changing, they are not universally keeping pace with changing requirements. All colleges are not the same though and change can be made to happen. We cannot blame the products of the education system for this. It seems likely, though, that graduates in increasing numbers will continue to question the necessity or desirability of a degree if it leaves them underemployed and in debt before they even attempt to reach their potential. The pressures created by the system as it is have a direct negative effect on creativity. If students are stressed, worried and carrying more psychological problems than ever, they cannot apply some of the Creative Traits such as Dreaming, Releasing, Playing and Relaxing. Wasn't Oxford University supposed to be the city of dreaming spires?

The 'always on' environment and its effect

03

In this chapter, we look at how much the environment has changed and what effect the new communications media has on it. We'll see how social media creates a hypercritical addition to the hyper-connected world. For those in public life, whether at school, university, serving in politics or on public boards, we'll look at how the channels have made their lives harder. We will also see that whilst IT has caused productivity to continue to rise, there's also been a cost to creativity and well-being. Indeed, these two can hardly be separated. We've ended up with lives that are so productive and fast, they've driven us further from what makes us balanced and rounded individuals.

There's no greater argument for why education needs to change than the way the world is for a large number of people. How people work has changed massively in 20 years. Given the changing nature of technology, it's safe to assume the pace will continue. Educational pressure has been piled on top of social overload. Then, employers come along and place yet more demands on an already overloaded infrastructure.

Let's look at some of the biggest changes in the last 20 years:

1997	2017
Work is a place	Work is a process
Work is stable and steady	Work is fragile and volatile
Technocrats in the back office	Technocrats in the board room
Work is 9 to 5	Work is whenever
Work happens in the workplace	Work happens wherever
Careers were for the long-term	Flexibility is everything
National	International
Experience is valued	Youth is valued
Newspapers	Websites
Market research data	Big data
Apply with CV/email	LinkedIn profile
Suits	Anything
One-way conversations	Total engagement
Annual	Quarterly

Our work environment has changed beyond all recognition. The biggest changes have been the cycle time, the increasingly technical nature, the competitiveness and the fact that it follows us around. This new environment has been very good for employers and business (see Figure 3.1).

Figure 3.1 Labour productivity in the business sector – 1947 (Q1) to 2012 (Q1)

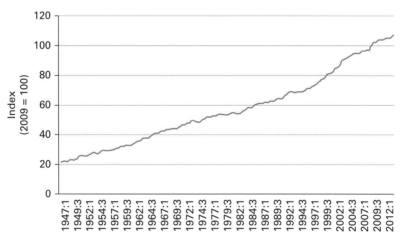

SOURCE US Bureau of Labor Statistics.

We analyse, compare and contrast more data than ever before. We compare year on year, month on month, department by department, country by country, etc. Our shareholders and employers are impatient and want measurable results. Because so much more *can* be measured, so much more *is* measured. This has led, in turn, to more and more requests for information and demands for attention. This data overload at work has been paralleled by the same process on social networks.

Most companies don't ban social media, so to the massive amount of more data the company imposes and requests, private networks must be overlaid. When people are under so much pressure to process information, the result is an unstoppable flow of data, an overloaded mind and consequently an analytical mindset. This has led to the phenomenon of people wanting to take mobile devices with them wherever they go, so they don't get left behind or 'miss out'. The constant bombardment of interruptions destroys and slows down the formation of ideas that could be vital to the process. This would be detrimental to well-rested minds but for the already distracted and time-deprived, work becomes an experience simply to be endured and minimized. When we dislike something so much, it's very difficult to get good at it. All competence follows preference.

This might be acceptable if it were not a chronic problem. Coping strategies do evolve, but there's no doubt that many feel overwhelmed. The cumulative effect of this over years becomes more profound. Graduates, who in many cases are deep in debt, who are not always the most psychologically stable, are then thrown into the world of work. Now some say that it's the graduates themselves who are at fault. You'll hear that 'They need to toughen up' or that 'They need to learn how to work'. That may be true but it ignores the environment they've been brought up in. They've been taught to pass exams, but in many cases not taught to talk to people.

Helayne Spivak is a former chief creative officer with many leading advertising agencies. She's created campaigns for Sears (Come See the Softer Side of Sears), Burger King, UPS, Club Med, Kraft, Kodak, Barneys New York and a US president, to name just a few. She's also written Super Bowl ads. So she knows a bit about creativity and education. She now spends time teaching at the Virginia Commonwealth University Brandcenter, a graduate programme which has won many awards for its creativity. Spivak identifies the lack of reading for pleasure as a problem: 'I used to binge-read like people binge-watch TV.'

One of the problems is that young people don't actually *speak* to each other. 'One told me that they thought that calling someone was rude. By sending a text the other person can deal with it in their own time.' They frequently want to talk in emojis, which Spivak describes as 'substitutes for humanity'.

Again, she says the output of the education system has been to produce people who are technically qualified, but lacking broader experience: 'They need to open themselves to the world. Read things they don't want to read. Study more history.' She points to a test that was done on a Texas campus where they asked who won the American Civil War and they struggled to answer. Their knowledge of contemporary TV shows, though, was excellent. Their thinking, she says, is: 'Fresh, but not deep.'

Could it be that the lack of actually speaking to people is part of the alienation and psychological problem? The Reverend Alasdair Coles says he makes progress by listening and trying to clarify what the person is saying. Frequently his advice is similar: 'Always talk to the people you trust. Share your concerns. Talk about what's good in your relationships.' This is a view also echoed by film director, Tony Palmer: 'Social media has been a catastrophe for the young. They're no longer reading, so they don't know what's been done before. This is why we're not seeing much originality.'

The social media environment has not only created a trivial environment. It's also created a vicious one, says Reverend Coles. People write things they would never say because of the 'disinhibition'. Sometimes this works in a good way – because of this loss of inhibition, some users may show more benign tendencies, including becoming more friendly, more willing to open up to others, and less guarded about emotions. But it's the bad behaviour which attracts the attention as internet-based commenters can frequently do or say as they wish, without fear of any kind of meaningful reprisal. In most internet forums, the worst kind of punishment is being banned from a particular site. In practice, however, this serves little use as the person can register using another username and continue the same behaviour as before.

It is difficult for creativity to exist in a blizzard of anonymous criticism. This is plaguing schools, universities and public life. Creativity, by its nature, is usually personally owned. Criticism in the age of social media is often anonymous. 'It's just become something you have to get used to', says one female politician. 'Where do you draw the line? Threats of sexual violence, rape, murder? Quite a few have just shut down some social channels to find that it comes back in official channels such as email.'

Psychologist John Suler calls this *toxic disinhibition*. Suler says there are six primary factors behind why people sometimes act radically differently on the internet from the way they do normally:

'You don't know me'

John Suler says that when a person remains anonymous, it provides a sense of protection that allows the user to move about without any kind of indication of identity or even distinguishing characteristics other than potentially a username. 'This kind of protection provides a meaningful release for people. They may feel free to say things they might otherwise be embarrassed by.'

'You can't see me'

Suler also says that because the internet provides a shield, a username or pseudonym may or may not have anything to do with the real person behind the keyboard. This allows for misrepresentation of a person's true self; online a male can pose as a female and vice versa, for example. The invisibility of the internet stops people reading standard social cues. Small changes in facial expression, tone of voice, aversion of eyes, etc, all have specific connotations in normal face-to-face interaction.

'See you later'

The asynchronous nature of the internet can also affect inhibitions because conversations do not happen in real time. It's therefore easier for someone to make a single post that might be considered personal, emotionally charged, or inflammatory and then 'run away'. In this way, the person achieves catharsis by 'voicing' their feelings, even if the audience is just as invisible.

'It's all in my head'

Lacking any kind of visual cue, the mind assigns characteristics and traits inserting imagined characteristics to the protagonist. The shadow of the thing becomes bigger than the thing itself. 'The user may construct an elaborate system of emotions, memories, and images; inserting the user and the person they are interacting with into a role-play that helps reinforce the "reality" of the person on the other end within the mind of the user.'

'It's just a game'

Because of the unreal environment, a feeling of escapism is produced. This is a way to throw off mundane concerns to address a specific need without having to worry about consequences. It seems that some people may see cyberspace as 'a kind of game where the normal rules of everyday interaction don't apply to them. In this way, the user is able to dissociate their online persona from the offline reality, effectively enabling that person to don that persona or shed it whenever they wish, simply by logging on or off.'

'Your rules don't apply here'

Suler points out that when online, a person's real status may not be known to others: 'If people cannot see the user, others have no way to know if the user is a head of state, a celebrity, or a regular private citizen.' This illustrates the fact that people can be reluctant to speak their minds directly in front of an authority figure. Fear of reprisal or disapproval previously inhibited a desire to speak out.

This has profound implications for the corporate environment because sites like Glass Door act as repositories for employees to describe their working environments, rate their boss and the firm. Some employees 'take this with a pinch of salt' but it is without doubt influential. These comments are made without any knowledge of the employer and it is highly unlikely for the reasons above that this feedback would be made in a face-to-face session. Put simply, exit interviews don't capture all the feedback.

One of the serious personal consequences of disinhibition is cyberbullying.

The website overcomebullying.org states that with 'the advent of modern communications such as email, chat, text messaging and mobile phones as well as the ability to publish online on websites, blogs and social networking sites such as Facebook and MySpace making their message instantly available to millions, the bully's reach and powers of social manipulation have been increased exponentially.'

The site says that bullies don't have to see their victims or answer for their actions. Cyberbullying may also include other offensive behaviours such as cyberstalking, revenge porn, and creating copycat accounts of others.

Some news sites benefit directly from this. The *Daily Mail* has become the largest online news site in the world, partly because of the entertainment provided by the online comment. For this reason, some have just chosen to quit sites like Twitter, including celebrities Kanye West, Miley Cyrus, Zayn Malik, Alec Baldwin and Adele. Numerous politicians have done the same.

Other organizations are trying to do something about this. Blogs like Stop Anonymous Online Comments claim that the anonymity granted to internet users leads to comments that are filled with exaggerations, outright lies, threats of violence and racism. The suggestion is that these sites have a responsibility not to foster an environment that tolerates, even encourages, comments and statements that tear at the fabric that holds our society together.

It's felt that the average internet user would just not make such comment without the cloak of anonymity.

The online disinhibition effect can also backfire on job security and future employment opportunities. According to the website thefacebook-fired.com, 16-year-old Kimberley Swann was fired from her job due to negative comments she made about her occupation on her Facebook page.

It's highly likely that as the technology develops, it will become increasingly difficult to avoid the consequences of illegal behaviour online. The FBI recently said that it had cracked an iPhone used by one of the gunmen in the recent San Bernardino terrorist shooting. It seems they had the help of an unnamed third party. Government officials did not go into detail about what was found on the phone.

The fact that the US Department of Justice was able to successfully access the phone without Apple's help is potentially bad news for the tech giant because it suggests Apple's encryption technology may not be as advanced as suggested.

In a statement, Apple said the case 'should have never been brought'. It reiterated its objection to the FBI's demand that the company build a backdoor into the iPhone, a step it said would have 'set a dangerous precedent'. However, Apple said it plans to continue to help police with other criminal investigations. For instance, the company currently provides police who have warrants access to customer iCloud accounts.

CASE STUDY: Set free only to be imprisoned again

Ilsa was a colleague of mine for many years. When she received her first Blackberry in 2002, the changes it wrought were initially liberating. 'At first, it was like being set free from my desk. I could easily impress clients by responding rapidly as the mails came in. But then as the volume of mail went up and everyone started to get mobile devices, I found it more problematic.'

Ilsa kept the device on at all times even at night, and found that she couldn't sleep if there was a flashing light indicating the presence of mail. 'As fast as I went I just couldn't keep up with the winking light. It was like being accused of not being on the ball.'

This behaviour can easily become obsessive. All people want to feel good at their job, but feeling that they are falling behind on processing information requests erodes this. In the company, as we rolled out these devices we saw them as a great utility – a service differential – but they came to dominate our lives. We started to feel rushed and to feel that there weren't enough hours in the day. The pace of the company accelerated.

Our experience was no different to many companies. People naturally rush when they feel short of time. This kind of condition, where one feels the need to rush without really having a reason, became known as Hurry Sickness, although we didn't know it then. This state of being seems like a normal adaptive mechanism to the busy world we live in today.

Ilsa's experience reflected this growing sense of obligation, becoming slave to the machine.

Let's look a little more at this condition and its effect on the individual.

In research reported by *Psychology Today* in 2013, it defined Hurry Sickness as: 'A behaviour pattern characterized by continual rushing and anxiousness; an overwhelming and continual sense of urgency. A malaise in which a person feels chronically short of time, and so tends to perform every task faster and to get flustered when encountering any kind of delay.'

According to Rosemary Sword and Dr Philip Zimbardo, writing in the magazine: 'We can try to sustain living at breakneck speed but sooner or later, physically, mentally and/or emotionally we fall apart. Our bodies – and minds – weren't meant to endure continual stress. Blood pressure spikes and eventually remains at an elevated level, hearts wear out, we become irritable and easily angered, and we get upset – sometimes to the point of weeping – from frustration and exhaustion.'

They listed some manifestations of the condition:

- Moving from one check-out line to another because it looks shorter/faster.
- Counting the cars in front and getting in the lane that has the least.
- Multitasking to the point of forgetting one of the tasks.
- Accidentally putting clothes on inside-out or backwards.
- Sleeping in daytime clothes to save time in the morning.

If it weren't so serious, it would be laughable. According to social psychologist Dr Robert Levine, in cities with the highest pace of life, men have the most coronary disease.

So this is a disease of the modern world. It wreaks havoc on the spirit, the mind and the body. Hurry Sickness can cause you chronic stress and many other health and emotional problems. This is exacerbated when you consider men sleep less than women (see Figure 3.2 overleaf).

Figure 3.2 Average sleep times per day, by age and sex

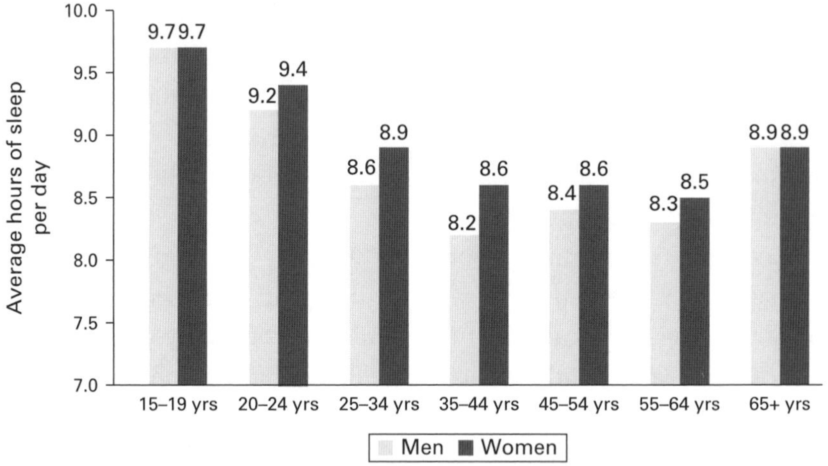

SOURCE US Bureau of Labor Statistics. American Time Use Survey.
NOTE Data includes all persons aged 15 and over. Data includes all days of the week and are annual averages for 2014.

So let's look at how the Hurry Sickness alters our brain processes. It changes our behavioural patterns on four main axes:

Physical

This is the most obvious dimension because it's usually when people get a physical problem that change is forced. One of the questions I've cheekily asked people is whether they've ever delayed going to the bathroom because of work. The surprising answer in most cases is 'Yes'. Again, this is laughable when considered, but it happens.

Perhaps the biggest and most obvious physical manifestation is sleep disruption. Because the body isn't physically active when processing the vast amounts of data, when the day stops, the mind doesn't. We'll cover this more later on, but one of the consequences of sleep deprivation is the production of ghrelin – the tiredness and hunger hormone. This is as a result of the brain interpreting the sleep disruption as a threat and commanding the body to seek out new resources in the form of fat, sugars and carbohydrates.

Emotional

The anxiety of not keeping up is not contained to the world of work because of mobile devices. Many people receive email and social updates on the same devices they use for work.

This creates the Fear Of Missing Out or FOMO. This is an apprehension that others might be having experiences from which one is excluded. It's characterized by 'a desire to stay continually connected with what others are doing'. In other words, FOMO perpetuates the fear of having made the wrong decision on how to spend time, as the alternatives can be seen and thus compared.

Rational (mental)

Rational problems should be easy to spot in someone suffering from Hurry Sickness (see above). We can see people juggling tasks, failing to meet deadlines, or looking as if they are unprepared. Some problems, though are more elusive – for instance, an unwillingness or inability to articulate verbally. The inability to concentrate may also be a key indicator.

Spiritual

This is perhaps the most elusive of all characteristics to spot. It's far more frequently experienced in the emotional dimension as frustration at a lack of inspiration and creativity. Other manifestations here are disorientation, confusion and amorality. Ironically, the spiritual deficit is most apparent when the individual gets centred and quiet enough to become aware of it.

We can map these axes as challenge dimensions (see Figure 3.3 below).

Figure 3.3 Axes of personal challenge

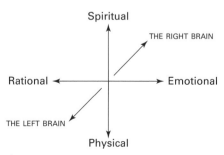

SOURCE LEWIS Rise Academy.

Overload places special emphasis on the bottom left quadrant. Unsurprisingly, balance is achieved with corrective action on the opposite quadrant. An example of this might be 'binge-watching' on box sets. The brain and balance crave a return to the balance (origin) of the axes. This can be what Russell Foster, Professor of Circadian Neuroscience at Oxford University, calls a 'homeostatic defence' or the ability of the body and brain to balance itself. The problem here is that the passionate never know where to stop, because they go on until they're exhausted. This is a typical entrepreneurial style and it can be difficult to work with such people.

Balance is near impossible to establish – however, recognizing the type of imbalance allows us to quickly apply the opposite response. Of course, some people just don't want the balance. Some people just love what they do so much that they want to do it all the time. Work is central to their lives and it defines them. Their work style is geared around lists and when they're immersed they can sometimes lose track of time. They sometimes even delay going to the toilet because they just wanted to get something finished. Their friends and family say they're always working and everyone who knows them considers them a workaholic. Psychologists have a name for these people – The Type A.

Understanding the Type A

Type A personality behaviour was first described by cardiologists Meyer Friedman and Ray Rosenman in the 1950s. After an eight year study of men aged 35–59, they estimated that Type A behaviour doubles the risk of coronary heart disease in otherwise healthy individuals. Subsequent analysis indicated that, although Type A personality is associated with the incidence of coronary heart disease, it does not seem to be a risk factor for mortality.

Type A individuals are ambitious, organized, highly status-conscious, sensitive, impatient, anxious, proactive, and concerned with time management. Type A personalities are often high-achievers that push themselves with deadlines and hate both delays and any lack of commitment. In short, these are the people that are 'always on'. When you email them, they take pride in responding immediately. They consider themselves to be hyper-productive. They are impatient and have limited attention spans. On the surface, they are high achievers, but tend to have long-term health risks.

Type As feel like everything in life is urgent. They feel like they should always be available. They even walk, eat, talk and drive fast. This means they can be difficult employees. They interrupt and they don't listen. You can see these people in the morning rush hour. They will be the ones doing make-up, taking calls and drinking coffee while shouting at the kids and driving. They have a pathological hatred of waiting in line for anything. These people never take a break and resting again is wasted time. This is what makes their creativity suffer. They don't allow time for ideas to incubate so their creativity tends to be fast and fresh, but ultimately shallow. This is classic tortoise and the hare territory.

Figure 3.4 Hurry Sickness curve

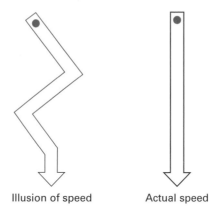

Illusion of speed   Actual speed

SOURCE LEWIS Rise Academy.

In Figure 3.4 above, the person is the dot on the line, feeling from their point of view that they are moving very fast. There is constantly changing scenery, frequent fads and changes of direction and, let's face it, even exhilaration.

Imagine being a dot moving down one of the lines above. The one on the left feels to be moving faster. On the other side, from their point of view, they're going more slowly. There is slowly changing scenery and no changes of direction, but undoubtedly the dot on the right will get there faster and more efficiently.

This is the essence of the philosophy in *Too Fast to Think*. By taking the time to think through the direction and process, less energy and time is expended and goals are achieved faster. Even though it feels slower.

The Type A

So there's always one, isn't there? The exception that proves the rule. Jacqueline de Rojas is talking to me from her home. It's unusual. How many people do you know that have a flip chart in their home? That's because she gets her best ideas when outside the office and her ideas are always visual: 'They're usually pictures and I need to draw them out immediately.'

Her background is also unusual. She's half Chinese and was brought up in a staunchly Catholic environment, so she felt like an outsider immediately. It made her want to break out into new horizons, so she decided to go to university in Germany: 'Survival is an interesting dynamic. I worked in male-dominated environments, so I realized that I couldn't smash the door in like all the Alphazillas around me. So I needed a different strategy to circumvent and create a better way.'

She thinks the hardship in her youth was key to making her more creative. She says that the imagination of the brain has a strange way of creating alternative approaches: 'You can't win in the long-term by putting your foot on people's throats. I wanted to build trust to play a long game. I discovered that process was my friend. I wanted to be consistently good.' She would always focus on *why* something was being done: 'We were trying to understand our customers' problems.'

She says it didn't always make her friends but: 'I didn't leave dead bodies around me like the other people. There will always be people that don't want to follow a process or engage in the process. You have to accept a 60 per cent fallout in transformational environments.'

She's clear that the leader is not the important one: 'It's not about the leader. It's always about the first follower. They're the ones that make the difference and allow you to create a movement. First followers are very different.'

And so is she. She runs marathons and enjoys other sports: 'The physical confidence is part of the mental confidence. Marathon running is 80 per cent mental, 20 per cent physical. You get physical reactions to mental blockages. Most of what constrains us is mental.'

There is always a price to leadership: 'I work myself like a dog sometimes. This just goes with women's territory. It's a lack of self-worth or a fear of failure. Women strive for perfection to such a degree that they don't want to fail and this misses the opportunity. It's important to be able to fail fast. It's still harder.'

One of the things she's had to work on is intolerance: 'Sometimes you need to give people space to be amazing. I don't need to be there to save them. Part of this is to put people in leadership positions before they're ready and give them coaches and mentors (these two are different things). In the past I might've fired someone for doing something stupid; now I give them time. I've learned that there's more than one route to success.'

This is what she does. She looks for alignment, especially with all players involved. This takes a lot of creativity: 'Being an outsider gives you more choices but you do have to be able to see them and then earn everything you get.'

Perhaps this explains her appetite for exploration. Was her upbringing a part of this? 'Yes. It made a huge difference. It was hard, but you have to look for the miracle and see what doors might open up. You also have to learn to hold out a hand to help other people. It's not that hard, but we seem to make it so.' So not typically Type A, after all.

Let's look at how moving too fast to think can be seen in the office environment.

The meeting

Many people complain about the number of meetings they have, because they feel they are interrupting an already badly interrupted day. This leaves people feeling resentful about the imposition of the additional workload they're likely to pick up as a result of the meeting. This means they seldom prepare as they should and seldom reflect on what was decided.

Meetings then can become 'the loudest voice is the dominant one' as people speak up loudly and quickly because they want the meeting over with. Much of this can be moderated by an enlightened chair. Some people's response to the shortage of time is to make all meetings shorter. This is Vanessa Brady's technique (see later) or make them meet standing up so they can't last long. This often creates the illusion of speed because people don't buy in. Meetings are there for all people to debate and decide on a course of action. This is fine, but, if all people are not unanimous, what looks like an efficient meeting can easily record decisions that simply fail at the implementation stage because of bureaucratic resistance.

This was sometimes the case with male-dominated meetings we had at LEWIS before we recognized the problem. They were typical of other organizations. There were frequently meetings which featured rapid, forthright, opinionated statements from men who make statements first, then use logic to back them up. The people that do this seldom ask other people for their opinions first. They don't gauge sentiment or objections. They normally wade right in. This is not leadership because it does not encourage other ideas. There's a saying that: 'If you're the leader and you're the smartest person in the room, then you're in the wrong room.' The leader's job is to make *everyone else* feel like they're the smartest person in the room.

Leaders in meetings should always speak last. In many meetings, though, the loudest voice will decide the course of action. Reticence or indecision can often be interpreted as approval, then a measure is quickly agreed and the meeting moves on. It's only much later that the decision fails to implement because it doesn't have the full support of those present. The leader doesn't look so smart and the meeting doesn't look so efficient now.

The greeting

Think about how you feel if your boss takes the time to come and say hello and enquire after your well-being. For a lot of people, this is much more than being about the transmission of information. It's more about what doesn't get said. Taking the time to say hello to people is not a luxury. It's essential for having personal as well as professional engagement. There's also an important creative element here. People who feel relaxed and part of a team are far more likely to contribute ideas without fear of criticism or failure. This culture comes straight from the top. What people see their boss doing (or being) is what they end up being like themselves.

Some people call this management by walking round. Others say it's vital for their research on gauging what they are being told by official representatives of an office. An experienced leader can soon sense problems with people if they can't make eye contact. Over the last three years I worked with a graduate called Emily who made a point of speaking whenever she saw me. This was not done in an obsequious type of way, but because she was just that type of genuine character. Not only did she advertise herself, but she showed that she was a great ambassador for a culture which encouraged her to treat her leader as just one of the team.

The status and hierarchies craved by many in management positions often unwittingly crush this natural openness of team structures. The lesson appears to be that if you want to encourage creativity in the workplace, get away from things that emphasize difference as much as possible. Incidentally, this does not mean that I choose to work in an open plan environment. I always retain an office for confidentiality and socializing. I do my real work outside the office in any case!

Office layouts

How offices are laid out can contribute enormously to outcomes. This is true of individual meetings as it is fixed seating. For instance, in a set piece meeting, it's seldom a good idea to put the two most senior people side by side. This just means that they spend their time talking, to the exclusion of the rest of the meeting. Senior people should always be placed at the extremities of a meeting.

Churchill said: 'First, we shape our buildings. Thereafter, they shape us.'

In a 2009 experiment, psychologists at the University of British Columbia, looked at how the colour of interior walls influence imagination. When people took tests in red rooms, they were better at skills that required accuracy and attention to detail, such as catching spelling mistakes or keeping random numbers in short-term memory. Apparently, this is because red is associated with danger, which makes them more alert and aware.

The colour blue, however, carried a completely different set of psychological benefits. While people in the blue group performed badly on short-term memory tasks, they did better on those requiring imagination, generating *twice* as many 'creative outputs' as those in the red condition. The colour of a wall doubled imaginative power.

Apparently, blue triggers associations with the sky and the sea. We think about expansive horizons, summer holidays and sandy beaches. This sort of mental relaxation makes it easier for us to dream and think of tangential associations. We're not thinking about what's right in front of us and we're more aware of the possibilities simmering in our imagination.

The psychologist Joan Meyers-Levy, at the Carlson School of Management, conducted an experiment that examined the relationship between ceiling height and thinking style. She demonstrated that, when people are in a low-ceilinged room, they are much quicker at solving anagrams involving confinement, such as 'bound', 'restrained' and 'restricted'. In contrast, people in high-ceilinged rooms excel at puzzles in which the answer touches on the theme of freedom, such as 'liberated' and 'unlimited'. According to Levy, this is because airy spaces prime us to feel free. Furthermore, Levy found that rooms with lofty ceilings lead people to engage in more abstract styles of thinking. Instead of focusing on the particulars of things, they're better able to zoom out and see what those things have in common.

The implication is that creativity works better in a more expansive space. Especially if it has blue walls...

The overachieving underachiever

'I never thought I was very clever. My parents were not educated. Even today, if I read a review of my work that's good, I don't believe it. I'm still trying to prove myself.' He has been published in 14 different languages and has been recently knighted. It's probably one of the best examples of mastery I've seen.

Professor Sir Cary Cooper was born in Boyle Heights, Los Angeles, to immigrant parents in 1940, but in an extraordinary career, he's ended up in leadership at Manchester Business School.

Suffice it to say, this is an unusual man. He's authored over 150 books. With the energy levels of a man half his age, he is both agile and modern in his approach. 'The drive is to prove that I'm up to it. This is also part fear for me.' His peer group, strangely, is full of lawyers. '80 per cent of them are lawyers. They're not enjoying life. They're doing what was expected of them, which was to become a doctor or a lawyer, rather than what they wanted to do.'

'My parents wanted structure for me. They wanted me to be a lawyer as well. My mother took me into the Bank of America and proudly told the desk clerk that her son was going to study law. Even when she found out I was going to be a pyschologist, she wanted me to be a "proper" doctor.'

Cary is what he calls an 'Industrial Social Worker'. 'I concentrate on what makes people happy at work. I like to translate the research into a common language so people can understand. I do an academic journal and 400 people read it. I write a book and 5,000 people buy it.'

'I get all my inspiration in the quiet moments. For me, I'm sitting on my tractor mowing the grass at my house. Either that, or I'm sitting on a train or an aeroplane. I consciously don't do my emails on the train. I want the time to myself.'

Even when he's working, he's playing. 'The vast majority of my time is fun. 70 per cent of what I do is having fun. I think that's why it works.'

Where are we going with mindfulness? 'If this was the world of cars, we're back in the 1960s.' He says the recession in 2008 changed everything: 'People got a lot of stuff. Flat screen TVs and 4x4s and then they lost everything. Then they asked whether they needed all this stuff. Oddly enough, I think we're entering a better age that's less materialistic.'

He relates one tale about a firm that had a long hours culture. They'd told Cary proudly that they had a nap room, so overworked people could get some sleep. Cary's response was scathing: 'This is tantamount to surrender. They expected to be congratulated for having something which only served to confirm what a terrible culture they had. Working environments must evolve into relaxed, aesthetically pleasing, biophilic, fun places.'

'I want to change the way people treat other people. I guess that comes from being an outsider. I know what it's like to be the wrong side of life.'

Cary's world now includes politicians, business people, academics and mental health charities. 'I've never felt uncomfortable being different. I guess that's why I find it easy to move among different people. I never use the knighthood and feel uncomfortable when people refer to it.'

'Is work culture dictated by capital structure? Does the separation of capital from deployment fundamentally change the culture of firms? The only company that survived the recession without lay-offs in the UK and continued to grow was John Lewis Partnership, an employee-owned business.'

'Scientists aren't like other people. If musicians or authors had never been born, then their unique music would be lost. Another scientist could easily come along and discover what I've discovered, so I need to move quickly. I'm bent on changing people's view of the world. In that respect, science is very similar to art.'

'Science needs art because scientists need artists' metaphors to explain what they're doing. Scientists are right at the edge of the darkness illuminating what's out there. We can't go into the future with trepidation. It must be done in playfulness.'

Conclusion

So we can see how the world we live in has been changed. Some business environments have recognized this and tried to change the physical surroundings to change some of the behaviour. It's OK to have an office that allows the Creative Traits of Dreaming, Releasing, Playing and Relaxing. All of these help individuals to Engage and focus. It's not just a matter of short-term productivity. Without long-term creativity, you risk well-being and long-term productivity. There are clearly some types of personality more at risk from overload than others. We can see the effects of left-brain process rationality and how it's applied in some business situations. We can see how this has affected the psychology and behaviour. Next we look at the physical provenance of the behaviour – the biology of the brain itself.

Your brain and   04
how to use it

In this chapter, we look at the biology of the brain, at the structures and what it needs to be healthy. Unless we understand this, we can't make it perform to the best of its ability. We also see how the plasticity of the brain allows it to physically change depending on the type of tasks we perform. We look at the two basic intellectual processes the brain performs of reductionism and conceptualization. We also look at some of the myths that have persisted about how the brain works. Chief among these is whether the left brain and right brain perform different tasks. We see how they deploy in the business context and how we tend to lead with our critical faculties. We look at what goes wrong when the balance of the brain is disturbed and introduce the concept of Flow and how it can be used for greater sustainability. In this chapter, you'll learn how to be more successful in presentation, interviews and business communications by understanding the disadvantages of only thinking in an analytical way.

So that's the environment that many of us are in – always on and highly pressurized. To understand the ramifications of this, we need to look more closely at ourselves. How much do you know about your own brain? Some of these facts may help you understand more. The weight of the human brain is about 3 lb and is made up of 75 per cent water – this is the reason that dehydration is a major problem for cognitive processes. It is also the fattest organ in the body and may consist of at least 60 per cent fat. It uses 20 per cent of the total oxygen and blood circulating in your body. For this reason, exercise is vital to cognitive processes, as is food. A study of 1 million students in the New York City school system showed that students who ate lunches that did not include artificial flavours, preservatives and dyes did 14 per cent better on IQ tests than students who ate lunches with these additives. In the March 2003 edition of *Discover* magazine, a report describes how people in a seven-year study who ate seafood at least once a week had a 30 per cent lower occurrence of dementia.

That the physical brain needs nutrients should come as little surprise, but in order to be healthy it needs something less obvious – it needs other people's input to learn and develop. Neuroscientist David Eagleman, in his book *Incognito: The Secret Lives of the Brain*, says that the ability to empathize with others is vital to shared experience: 'It's why we can go to a horror movie and feel the same terror as the people in the film. Empathy is a classically right-brained skill.' Eagleman means that this is the brain processing illogical emotions such as faith, trust and belief.

Of course, all brains are individual and each perceives information in a different way. The ways two brains can interpret the same information can differ wildly depending on age, cultural or experiential behaviour.

Empathy and botox

Just looking at another person smiling can make us smile and feel good – how does this work? Well, it seems that humans have a deep natural ability to mirror other people. In communications training with a hundred people over the last few years, I've seen this characteristic first hand. What you put into people is what you get out. If you approach them in a calm and respectful way, the subject will be calm and respectful. This is most important when dealing with inexperienced creatives, because they can be more fragile. Experienced creatives are more used to having ideas shot down at the point of conception.

In the most telling piece of research, Eagleman relates a group of subjects that had been given Botox as part of a cosmetic surgery procedure. They were asked to look at pictures of people smiling. No surprise that this group's facial muscles didn't respond to the smiling pictures. They had been given Botox, after all. But what's really surprising, is that when asked to write down the emotions they were seeing, they more frequently got them wrong. Their muscles were so deadened that not only were they unable to manifest emotion, but they also had no feeling in these muscles to allow them to autonomically read emotions in others. This suggests that we rely upon the interpretation of our own facial muscles to interpret behaviour in others.

This highlights that empathy in brain health and well-being cannot be taken for granted. It's important in both creative provenance and well-being for the individual and team. Human contact is a vital way of maintaining neural health. In a vacuum, you can lose your sense of self. When people are placed in solitary confinement, they start to become like caged animals, but this stage dissipates and they start to become more passive and they report their life slowing down. People released from solitary confinement frequently suffer post-traumatic stress disorder.

The brain is capable of sustained and extraordinary feats of creativity, if we understand its requirements. The structure of the brain is therefore worth further investigation. There are physically two hemispheres to the brain. What's not widely understood is how physically separate these halves are. They are almost completely separate organs, connected together by a structure called the corpus callosum. (Neuroscientist Jill Bolte Taylor's TED video illustrates this graphically.)

According to psychiatrist Iain McGilchrist, the relative size of the corpus callosum to the volume of the hemispheres has been shrinking with evolution. The main function of the corpus callosum is to inhibit the other hemisphere. McGilchrist says: 'Something very important is going on here about keeping things apart.' It used to be thought that the two sides did very different things – that typically the left side did all the comparison, contrasting and analysis and the right side did all the illogical stuff – faith, love, belief, trust, belonging, etc. The truth is more complex. McGilchrist again: 'If I had to sum it all up, I'd get away from all those old things we used to say – reason and imagination (for left and right). For reason, you need both hemispheres. For imagination, you need both hemispheres.'

Where did this notion come from?

The right brain, left brain theory originated in the work of Roger Sperry, who was awarded the Nobel Prize in 1981. While studying the effects of epilepsy, he discovered that cutting the corpus callosum could reduce or eliminate seizures. The problem, though, was that these patients also experienced other problems after the operation. For example, many split-brain patients found themselves unable to name objects that were processed by the right side of the brain but were able to name objects that were processed by the left side of the brain. Otherwise, they functioned normally.

Based on this information, Sperry suggested that language was controlled by the left side of the brain. There's no doubt that the left side of the brain tends to control many aspects of language and logic, while the right side tends to handle spatial information and visual comprehension.

Later discoveries showed the brain is not nearly as dichotomous as once thought. For example, recent research has shown that abilities in subjects such as maths are strongest when both halves of the brain work together. Today, neuroscientists know that the two sides of the brain collaborate to perform a broad variety of tasks and that the two hemispheres communicate through the corpus callosum.

A bit more complex than just left and right

It's quite possible for the brain to work almost simultaneously on the physical left and right sides, but, no matter how split the activity becomes, they still work together. When looking at an MRI brain scan in real time, it's clear that both sides of the brain are lighting up simultaneously. Science writer Carl Zimmer wrote about this in an article for *Discover* magazine. He says that the notion of a left-brain and a right-brain process doesn't really capture their intimate working relationship: 'The left hemisphere specializes in picking out the sounds that form words and working out the syntax of the phrase, for example, but it does not have a monopoly on language processing. The right hemisphere is more sensitive to the emotional features of language, tuning in to the slow rhythms of speech that carry intonation and stress.' So it's really a misconception that these two hemispheres of the brain do different tasks. There are some tasks which are performed on either side, but the physical processing sometimes flashes from one side to the other as they act in concert.

Processes rather than hemispheres?

If we can get away from the anatomy of the brain, we can definitely say there are two directions of travel or processes for thinking. We can analyse something. We can reduce it down into its constituent parts, then analyse those parts further. Or we can do the opposite. But what is the opposite of analysis? Is it conceptualizing? Is it 'not analysing' – not doing anything? It's clear both of these directions exist, so in a need for simplification, they have become known as left-brain thinking and right-brain thinking. It's not based in the right-hand side or left-hand side – it's a discrete process which is carried out by BOTH sides of the brain simultaneously.

The right-brain process

According to the left brain, right brain theory, the right-brain process excels at expressive and creative tasks. Some of the abilities popularly associated with the right-brain process include:

- recognizing faces;
- expressing emotions;
- music;
- reading emotions;
- colour;
- images;
- intuition;
- creativity.

The left-brain process

The left-brain process is considered to be best at tasks that involve logic, language, and analytical thinking. The left-brain process is described as being better at:

- language;
- logic;
- critical thinking;
- numbers;
- reasoning.

We also know that the different hemispheres control opposite sides of the body. Typically, the majority of humans are right-handed, but there are few convincing reasons for this. Could it be that the dominance of the left brain is a factor?

In the early part of my life I did a lot of manual work. I worked on a farm, in factories and in car and motorbike shops. Later in my life after going to university, I worked with highly educated people. Some you might even describe as intellectuals. I noticed the body language between educated and so-called 'uneducated' was profound. When I worked in a factory my colleagues would seldom cross their legs. There was a way that educated people sat and stood. They would frequently cross their legs. They would fold their arms. They would frequently touch their face.

Could it be that the more educated people are, the more left-brained they become? Worse, could it be that this mental imbalance was echoed by a physical separation which the body sought to balance? Examples of this could be the endless hair-ruffling, face-touching, hand-clasping, leg-crossing and arm-folding that educated people frequently perform.

A further illustration is the 'Hand Clasp Test'. Clasp your hands together. Which thumb is on top? If it's the left thumb, you're protecting your right thumb which indicates that the right brain is dominant and you have a tendency to be more conceptual and empathetic. The other way around suggests you are more analytical. Now this doesn't mean that you are either Picasso or a Dalek, but it may be useful when building a bigger picture.

Another test that challenges the processes is in colours and words. Think of the word BLUE in a red font or vice versa? Try it. How comfortable does it feel?

We know definitely that both the left and right brain perform different tasks. It's clear from the work by Jared A Nielsen, Brandon A Zielinski, Michael A Ferguson, Janet E Lainhart and Jeffrey S Anderson that each hemisphere does not exclusively perform creative or analytical tasks (from 'An evaluation of the left-brain vs right-brain hypothesis with resting state functional connectivity magnetic resonance imaging, *PLOS ONE*, Volume 8, Issue 8).

It's clear though that the creative and analytical processes are quite distinct, irrespective of what part of the brain they are performed in. We also know from Dr Jill Bolte Taylor's work that damage to one side can cause great imbalance to the processing capabilities. Her book *My Stroke of Insight* describes what happened. One morning, a blood vessel in her brain exploded. As a brain scientist, she realized she had a ringside seat to her own stroke. She watched as her brain functions shut down one by one. This included motion, speech, memory and self-awareness. Amazed to find herself alive, Taylor spent eight years recovering her ability to think, walk and talk. She has become a spokesperson for stroke recovery and for the possibility of coming back from brain injury stronger than before. In her case, although the stroke damaged the left side of her brain, her recovery unleashed a torrent of creative energy from the right.

Her experience was useful because it allowed her to mix scientific with the anecdotal observations to show brain biology in real-time. As a neuroscientist, there's no doubt that Taylor experienced both an analytical view of the world plus a holistic one during her extraordinary episode. The narration though has all the more credibility because of her scientific background. One wonders whether this would have been considered so credible had she been an artist or musician.

This does illustrate one of the problems of exploring this area. Any discussion of the merits of the right-brain process among highly left-brained people is going to be immediately challenged with logic and analysis, but hey, you can't be a prophet in your own land. Often, the very people that pour scorn on the idea of the right-brain process are those who salve the ends of their working days with walking, theatre, music and alcohol.

What you are capable of

This is perhaps one of the most surprising areas of brain behaviour for good and bad. It seems the brain is capable of remarkable detachment as well as attachment. There are several instances of this. Nazi behaviour during the Holocaust is well documented. In the 1960s, Yale University psychologist Stanley Milgram conducted an experiment on the obedience to authority figures. He measured the willingness of study participants, mainly students from Yale, to obey an authority figure who instructed them to perform acts conflicting with their personal conscience. The experiment found, unexpectedly, that a high proportion of people were prepared to obey, albeit unwillingly, even if apparently causing serious injury and distress. Milgram devised his study to answer the popular question at that particular time: 'Could it be that millions of Nazi accomplices in the Holocaust were just following orders?' 'We need to understand genocide as a neural phenomenon', says Eagleman ominously. You can make people murder others by simply telling them to follow orders.

The impact of overload on the structures

We know information overload specifically forces greater left-brain process centricity. This is where the compare, contrast and analyse functions are in full deployment. The persistence of this state has profound behavioural implications as the qualities of the left-brain process become over-employed and hyper-developed.

This looks like someone who is obsessed with details, critique, complaint, anxiety and worry. The qualities of the illogical right-brain process – trust, faith, hope, belief, belonging and optimism – are consequently hyper-diminished.

Although there is still debate about the tasks actually performed by the two physical sides of the brain, there is consensus on one issue – the brain is profoundly divided between left and right hemispheres. We know, for instance, that the left side of the brain is associated with the right-hand side of the body and vice versa. This is especially true of the ocular systems. Information from the left eye is processed by the right hemisphere. We also know that both sides are needed for a reason, because the two sides do different things. The way the processes are deployed, though, is worth understanding.

We know the brain responds to any prolonged stimulus. It devotes resources to growing itself wherever it's used most. In the case of London taxi drivers, this has been shown to have a direct impact on the size and shape of the brain. When we devote more resources to 'now' and less to planning or remembering, we become obsessed with the short-term. In research funded by the Wellcome Trust, 'the Knowledge' – the complex layout of central London's 25,000 streets and places of interest – was shown to cause structural changes in the brain and memory in the city's taxi drivers. The study supports the evidence that learning can change the structure of the brain, offering encouragement for lifelong learning and the potential for rehabilitation after brain damage.

Led by Professor Eleanor Maguire from the Wellcome Trust Centre for Neuroimaging at University College London, the research showed 'a greater volume of grey matter – the nerve cells in the brain where processing takes place – in an area known as the posterior hippocampus and less in the anterior hippocampus relative to non-taxi drivers. The studies also showed that although taxi drivers displayed better memory for London-based information, they showed poorer learning and memory on other memory tasks involving visual information, suggesting that there might be a price to pay for acquiring the Knowledge. The research suggested that structural brain differences may have been acquired through the experience of navigating and to accommodate the internal representation of London.'

The method for this was interesting in its own right. Professor Maguire and colleague Dr Katherine Woollett researched 79 taxi drivers and 31 controls (non-taxi drivers), taking snapshots of their brain structure over time using MRI scans and studying performance on memory tasks. Only 39 passed and went on to qualify as taxi drivers, giving the researchers the opportunity to divide the volunteers into: those that passed, those that trained but did not pass, and the controls who never trained. The researchers examined the structure of the brains at the start of the study, before any of the trainees had started. They found no differences in the structures of the hippocampus between the groups, and all groups performed equally well on the memory tasks. A few years later, when the trainees had either passed the test or failed, the researchers again looked at the brain structures. This time, they found significant differences in the hippocampus – those that qualified had a greater volume of grey matter than they had before they started their training. This change was not found in those who failed to qualify or in the control groups.

On memory, both qualified and non-qualified trainees were better at tasks involving London landmarks than the control group. However, the qualified trainees were worse at other tasks, such as recalling complex visual information.

The research shows something interesting. The human brain remains malleable, even in adult life, allowing it to physically adapt when we learn new skills. By following the trainee taxi drivers over time, Maguire saw directly within individuals how the structure of the hippocampus changed. This offers encouragement for adults who want to learn new skills later in life.

In the research paper, Maguire and Woollett speculated on the biological mechanisms that may underpin the changes to the brain. One theory suggests that there is an increase in the rate at which new nerve cells are generated and survive. The hippocampus is one of the few brain areas where the birth of new nerve cells is known to take place. Alternatively, it could be that the synapses, or connections, between existing nerve cells grew stronger in the trainees who qualified. So the brain actually grows and develops differently according to the way it's used. The implication is clear – the more you do something, the better you get, because your brain not only opens new neural pathways, it physically adapts to its functions. This is also not counting other physical effects such as muscle growth. The brain also grows to accommodate information overload and creates more resources to cope. This is both good news and bad. If the brain develops physical resources to cope with overload then it's not strengthening its ability to conceptualize and creatively think. This capability like all others, needs to be practised and developed.

The left-brain process

There's little doubt that the left-brain process exists as far as the 4 Cs of its processes are concerned: the convergent, the committed, the concentrated and the critical faculties. This is what we referred to before as the tendency to Compare, Contract and Analyse. These are highly developed in fresh graduates, sometimes to their detriment.

CASE STUDY: Flavio

Flavio was a delegate at Rise. His line managers had sent him with the specific guidance that 'he overanalyses everything'. Sure enough, as soon as the course began, Flavio questioned everything – Why was the course designed in this way? Why was the team structure the way it was? How was the course to be marked? The questions were incessant.

Flavio was experienced, knowledgeable and committed to the task, but the reliance on logic was not motivating for his team or anyone around him. He was an impressive leader – though perhaps in the way that the character Spock is from *Star Trek*. Nonetheless, Flavio could also be charming and funny when he was not working. It's just that as soon as work began, he switched formally and reverted.

Rise involves a group painting exercise where Flavio had even cornered off his own section of the painting so he could concentrate on 'his part'.

Funnily enough, it's usually the most sceptical 'left-brain' thinkers that benefit from Rise. It's not something you can tell people – they have to experience it.

Although the course did not cure Flavio of his analytical tendency, it at least made him aware of it and occasionally caused him to laugh at it. He began to call it 'the beast' and started to make allowances for it. This allowed Flavio to make allowances and corrections for what had been, up to that point, an unconscious problem blocking creativity in both himself and in others.

The right-brain process

The right-brain processes are also clear as per McGilchrist – these are the divergent, the synthetic, the surrendered, the sense of absence. These behavioural processes are clear and verifiable, but the anatomical analysis again, does not appear to support the processing in the physical right brain.

We need to refer to neuroscience again here. Professor Russell Foster: 'The idea is not generally supported by the neuroscience community. I do think it's a useful metaphor though which is probably why it became so popular – but the idea that we use one side of the brain more than the other in everyday life – and that "left-hand users" are analytical vs "right-hand users" are more intuitive and artistic is probably incorrect.'

The myth is thought to stem from social stigmatization of left-handed people and the misunderstood Nobel Prize-winning research project put together by Roger Sperry.

So the main conclusion is that the brain is really two completely separate structures which do completely separate things. The physical left hemisphere doesn't do all the analytics. The right hemisphere doesn't do all the belief and faith. The two sides share the process BUT the processes themselves are identifiable and discrete.

As Sperry himself summed it up: 'The great pleasure and feeling in my right brain is more than my left brain can find the words to tell you.'

CASE STUDY: Anika

Anika was known to be a creative. She was frequently late for meetings, her desk was a mess and some days she just couldn't function. The thing is though, on her day, she could be better than anyone by turns lucid, logical, charming, organized, visionary and dependable. I asked her why she felt she had this range: 'I've always been moody and unable to maintain consistency', she told me. 'It's not that I don't want to be. It's just that I've never mastered it.'

Anika's creativity was beyond doubt, but it was clear that she put herself under a great deal of pressure, often waiting until a deadline approached before delivering. It was clear to me that the barrier to her sustained creativity was not a mental, but a physical one.

There are limits to the places you can go as an employer and a coach. You have to ask permission. We'll hear more from an expert management coach later, but building trust is particularly important (something also referred to by George Zambellas, the former head of the Royal Navy who we'll hear from later).

In this case, I asked whether Anika would mind if I reviewed her diet. She accepted and kept a food diary for a short time. The results were clear. Although a vegetarian, Anika was sustaining her entire output with caffeine and carbohydrates allied to virtually no exercise. She was jacking herself up in the morning to get going, then crashing mid-morning then eating cookies, missing lunch and then into chocolate in the afternoon followed by a drink (or several) after work.

Sometimes it's just not enough to look at the intellectual processes, you have to look wider. In this case, the creative problem was a subset of the physical one.

I introduced Anika to an old text, *Food Combining for Health: Get Fit with Foods That Don't Fight* by Doris Grant and Jean Joice.

Over 50 years ago, Dr William Hay concluded that the body uses acids to digest proteins and alkalis to digest carbohydrates and starches. If they are both eaten separately, the theory runs, they are digested faster at the optimum level of pH. If they are mixed, the pH levels in the stomach are suboptimal for both. This means that food leaves the stomach undigested to be dumped into the next stages still fermenting and unprocessed. The simple diet involves little change in the main inputs, just the combinations. So bread can be had with soup, fish, beef or chicken with salad, but not with potatoes.

Some believe that the isolation of the starches can be done by colour. Potatoes, pasta and bread are all white and and break down into sugars. Reducing these can improve digestive performance and cut calorie intake.

Hay was a New York doctor, author and lecturer on health. A traditional physician for the first 16 years of his career, he introduced the world to food combining and ran a successful sanatorium. He spent 16 years in regular medicine and surgery, specializing in the latter. He later discovered he had Bright's disease, and was unable to cure it using the medical methods of the time. This led him to find alternative methods to rid himself of disease. He came up with the concept of food combining (also known as the Hay diet) – the idea that certain foods require an acid pH environment in digestion, and other foods require an alkaline pH environment, and that both cannot take place at the same time, in the same environment.

Hay observed that mixing the two might lead to painful indigestion and more serious problems such as ulcers, allergies and obesity. Though criticized at the time, the Hay System has been supported by more recent research such as that done by Dr Gerald Reaven on insulin resistance, and provides essentially the healthy, wholefood diet of mostly alkali-forming foods such as fruits, green vegetables, and salads advocated by many leading nutritionists today. I chose this book for Anika because the end point is essentially a healthy vegetarian dietary regime.

The book shows how to separate incompatible foods and explains how the Hay System alleviates the symptoms of chronic diseases such as arthritis and diabetes, while increasing energy and well-being in those without specific health problems. The effect of diet on Anika was almost instant. A lot of her symptoms disappeared and she became much more even-tempered. She also reported that her energy levels and skin improved and the Irritable Bowel Syndrome which plagued her had improved dramatically.

The alarming conclusion that the neuroscience suggests is that the two sides of the brain are really quite separate and, although they work in unison, they are really self-contained.

A scientist at the University of Utah, Jeffrey Anderson, took this further. He researched more than a thousand people's brains to compare how different sides operate. He told *BBC Trending* that his research has confirmed that the left-right, creative-logic dichotomy is simply a myth. He said: 'It is certainly the case that some people have more methodological, logical cognitive styles, and others more uninhibited, spontaneous styles. However, this has nothing to do on any level with the different functions of the [brain's] left and right hemispheres.' So Anderson says that, while the brain processes are recognizable and universal, the brain biology does not support the idea that these processes reside in any one place. One answer to where the whole left brain/right brain idea comes from might be the left-brain process itself. It prefers simplistic 'either/or' binaries through which to see the world.

Are you confused yet? You should be. Your left-brain process is trying to digest all the logical information, while your right-brain process just intuits that it's believable! The main reason for understanding the science here is to overcome the roadblock that these models of thinking run into – for example, there can't be a left- or right-brain process because they don't happen in the left or right brain. Quite the contrary; one of the big problems here is you're subjecting intuition to rational scrutiny. No wonder it's confusing!

The left and right in history and culture

Another reason could be the stigma associated with left sides and left-handedness. Historically, it was not uncommon for children to be punished if they wrote with their left hand instead of their right one, due to social stigma of the unknown which was often affirmed through religious beliefs. In the English language, the word 'left' derives from the Anglo-Saxon for 'weak' – *lyft*.

It gets worse. The Latin for right is *dexter*, where we get the word dexterous or skilful. The Latin word for left (*sinister*) was used in augury (omens portending misfortune) in the sense of 'unlucky, un-favourable'. Thus, sinister acquired a sense of harmful, unfavourable or adverse.

The right-hand side is quite important in culture. The British drive on the left because horsemen and carriages would always pass on the left to keep the stronger right arm free to use a sword. The Vikings when navigating used the 'steerboard' always on the right, controlled by their stronger arm. This is where we get the word star-board. Hence, ships are usually docked on their left side, the port side. Pilots always sit on the left-hand side of the cockpit to keep their right arm free to interact and so they can see the runway out of their left-hand side window. Most traffic patterns at airports are left-hand circuits.

Anderson again: 'It's absolutely true that some brain functions occur in one or the other side of the brain. Language tends to be on the left, attention more on the right. But people don't tend to have a stronger left- or right-sided brain network. It seems to be determined more connection by connection.' Jared Nielsen was a student that worked on the research as part of his coursework. He said that everyone should understand the personality types associated with the terminology 'left-brained' and 'right-brained' and how they relate to him or her personally. The problem, he said, was that 'we just don't see patterns where the whole left-brain network is more connected or the whole right-brain network is more connected in some people. It may be that personality types have nothing to do with one hemisphere being more active, stronger, or more connected.'

So is the left brain, right brain a dead end?

Even though the MRI scans of the left and right hemispheres of the brain done by Nielsen *et al* do not yield the evidence for physical separation of the thought patterns, the processes themselves remain valid. Even if there is an alternating physical location for the processes, this in no way invalidates the taxonomy of the convergent, reductionist thinking juxtaposed with the divergent and synthetic processes.

Perhaps the problem with creativity is that it works in the same way, drawing upon both sides of the physical brain, but for different tasks. The rule appears to be that the most resistant to right-brain thinking processes are the left-brained process people, but they are also often the ones that become the most evangelical about the epiphany or breakthrough. Sometimes, if people like Flavio don't believe that there is an equal and opposite process from convergence called divergence, then the pursuit of alternatives quickly becomes a dead end.

Let's look at how we interact and exchange ideas. For this we can use the example of the job interview, although the process repeats at any time when meeting for the first time.

The awkward interview

Ever sat in an interview where you've made your mind up about a candidate in the first 10 minutes then had to go along for a decent amount of time to complete the session? This normally happens because the candidate inadvertently makes you notice something repeatedly. What's the first thing you notice about a candidate? Would you notice a poor handshake? How about sweat patches? Or a lack of eye contact? Whether you make a value judgement about any of these things, the fact is you noticed. As soon as you notice, you are in analytical mode and the compare–contrast–analyse functions are switched on. We are innately cautious. We deploy our left-brain processes first. This is a bit like the sleeping dragon. Once it's awake, it can be a terrible thing. More successful interview candidates creep past the sleeping dragon by being careful to get through the first 10 minutes to allow the left brain to scan and not see anything dangerous. This first phase is what psychologists call empathy. When politicians speak they report something similar. 'I always try to get the audience on my side in the first 10 minutes', says one UK Government Cabinet minister. 'You have to tell them first how special they are', says another.

Salespeople are often taught to create empathy with the old AIDA model:

Awareness

Interest

Desire

Action

Have you heard about the latest pen from x? Here try this and see how it fits in your hand. Can you see yourself signing a contract for your new car with this? How would you like to take this forward?

The hypnotist talks about:

- empathy;
- rapport;
- control.

Pick an armchair to sit in. Relax, sit back and get comfortable. Take a few deep breaths and let yourself completely relax. Now let yourself sink into the chair and close your eyes. Feel yourself slowing down as you begin to relax completely. Just concentrate on your breathing. As you slow down, let all thoughts of anxiety go and be at peace. And as you relax and feel more comfortable, concentrate on each breath. Breathe deeply and relax. Now as you relax and let everything go...

Still there? Good.

These techniques revolve around calming the left-brain process, so the right-brain process – belief, trust, belonging and faith – can come through. The working of the left- and right-brain processes here are particularly interesting. When we're trying to persuade people, we need to be aware of how the mind works. In an interview situation, the initial deployment is always with the left-brain process. I hasten to add, there are strict rules concerning discrimination and these are not being questioned here.

Let's take for example Carl. He's a fresh design graduate coming for an interview. He's not smiling and is clearly nervous. His hand-shake is clumsy and clammy. Carl is wearing chinos and a shirt with a jacket. His shoes are shined. He looks a little bit smarter (and more awkward) than most people in your office. But he's wearing white socks. Would you notice? If you did, would it make you more or less likely to offer him a job? No matter. Carl takes his suit jacket off and, because of his nerves, has quite large sweat patches under his arms. Would you notice? If you did, would it make you more or less likely to offer him a job? No matter. His shirt is a short-sleeved shirt and you notice he has a swastika tattoo on the back of his right hand. Would you notice? If you did, would it make you more or less likely to offer him a job? No matter. Carl smiles nervously and you say: 'Let me start off by telling you a little about the role.' Now, whatever your conclusions about Carl, the point here is that you *noticed* these things and every time you did, it became just that little bit harder for your right-brain process to deploy because the left-brain process was in its way. You can't consider whether Carl belongs in your office or whether you believe and trust him, when your brain is occupied by his socks, sweat patches or tattoos. Consciously, of course, you may be fine with sweat patches. And that all happened within the first minute. So there are a number of questions this raises.

What's the first thing someone would notice about you when meeting *you* for the first time? How often do you take time to introduce your-self properly and get someone on your side before you hit them with an idea? Are you smiling at them?

If we change the above situation and now Carl has read *Too Fast To Think* – he is now dressed similarly to the other people in your office. He knows that he needs to establish empathy. He doesn't look unnaturally smart and the sweat patches and tattoo are gone. He sits down at your invitation, smiles and says: 'Hello, I'm Carl. How would you like to start? Shall I show you some of my work, or would you like to tell me a little more about the role?'

The left-brain process kicks into life as soon as you meet someone new. If, after the first five minutes it meets with no evidence of contrast or concern, it presses on. If, after another 10 minutes, it's still the same, it relaxes further. If it then finds qualities it likes or aspires to have – empathy, friendliness, openness – it proceeds to respond with the same. It's often said – what you put in is what you get out.

But we have to remember that our ideas are often rejected or accepted before we get beyond the first 10 minutes of presenting them, because of the power of other people's left-brain processes. This is as true in a presentation as when in an interview.

In Malcolm Gladwell's book *Blink: The Power of Thinking Without Thinking* he talks about the power of first impressions. He also says that it can sometimes be better to trust the subconscious mind rather than rely on deliberation and detail.

The boring presentation

The need for simplicity in communications is paramount and this is not just for efficiency or accuracy. It's also because Millennials have the lowest attention span of all. They're not impressed by clip art on PowerPoint and they expect presentations to be natural, lively, interactive, unpredictable and unscripted. The left-brain process has a thick carapace. They have high expectations.

Now some people are concerned about not being too spontaneous in a social media environment, just in case something gets taken out of context or someone says something dumb. But which is worse – being so dull that no one wants to share, or people sharing a mistake that makes them comment about what you said? On balance, take the risk, make a mistake and learn from it.

Many presentations become interesting because something happens and the speaker has to respond spontaneously. This can provide humour which bounces people into their right-brain process. One of the best ways to ensure this is to speak without notes (see Appendices). Another way is to keep simplifying. As Henry David Thoreau said: 'Our lives are frittered away by detail; simplify, simplify. Concentrate on a small number of things and do them well. Is this relevant? Everything is too long.'

One thing is clear – your audience is approaching you with their left-brain process well and truly engaged, so you'd better be prepared.

When things go wrong: the link between creativity, mental illness and depression

Irrespective of the neuroscience, creativity is associated with depression. We'll hear more from author Elizabeth Gilbert on this later, but high levels of creativity are often associated with mental health problems. The notion of 'suffering for one's art' is ingrained.

Writing in *The Guardian*, Science Editor Ian Sample said: 'The notion of the tortured artist is a stubborn meme. Creativity, it states, is fuelled by the demons that artists wrestle in their darkest hours.' Sample says this idea is fanciful to many scientists but points to a study that claims the link may be well-founded after all, and written into the molecules of DNA.

A 2015 report from scientists based in Iceland reported that the genetic factors that raise the risk of bipolar disorder and schizophrenia are found more often in people in creative professions. Painters, musicians, writers and dancers were, on average, 25 per cent more likely to carry the gene variants than professions the scientists judged to be less creative, among which were farmers, manual labourers and salespeople.

Kári Stefánsson, founder and CEO of deCODE, a genetics company based in Reykjavik, said the findings, described in the journal *Nature Neuroscience*, point to a biological link between some mental disorders and creativity. 'To be creative, you have to think differently', he told *The Guardian*. 'And when we are different, we have a tendency to be labelled strange, crazy and even insane.' The scientists drew on genetic and medical information from 86,000 Icelanders to find genetic variants that doubled the average risk of schizophrenia, and raised the risk of bipolar disorder by more than a third. When they looked at how common these variants were in members of national arts societies, they found a 17 per cent increase compared with non-members.

The researchers went on to check their findings in large medical databases held in the Netherlands and Sweden. Among these 35,000 people, those deemed to be creative (by profession or through answers to a questionnaire) were nearly 25 per cent more likely to carry the mental disorder variants. Stefansson says that scores of genes increase the risk of schizophrenia and bipolar disorder. These may alter the ways in which people think, but, in most people, do nothing very harmful. But for a small percentage of the population, genetic factors, life experiences and other influences can end in problems and a diagnosis of mental illness.

'Often, when people are creating something new, they end up straddling sanity and insanity', said Stefansson. 'I think these results support the old concept of the mad genius. Creativity is a quality that has given us Mozart, Bach and Van Gogh. It's a quality that is very important for our society. But it comes at a risk to the individual, and 1 per cent of the population pays the price for it.' Results imply creative people are 25 per cent more likely to carry genes that raise risk of bipolar disorder and schizophrenia.

The ancient Greeks were first to make the point. Shakespeare raised the prospect, too. But Lord Byron was, perhaps, the most direct of them all: 'We of the craft are all crazy', he told the Countess of Blessington, casting a wary eye over his fellow poets (Kay Redfield Jamison's book *Touched with Fire* (1993)). Most of the artist's creative flair, then, is down to different genetic factors, or to other influences altogether, such as life experiences, that set them on their creative journey. For Stefansson, even a small overlap between the biology of mental illness and creativity is fascinating. 'It means that a lot of the good things we get in life, through creativity, come at a price. It tells me that when it comes to our biology, we have to understand that everything is in some way good and in some way bad', he said.

Albert Rothenberg, Professor of Psychiatry at Harvard University is not convinced. He believes that there's no good evidence for a link between mental illness and creativity. 'It's the romantic notion of the 19th century, that the artist is the struggler, aberrant from society, and wrestling with inner demons', he said. 'But take van Gogh. He just happened to be mentally ill as well as creative. For me, the reverse is more interesting: creative people are generally not mentally ill, but they use thought processes that are of course creative and different.

'The problem is that the criteria for being creative is never anything very creative. Belonging to an artistic society, or working in art or literature, does not prove a person is creative. But the fact is that many people who have mental illness do try to work in jobs that have to do with art and literature, not because they are good at it, but because they're attracted to it. And that can skew the data', Rothenberg said. 'Nearly all mental hospitals use art therapy, and so when patients come out, many are attracted to artistic positions and artistic pursuits.'

History is full of anecdotal evidence of artists that have suffered, often at their own hands such as Tony Hancock and Robin Williams. The comedian Spike Milligan's depression was so severe it led to him being hospitalized regularly. The composer Edward Elgar wrote 'Nimrod' for his friend Augustus Jaeger, who encouraged him to continue when about to give up composing after a fit of depression. If the ultimate aim of creative maximization is to live at the extremities of left- and right-brain processes, then perhaps we should not be surprised if what we find is unsettling.

Flow and pulse: the way to sustainable creativity

In positive psychology, Flow, also known as the zone, is the mental state when a person is immersed in a complete energized focus. It was named by Hungarian psychologist Mihály Csíkszentmihályi. According to him, in Flow, the emotions are not just contained and channelled, but positive, energized, and aligned with the task at hand. The hallmark of Flow is a feeling of spontaneous joy, even rapture, while performing a task, although Flow is also described (below) as a deep focus on nothing but the activity – not even oneself or one's emotions.

Csíkszentmihályi says: 'Regardless of the culture, regardless of education, there are seven conditions that seem to be there when a person is in Flow. There's this focus that, once it becomes intense, leads to a sense of ecstasy, a sense of clarity: you know exactly what you want to do from one moment to the other; you get immediate feedback. You know that what you need to do is possible to do, even though difficult, and sense of time disappears, you forget yourself, you feel part of something larger. And once the conditions are present, what you are doing becomes worth doing for its own sake.'

This perhaps explains the story behind two online encyclopaedias. The first was developed at a cost of millions of dollars by a major corporation. The second was created by volunteers who were unpaid. Which do you think succeeded? Yes, the former was Microsoft's Encarta which was closed in 2009 and the latter was Wikipedia which continues to thrive today. The concept of Flow partially explains this. Csíkszentmihályi also points out that increases in material well-being does not correlate in a linear sense with happiness. He points out that above a basic level of income, the number of people who call themselves happy is fixed at around 30 per cent. What he illustrates is that happiness is indeed a choice. You can't make someone happy. They have to choose to be happy.

This sense of ecstasy, he says, is a step into 'an alternative reality'. Although his research was based on 8,000 interviews of people from all types and backgrounds, the truth would appear to be deceptively simple – when people are in Flow, their left-brain processes are suspended. They are in habit mode and their 'existence is temporarily suspended'. They have reached unconscious competence in the learning cycle.

The learning cycle

State	Confidence level
Unconscious incompetence	High (they're not aware they're incompetent)
Conscious incompetence	Low (they're aware they're incompetent)
Conscious competence	Medium (they're aware they're competent)
Unconscious competence	High (they're not aware they're competent)

When people are good at something, they're often unaware of how good they actually are. His research also points out a link between ethics and success. This is no surprise when some of the best leaders are always considering the whole community they serve, not just the narrow interests of shareholders. The purest passions produce the highest returns, although they may not be long-term or measured monetarily. If you set out with your skills just to make money, you might make some. The most successful leaders are successful because they make everyone in their business feel successful. You might be able to measure this at the bottom line, but it's definitely an indirect link.

American philosopher and psychologist John Dewey argued that the rhythmic highs and lows of life are essential to its creative completeness. Almost a century later, artist Maira Kalman observed: 'We hope. We despair. We hope. We despair. That is what governs us. We have a bipolar system.' This is also pointed out in Tony Schwartz's *The Way We're Working Isn't Working*: 'We find ourselves in an energy crisis. This one is personal. We have to learn to manage our energy rather than our time.' He argues that if time is finite, the only way to boost performance is by managing personal energy. He states there are four kinds of energy:

- Physical – the quantity of the energy.
- Emotional – the quality of the energy.
- Mental – the focus of the energy.
- Spiritual – your sense of purpose – if this is high, the energy is maximized.

This is echoed by the axes of personal challenge in Chapter 3.

In the physical layer, Schwartz says we tend to treat ourselves like machines working linearly until they are switched off. He argues that humans don't run like this as they breathe in and out – they pulse. 'We value the expenditure of energy and dismiss the renewal of energy.' He argues that the latter is just as important as the former. 'The more you spend energy in a focused way followed by intense renewal the more productive you become.' Emotional energy, he says, is often based on false confidence. 'We believe certainty is power' and this makes us feel strong. But strength does not create interdependence. Vulnerability is more likely to do this.

The overload is directly implicated here because people shut off news and information which they don't agree with, so their world becomes an echo chamber. They increasingly feel cut off and alienated. They don't need anyone and no one needs them. This leads to spiritual disconnection.

Schwartz points out that the left-brain processes has become dominant because of the need for certainty, but repeated success does not add further to mastery. At its root, mastery involves recognizing vulnerability and that which has yet to be completed. Although this oscillation might be a part of the human condition, its clinical illness – bipolar disorder, first termed manic depression for its alternating extremes of elation and depression – is a form of mental illness. Alongside clinical depression, it is also one of the most commonly occurring conditions affecting the relationship between creativity and mental illness. If we want creativity to be sustainable, we have to understand the structures of the brain, how they work and to understand that we aren't machines.

It's still surprising that we don't routinely teach the structures and functions of the brain in detail in the early stages of secondary education. If we drive a car, we don't have to know how it works, but it helps. If we ride a bicycle, we don't have to know how it works, but it helps. What other form of human endeavour would try to optimize the performance of something without studying how it works? That's also why we need to understand what happens when the brain is sleeping.

The final word from the brilliant Iain McGilchrist: 'The intuitive mind is a sacred gift and the rational mind is a faithful servant. We have created a society that honours the servant, but has forgotten the gift.'

Conclusion

We need to understand how the brain physically works to get the best out of it. We've established that the right and left brain do not physically house logic and intuition. The processes, however, still exist independently. If we understand this, we can be more successful in presentations and interviews in the commercial and personal world. If we want extraordinary and sustained creative output, maintaining balance is also essential. This means that we need to know that slowing down is part of the Creative Traits. Relaxing, Playing and Engaging (especially in face-to-face situations) is critical to our success. Next, we find out about the role of Dreams.

Sleep matters   05

If we want our creative minds to function properly, we cannot just assume they are healthy and balanced and ignore sleep. To do that would be a classically left-brained mistake – we would ignore the wider context of the brain function. It's not just about the quantity of sleep, it's about the quality, too. And a lack of sleep can have profound short- and long-term implications. We look at these and the link between sleep and cognitive performance and how this affects different people. We investigate the links between sleep deprivation, obesity, diabetes and cancer. We also investigate the link between the technology we use and sleep disruption. By the end of this chapter, you'll understand that you can improve creativity by simply sleeping better. You'll also be aware that when we work to excess using modern IT, that can make the problem significantly worse because of the light emissions from the screens we use. You'll also learn that sleep disorders are surprisingly common among many public figures.

I thought carefully about whether this area warranted a separate chapter. Why? Because ALL of the Creative Traits: Quiet, Engage, Dream, Relax, Release, Repeat, Play and Teach depend on sleep for their effectiveness. I've never seen anyone be able to function well creatively without sleep. You might even call sleep the parent of all creative traits in the same way that courage is the parent to all virtues.

Many of those interviewed for this book have reported sleep as a key issue for them. Some like Dror Benshetrit and Ray Kurzweill head to sleep with a problem to solve. Others like Vanessa Brady will sleep 12 hours a night if she could. Some, like Margaret Thatcher, were famous for not needing much of it. The requirements and habits for sleep are as diverse as people themselves, but one thing remains the same for all – its importance. Few, however, are taught about sleep and even less learn about it, yet we will spend a third of our lives doing it. There is no endeavour in our busy lives which receives such poor consideration and it's vital to the premise of this book that we understand how it works.

Not only will this make you a better creative, but it might also save your life. Sleep deprivation is implicated in many medical conditions and accidents. Worse, you may not be aware that you may be affecting your partner's ability to sleep and vice versa. This is especially the case for couples with young children. This time is frequently remembered as being the worst of the marriage to date with both parents being chronically sleep-deprived for years at a time.

Understanding sleep hygiene for yourself may also have profound benefits for understanding children's sleeping behaviour as this changes as they enter adolescence typically with teenagers becoming late chronotypes. We heard earlier how innovators like Steve Frampton at Portsmouth College are using their understanding of this to rebuild the academic day and deliver better results.

It actually requires a separate book, but fortunately there's already been one written that I highly recommend (see below). The issue of sleep is so frequently overlooked in terms of improving not only creativity but also quality of life. It's because it's passive. How could you ever possibly improve something by simply not doing it? Well, that's what sleep involves. It warrants an entire chapter because it touches *everything*.

I first met brain biologist, Professor Russell Foster, while browsing in an art gallery on a cold wet winter's night in London's Mayfair. It's an unusual place to meet a scientist. Especially a circadian neuroscientist. He was gazing at a picture that I was also drawn to. It was a beach scene by artist Sarah Butterfield. It was about as far away from the miserable streets of London as you can get. I asked him what he liked about the painting. 'It's making my mind work', he said, without looking at me. 'Which part?' I asked. 'Nearly the entire caudal half of the cerebral cortex is dedicated to processing visual information. It could be the precentral gyrus which is the primary somatosensory receiving area. But I think I just like it', he said, turning to me and smiling.

A lot of professors don't smile, but he does. He smiles a lot. He is always enthusiastic. He doesn't walk. He bounces along like a ball. It's almost as if he has been inflated to twice the normal recommended human pounds per square inch inflation for enthusiasm to the point that he may well burst. His capacity to immediately understand something at a hugely complex level, and then to want to share it, is probably the reason why he's the leading neuroscientist in the world. He teaches and researches at Brasenose College, Oxford University. Just so you know he's qualified.

Foster does something for me which borders on the definition of genius. He is able to comprehend great complexity, then simplify it, without any fear that oversimplifying will in any way undermine his credibility or the meaning. He doesn't gain credibility from making things sound complicated. He is one of the few academics I've met that has this gift. He needs very few syllables to transmit meaning. I wish we had more academics like that. The first thing you notice about this man is his enthusiasm and love for his subject matter. His concentration on the matter in hand is intense. Yet he's never far away from a smile.

So here's Professor Russell Foster, CBE, fellow of the Royal Society and head of Circadian Neuroscience at Oxford University. And remedial child. Shortly after his 11th birthday, his father left and this coincided with him being put into a remedial class for talking too much. 'I just simply had to finish a *very* interesting conversation and my teacher kept on interrupting. She told me to stop, but I needed to finish the conversation.' He says this gave him the secret of his success, which he describes as: 'A deep and profound insensitivity. People have been rude about me all my life and I just haven't noticed! I've just kept on pursuing my ideas.' He says it just doesn't matter if you put your foot through the rung: 'You just have to have the determination or the psychological robustness to keep climbing', he adds. Foster is passionate about, well, just about everything.

There seems to be a common thread here with many profoundly creative people that a trauma in early life is a key inflexion point to developing creativity. Sometimes the horror of this is transformational. When things are so bad at an early age, could there be a simple emotional defence mechanism that creates an alternative and imaginary world? J K Rowling's early hardship as a provenance for Harry Potter and the wizarding world might support this theory. All worlds need to be imagined before they are inhabited. There frequently seems to be a linear relationship in some cases between childhood hardship and creative response.

In Foster's book *Sleep: A Very Short Introduction*, he explains what sleep is for. 'It's the single most important behavioural experience we have. If you live to 90 then you'll spend almost 32 years asleep. At most we tolerate the need for sleep and it's because we don't do anything while we sleep. Or we think we don't.' There are a few fans of sleep but it seems the 'Greed is Good' Eighties left us with a legacy that sleep is 'self-indulgent, indolent, lazy, sybaritic… and something vaguely suspect', as India Knight said in her column in *The Sunday Times Magazine*. She says that this is 'to do with a puritanical, Anglo-Saxon conflation of bed and sex.'

Many think sleep is a complete waste of time, until something goes badly wrong. There are many reformed insomniacs – Arianna Huffington, for example. The founder of *The Huffington Post* has earned fame as both a workaholic and an insomniac, but ever since she passed out from exhaustion, broke her cheekbone, and got five stitches over her eye, she's become a fervent, anti-insomnia crusader. In the past, she's declared lack of sleep a feminist issue and is encouraging women to get at least seven hours a night. Van Gogh treated his mattress and pillow with camphor, a relative of turpentine, to help him sleep. Some believe the camphor slowly poisoned him and was one of the factors that pushed him to suicide. Bill Clinton long claimed to get by on five hours of sleep a night, but he's later tried to extend that after a heart attack that he partly attributed to fatigue. 'Every important mistake I've made in my life, I've made because I was too tired', he was quoted as having said.

According to the National Sleep Foundation, 60 per cent of Americans between the ages of 13 and 64 experience a sleep problem almost every night. It's a problem that dogs people irrespective of their status or fame. The singer Rihanna sends Twitter messages that she's having trouble sleeping. After completing a world tour in 2011, she tweeted: 'Suddenly all the silence is being drowned by my thoughts! No sleep.' George Clooney, the Oscar-winning actor told *The Hollywood Reporter* that he has trouble falling asleep without the TV on. Lady Gaga told *OK!* magazine in 2010: 'My passion is so strong I can't sleep – I haven't slept for three days. 'I lie in bed and try to pray and breathe. I have a very overactive mind.' After adopting her son, Louis, Sandra Bullock, the Oscar-winning actress, drastically cut down on sleep. She told the UK's *Now* magazine she was surviving on just three hours a night.

Groucho Marx's sleeping problems were triggered by the 1929 stock market crash, in which he lost a fortune. At night, he would reportedly call strangers with such classic jokes as: '*Q*: What do you get when you cross an insomniac, an agnostic and a dyslexic? *A*: Someone who stays up all night wondering if there is a Dog.' Margaret Thatcher survived her long tenure as British prime minister on only four hours of sleep a night. Her motto was: 'Sleep is for wimps.' She lived a long twilight suffering from Alzheimer's disease, something Foster is currently investigating.

The idea that the brain is doing nothing while sleeping is a common misconception. Foster has shown that the brain is actually working very hard while we sleep.

Strangely, there is no consensus on why we sleep. He believes there are three main reasons:

- Restoration – some genes are only turned on when the brain is sleeping.

- Conservation – some say it's to save energy. This is unlikely because the difference between sleeping and staying awake is around 110 calories.

- Brain process and memory consolidation – people who sleep are more than three times more powerful cognitively and creatively.

Foster says that in the 1950s people regularly slept more than eight hours: 'Nowadays it's closer to six and a half hours. Teenagers need more than nine hours, but they're frequently getting less than six

hours. It's nowhere near enough.' The lack of sleep is now implicated in car accidents, illnesses, industrial injuries and even with the
nuclear explosion at Chernobyl, where sleep-deprived engineers
were partially held responsible. They'd worked a shift for more than
13 hours.

'Sleep is the best cognitive enhancer we know. I've no idea why
leaders don't recognize this. It's not just a matter of enhanced performance, it's about safety as well.' And it's not just short-term cognitive
functions that are at risk: 'Just one night of disrupted sleep can lower
the effectiveness of killer (immune) cells by 24 per cent. That's probably
because of the elevation of stress caused by the internal desynchrony.

'The brain is like a net – held tight during the day. Sleep then
loosens this net and things begin to mingle. Part of the creative process is these free-ranging associations. This is what happens when the
brain develops theta waves. These are the brain state of REM sleep
(dreams), hypnosis, lucid dreaming, and the barely conscious state
just before sleeping and just after waking', he says. These brain waves
have big implications for behaviour, because without them the body
can't regulate itself. 'The wake state overwhelms us as does the sleep
state', he says. 'This is what's called Homeostatic defence or the
ability of the body to rebalance.'

How does he maintain his creativity and passion? 'I'm afraid I
can't help myself. This is an immensely exciting time – we're on the
threshold of a pill to cure jet lag. It's a bit like the final stages of
Around the World in Eighty Days – I end up burning bits of the infrastructure in order to maintain the speed.' Foster says tired
brains crave coffee and nicotine to stimulate them. He even admits
to this himself. Then alcohol is used to slow the brain down. This
causes what he calls the short-term stimulus–sedative cycle. 'If you
sleep less than five hours a night you have a 50 per cent likelihood
of being obese. This is because of the hunger hormone ghrelin.
This causes the body to seek out carbohydrate and sugar and can
also lead to diabetes.'

Night shift workers are frequently getting less than six hours a
night. In one test, nurses on night shift were shown to have a statis-
tically higher incidence of breast cancer (*Journal of the National
Cancer Institute*, Volume 93, Issue 20).

Foster's tips for sleeping health are simple:

1 Reduce the level of light as you head towards bedtime. Do not clean your teeth in a brightly lit bathroom immediately before bed.

2 Turn off all computers. The blue light they give off stimulates the brain.

3 Keep the bedroom cool. Most are upstairs and therefore warmer.

4 Do not take stimulants like coffee after lunch.

5 Seek out morning light – this helps synchronize your system.

Many mental disorders often begin with a lack of sleep like bipolar disorder. He even suggests that some of the anti-toxins released during sleep are useful in attacking the amyloid plaques that cause Alzheimer's disease.

In an article in the *Harvard Business Review* (February 2016) about sleep, two McKinsey staffers, Nick van Dam and Els van der Helm made the link between leadership effectiveness. Their survey of more than 180 business leaders found that 43 per cent say they do not get enough sleep at least four nights a week. Sleep deprivation impairs the ability to focus attention selectively: studies show that after roughly 17 to 19 hours of work, cognitive performance is equivalent to that of a person with a blood alcohol level of 0.05 per cent (the legal drink-drive limit in many countries). After roughly 20 hours this rises to 0.1 per cent, which meets the legal definition of drunk in the United States. Sleep appears to be beneficial for a range of cognitive functions to help solve problems, including insight, pattern recognition, and the ability to come up with innovative and creative ideas. One study has shown that a good night's sleep leads to new insights: participants who enjoyed one were twice as likely to discover a hidden shortcut in a task as those who didn't. Other scientific studies have shown the beneficial impact of sleep on all three stages of the learning process: before learning, to encode new information; after learning, in the consolidation stage, when the brain forms new connections; and before remembering, to retrieve information from memory.

To help other people, you need to understand them. This requires interpreting emotions and tone of voice. But, when sleep-deprived, the brain is more likely to misinterpret these cues and overreact. Nick van Dam and Els van der Helm also claim that recent studies have shown that the sleep-deprived are less likely to trust someone else. Is this a corporate or personal problem? Well, it's both.

The last part of the brain to evolve was the neocortex. This is responsible for sensory perception, motor commands and language. The frontal part of the neocortex, the prefrontal cortex, directs what psychologists call executive functioning. This includes all higher cognitive processes – problem-solving, reasoning, organizing, inhibition, planning, and executing plans. These processes help leaders get things done. Neuroscientists, like Foster, know that although other brain areas can cope relatively well with too little sleep, the prefrontal cortex cannot. Basic visual and motor skills deteriorate when people are deprived of sleep, but not nearly to the same extent as higher-order mental skills. Perhaps this is why research funding is pouring into Foster's team.

It's beyond doubt that sleep-deprived leaders are bad leaders, so many organizations have responded by implementing policies that are mindful of time off. These might include a cut-off time on email, follow the sun operations, work-free vacations, napping rooms and training to encourage better use of sleep apps. This is about a cultural change rather than a series of techniques. It's clear that leaders that are more rested are more effective. The relationship between sleep and stress is clearly understood. You don't need laboratory research to confirm this. The problem is that we live in an empowered age. Top down edicts don't always help change cultures. Part of the process of treating colleagues like adults, is to assume they know where the off switch is and can use it when they need it.

Some people just feel better to be always on. For others, it's the worst thing imaginable. However it's brought about, sleep must be considered one of the biggest determinants of success. Many employers have a growing interest in this area, like airlines, 24 hour retailers and emergency services. As the link between sleep and injury becomes better understood, we can expect that it will not only be grossly unproductive to continue in this way – it may even become illegal, too. Proper sleep may be easily recognized as a critical factor in effective and high quality creative thinking, but its absence has more significant implications.

Why don't employers wake up to the massive liabilities that are going to occur in this area? 'Undiluted terror of the implications', Foster says. 'I think some would rather bury their heads in the sand.' The biggest battle, though, is at the individual level because the sleep-deprived are the last to recognize the problems with their own state. Foster agrees: 'Oh yes – the tired brain is so compromised it cannot appreciate how compromised it is!' This is because the left-brain process is not monitoring permanently – if it doesn't meet divergence it carries on until it moves on to something else.

Back from the future

Ray Kurzweil is from the future. He's been described as 'the restless genius' by *The Wall Street Journal*, and 'the ultimate thinking machine' by *Forbes* magazine. In 1999, he received the National Medal of Technology, the nation's highest honour in technology, from President Clinton in a White House ceremony. In 2002, he was inducted into the National Inventors Hall of Fame, established by the US Patent Office. He has received 20 honorary doctorates, and honours from three US presidents. Kurzweil has authored seven books, five of which have been national bestsellers. *The Age of Spiritual Machines* has been translated into nine languages and was the number one best-selling book on Amazon in science. Ray Kurzweil's book, *The Singularity Is Near*, was a *New York Times* bestseller, and has been the number one book on Amazon in both science and philosophy.

We start by a gallop through known history: 'Human creativity is at the top of the neocortical hierarchy. The neocortex is a series of modules – we have 300 million of them – that can recognize a pattern of information. The neocortex started 200 million years ago. Then 65 million years ago there was the Cretaceous extinction event – a catastrophic change when 75 per cent of all species were destroyed. Mammals adapted and got bigger and developed the neocortex of curvatures and ripples. This is 80 per cent of the brain and that's where we do our thinking.'

He describes the hierarchy of the neocortex: 'At the bottom, we can see physical dimensions. At the top, we can see whether something is funny or artistic. No other primate can do this. They don't tell jokes. They can't pick up the beat. Every human culture has music. This is at the top of the neocortical hierarchy. This is the biological basis of creativity.'

Kurzweil says the main reason we have a brain is to predict the future, but that a lot of extrapolation is linear, not exponential: 'So we were told that sequencing the genome was going to take a hundred years because only 1 per cent had been done after seven years. But 1 per cent is only seven doublings from 100 per cent. It cost a billion dollars to do – now you can do it for a few thousand.'

Kurzweil believes we got a one-off qualitative improvement in the neocortex allowing us to handle abstract thinking: 'Our skulls now can't get any bigger in evolution, otherwise childbirth would become impossible.' But he points out that the law of shrinking technology will address this. By 2030, he says, we'll have nanotechnology machines smaller than single blood cells. They will be introduced non-invasively. They will augment our immune systems; currently they're not programmed to destroy cancer or carry retrovirus – it will go inside the brain and link to exterior synthetic neocortex to allow it to access the Cloud, wirelessly and seamlessly. This will give us internal virtual reality. This won't be a one-shot deal – this will be the big trigger to exponential development of the neocortex. This will give us answers to questions which are too profound for us to handle today.

This opens up the potential for the brain to handle greater complexity and pattern recognition: 'The use of metaphor is key to creativity and that's all about being able to recognize patterns in a different context.' He points to Charles Darwin's theory of evolution that came directly from a metaphor he took from geology. He studied Charles Lyell's work on geology who noticed that features like the Grand Canyon always had small trickles of water in them. People thought that idea was ridiculous, but Darwin did the mathematical work and showed that a small amount of erosion over a long period of time could create the features and that gave him the confidence to write *The Origin of Species*. The small trickle of water was a direct metaphor for the small trickle of genetic change.

This is why the creativity of others is so important to your thinking. It may provide the metaphor which enables your epiphany.

Kurzweil points out that art and music is full of metaphor expressing ideas about society or relationships in a different way: 'The neocortex is, in effect, a great metaphor-generator. It can recognize patterns in really different contexts. The more it gains exposure to metaphor, the more creative it can become. When the modules of the neocortex are synthetically enhanced, so the creativity will expand exponentially.'

He adds that Garry Kasparov was defeated by Big Blue in 1997 because the computer could analyse 300 million move sequences a second. Kasparov could only process one, but he held his own because he had deep powers of pattern recognition. Kurzweil says that most experts can recall and master about 100,000 patterns. That shows the power of the neocortex to recognize patterns and metaphor. That really is the definition of how creativity works.

His point is clear – we're exposed to vast amounts of information, but taught to look at it in a professional way so we can easily miss the metaphors. That can come from looking at data in a less structured way.

He also uses sleep and dreaming in a disciplined way – part of what he calls 'creative due diligence'. He programs himself, then goes to sleep. He often dreams about the problem. He points out that Freud said two things about dreams – firstly that the censors are turned off, for example, so dreams can be about the culturally taboo or sexual urges that would not ordinarily be acceptable. Secondly, rationality is also suspended: 'So when an elephant walks through the wall, the strange thing is that you don't think it's strange.' He says the most fertile part of the sleep process is the interface with waking. 'This doesn't happen when the alarm goes off but when you wake naturally. You can be in the dream but still be aware that you're in bed. You're semi-conscious. That's when I spend 20 minutes "lucid dreaming" evaluating the metaphor before they disappear. Very often, not always, this is where I get my key insights.' This is very much a hybrid solution.

How does he explain the universal dystopian view of the world? 'A century ago you could count the democracies on the fingers of one hand. Two centuries ago it was even less. By any standard the world is getting healthier, safer and wealthier. But, we have exponential better news about everything bad happening.

'People instinctively fear change, but the United States is very good at this. He says this is partly down to the fact that even today many Americans are second or third generation offspring of people that risked everything to come to the United States. They embraced change, and because they were from all over the world, they brought a small part of that culture with them. This is the essence of Silicon Valley. We have a word for failure. We call it experience.' This explains why US innovations are so readily adopted by world cultures. When you embrace cultural change, you embrace all types of change.

'There's one thing about the future which is amazingly predictable and that is the price-performance of computing calculations per second per constant dollar. It's been a perfectly smooth exponential curve. Nothing has stopped this. It's true of every form of information and biotechnology.' He calls this the law of accelerating returns.

One of the best methods he has for creativity is to invert the direction of the problem-solving from reductionism to conceptualization: 'I imagine giving a speech many years hence as to how I solved the problem and then I work back logically to where we are now.' In short, he works back from the solution and dreams up the way it was solved. This is how he comes back from the future.

The link between technology and sleep

We know that there is more disruptive communication from the information media. We know much of this is delivered by mobile devices. We know that mobile use is increasing dramatically. We also know that sleep is suffering, but is there a connection between these facts?

There's evidence that blue light, emitted by smartphones, tablets and laptops, is affecting the quantity and quality of the sleep we are getting. Darkness is a natural cue for sleep, but we're disrupting that by staring at bright screens for hours after the sun has gone down. 'There are about 30,000 cells inside your eye that are reactive to the wavelength of light which would be considered blue', says clinical psychologist and sleep therapist, Dr Michael J Breus. 'Blue runs in about the 460 nanometer range, in terms of the spectrum of light. That particular spectrum of light hits these cells and makes them send a signal to an area of the brain known as the suprachiasmatic nucleus and tells it to turn off melatonin production. Melatonin is the key that starts the engine for sleep.

'There's nothing wrong with blue light for most of the day', says Dr Breus. 'You just don't want to have it about 90 minutes or so before bed.' It seems that blue light has been well-known to sleep researchers for many years. Our circadian rhythms determine our internal clocks. In line with Foster's comments, he points out that: 'In the past 50 years, there has been a decline in average sleep duration and quality, with adverse consequences on general health.' In his research he assessed two groups: half read a normal printed book for four hours before bedtime for five consecutive nights; the other group read a light-emitting eBook reader for the same period. The subjects using the eBook reader showed suppressed levels of melatonin. On average, they took 10 minutes longer to fall asleep and displayed significantly less rapid eye movement (REM) sleep than the group reading printed books. There are also some scientists linking blue light to age-related macular degeneration, though the evidence doesn't seem to be con-clusive. Overexposure could be playing a role in the rise of cataracts and even blindness.

'We are seeing a much greater number of age-related macular degen-eration patients, even back correcting for the aging population, so the risk factors are clearly changing', explains Professor John Marshall, Frost Professor of Ophthalmology at the Institute of Ophthalmology in London. 'If you look at cataracts there's a very good correlation between the age of onset of cataracts and the degree of ultraviolet where you live in the world – that's why people close to the equator tend to get their cataracts 5 to 10 years earlier.' It also seems like blue light might be the least of our worries.

'Light bulbs are much brighter sources', explains Professor Marshall. 'When was the last time you got an after image from looking at your iPad? When you look at a light source, especially an LED, you've got that multicoloured image on your retina which takes a long time to fade.

'Until recently, we lit our homes with incandescent bulbs and they were relatively biologically friendly, in that there was very little blue', says Marshall. 'More commonly now they're LEDs, and these light sources have a lot of the potentially damaging blue, to the extent that I don't use them.'

The blue light isn't unnatural. Sunlight, for instance, has a tremen-dous amount of blue light in it. We need blue light to wake us up in the morning, and it has been correlated with higher levels of alertness. 'When we wake up in the morning our circadian rhythm is a little off, our in-ternal biological clock runs on a slightly longer schedule in many cases than 24 hours, and so to reset that clock every morning we need sun-light', says Dr Breus. 'One of my biggest recommendations for patients is every morning go outside and get 15 minutes of sunlight.'

In the evening, we need to be more mindful of our blue light exposure. Proximity is an important factor. That's why smartphones, tablets, and laptops are perceived as a bigger risk than light bulbs or TV screens. Though, it's worth remembering that the impact on sleep is about more than just the blue light exposure.

Some hardware manufacturers have taken on the problem with software like F.lux. It changes display according to the time of day, so it gets warmer at night and has more blue during the day. It's free and available for Windows, Mac, Linux and iOS devices. There's an app called Twilight on Android that does the same thing. 'I think there's a second factor that people aren't really talking about that much, and that is the level of engagement in whatever the device is', explains Dr Breus. 'If you're playing your favourite game, or whatever it is you like to do before you go to bed, you're mentally engaged in that act.'

So we know that information overload is soaking up free time. We also know the devices can make it harder for us to sleep. At best, sleep deprivation gives us decreased creativity. At worst, the combined impact of all these conditions chronically could result in a class action suit and an early grave. Fortunately, at the time of going to press, Apple announced that iOS 9.3 allows users to automatically dim the emissions closer to bedtime.

The role of light

In a piece written by Russell Foster and Ron Douglas (CET, 'The eye: organ of space and time') they discuss the role of light: 'Life is like an opera, which involves a number of soloists, an often large chorus and many musicians playing a variety of instruments. To produce something worth listening to they all need to produce the correct notes, at an appropriate volume, in the right order, at the appropriate time. If everyone did what they wanted, whenever they felt like it, the result would be an uncoordinated cacophony. A conductor is needed to bring order to this potential chaos.

'The many complex physiological and biochemical processes responsible for an organism's life must be similarly coordinated. You wouldn't want to eat, sleep and urinate at the same time after all. In all organisms the conductor of life's complex orchestra is a biological clock that ensures all the body's processes happen in the right order and at an appropriate time across the 24-hour day' (*Journal of the National Cancer Institute*, Volume 93, Issue 20). Such is the importance of light and its effect on the body clock. Many other aspects of the human metabolism change in tune with the light/dark cycle. This includes body temperature, blood pressure, alertness, cognitive function and the levels of many hormones such as cortisol. This increases prior to dawn in anticipation of daytime activity and then declines in the evening in preparation for sleep. Hormones, such as pineal melatonin and growth hormone (from the pituitary) are normally only released at night. 'Even our libido waxes and wanes across the 24-hour day, with a notable increase in males associated with the morning rise in testosterone', says Foster.

The light and dark cycle is a vital process in the body because the cycle itself is not constant. As the days gradually shift through summer and winter, the system needs constant adjustment. Most people only notice this when they have jet lag. He adds, 'Most, if not all, cells of the body have the capability to generate autonomous 24-hour rhythms of activity.'

The link between technology and general well-being

Writing on the biology of technostress, Professor René Riedl at the University of Linz in Austria said that both the use and ubiquity of technology has a dark side: 'Despite the fact that human society has benefited from the availability of information and communication technologies (ICT) it may lead to notable stress perceptions, a type of stress referred to as technostress.' He said this has hardly been addressed from a biological perspective and it could easily be measured by looking at stress hormone levels and cardiovascular activity as predictors of health. From what work had been done, his review revealed 'significant negative biological effects that develop from human interaction with technology such as increased activity of the cardiovascular system, or elevated levels of stress hormones such as adrenaline and cortisol.'

Working while sleeping

Dror Benshetrit, is a designer, thinker, dreamer, and futurist whose ingenuity runs through an unusual range of unconventional work – interiors, exteriors and luxury goods. His work is included in the permanent collections of major museums in the United States, Europe, and the Middle East. An engaging storyteller, Benshetrit has lectured at the University of Pennsylvania's School of Design, University of Nebraska, and the Wolfsonian – Florida International University museum and research centre. He currently serves on the board of the Museum of Arts and Design in New York.

Benshetrit is also an outsider and a mixture of contradictions. Although he now lives in New York City, he's from Israel. He loves the peace of the countryside, but spends so much time in the city. He is a designer who has also served as a soldier. He's working on a book, but is also a dyslexic: 'At school, I just found creative ways of hiding it. But nobody treated me as if I was different.'

A lot of creative people seem to have this range of seemingly irreconcilable experiences.

He needs a lot of sleep, but he uses it productively: 'I guess I'm always working even while I'm sleeping. It is exhausting.' Does he ever try consciously not to work while sleeping? 'No. I'm always working. I guess I'm addicted to the pleasure of creativity and new realities. It's just worth it even though you're exhausted.' As a schoolboy, he says he tried to remember his dreams and return to them every night when sleeping.

He says that time seems to stand still and it feels like he's playing: 'It's fun and sometimes it almost feels idiotic.' Can it be that simple? 'From the creative aspect I'm never intimidated by scale. Whether I'm working on a vase or on a city it's all the same.'

Fear is also a factor. He says he gets scared balancing clients' demands and budget. 'That's my major duality. Sometimes you hold back because you have to rationalize. There's a danger in that you are intimidated by these things. You sometimes feel a need to make it more complex, but you have to resist this to keep it pure to maintain the core integrity. You have to create the poetry but you have to solve the problem as well.'

Sometimes, he says he is so immersed, his wife has to remind him where he is. Once he gets stuck into a big idea, sometimes it's difficult for him to zoom out: 'I try to avoid small talk. I try to spend my time with artists, with other dreamers.'

Benshetrit says he can't get enough of artists like Buckminster Fuller, Isamu Naguchi, and Giovanni Castiglione. 'If the three of them had been one person, it would have been magical.'

Although these artists have the ability to transport him, the other source of provenance for him is exercise: 'A lot of my ideas come when I run. It's just like a drug. It generates ideas, but they're not necessarily *great* ideas.' How does he induce creativity in others? 'I need to get them to feel, imagine, do and share. It's about provoking the individual sensitivity and their own imagination. It's never about what I like. I want them to come up with ideas. These are the starting points not the end.'

Conclusion

I wanted to look at the link between creativity and sleep and found that the problem was more complex. Not only does sleep play a key role in cognitive ability, but it also deeply affects health in areas such as weight gain and diabetes and, if allowed to become chronically disturbed, is implicated in mental health and more serious conditions like cancer and schizophrenia. This is perhaps the one area universally, where an improvement in sleep quality and quantity can bring immediate creative results. The reason that it's ignored, though, is emblematic of the problem that exists between the right- and left-brain processes. We look at the output of one part of the system and ignore the whole. Like a sports coach that concentrates on building endurance and muscle while ignoring diet. How can we become better creatives when we are so sleep-deprived that life becomes a monotone chore? This is no longer a matter of being more effective creatively or not – it's simply a matter of self-preservation. The greatest tools for suicide could be said to be a knife and fork and a light bulb. We eat the wrong things and forget where the off-switch is.

Next, we look at the flashpoint of creativity itself – where ideas come from.

Where great ideas come from 06

So we've looked at the changed environment and how this is affecting behaviour in the world around us. We've looked at how this came about and how it could be different. We've also looked at the structures of the brain, how they work and what can optimize performance. Now we need to look at the narrow process of how, why and where ideas come to us. By the end of this chapter you will have learned where your best ideas come from and what process works most effectively for you. We'll look at how the creative arts can stimulate the mind and we'll look at what inhibits the process and how we can get round that. This will help you make the first step towards unblocking or enhancing your own creative flow. This, of course, cannot just be a one-off. All excellence is a habit and this underlines one of the most important of the Creative Traits: Repeating the process.

There's a lot of talk about ideas. There are books about ideas. There are TV programmes about them. Many professions are all about ideas. Sometimes these are very different. Political ideas are very different from design ideas. People seek new ideas and argue about ideas. It's generally thought that ideas are quite important, especially when solving problems and creating progress. But nobody talks about where the ideas come from. Some would argue that having ideas is easy, it's the implementation that's hard. Of course, that's true. The better the idea, though, the easier it is to implement. It's half-baked or bad ideas that prove difficult to activate. If ideas are so central to what we do, then why do so few of us talk about where ideas come from? When you ask people they often look a bit embarrassed as if you'd asked something quite personal or intimate. Like it was a forbidden secret.

Some have attempted to define creativity. 'Previously unconnected matrices of thought' is one. 'Any thinking process in which original patterns are formed and expressed', is another. This is what happens when we use our left brains to analyse and define something. If we want to understand creative provenance, we have to understand the limits of 'left-brain process' rationality. As Iain McGilchrist suggests, if we can understand the limitations of analysing and defining something, we might get another insight. For instance, we might define ideas as what happens when your analytical capability is otherwise occupied with the habitual or routine.

In Tony Schwartz's excellent book *The Way We're Working Isn't Working*, he asks a great question: 'So where are you and what are you doing when you get your best ideas?'

You know the ones he's talking about. The real epiphanies. When you get hit with such a good thought, you simply know it's brilliant. It doesn't have to be about work. It could be about your health, your relationships or your long-term planning. I've been asking this question for 20 years. During that time, I've asked hundreds of people. Here's what they say:

- waking/about to fall asleep;
- in the bathroom/shower/toilet;
- driving;
- running;
- sitting on a train or bus or aircraft;
- walking the dog;
- dancing.

What do these places have in common? Well, no one is using an iPhone for a start! This, of course, is bizarre. It hardly bears rational examination. No wonder people are embarrassed to admit it. No wonder educators don't like to talk about creative provenance. In the great places of endeavour, at work, at university, in the lab, people are not coming up with ideas. As one leader put it: 'Well, we all have shower ideas, but we don't bring them to work.' Why not? Is the worth of any idea dictated by where it was born? You might as well say the same of people. It would be wrong in both cases. This has huge implications for how we organize our places of work, because creativity is now part of our work. Therefore our work is no longer a place. It's a process.

This illustrates a fundamental problem. If we're so busy all the time, how will the ideas come to us? We seem to have created lives where we are too busy to think deeply and creatively. It's become something that occurs when we stop and we seldom do that. When so much is crammed in, the machinery can't work properly any more. The responses of people on the subject of creative provenance have much in common. For instance, seldom did anyone ever say they had these thoughts at work. Additionally, most people report these epiphanies only when they are on their own. This type of creativity at least is a solitary exercise. When probed further, people usually describe places which are familiar, habitual, maybe even boring. They are as close to neutral or untroubled as they could be. Importantly, the idea can come when people are either quiet or involved in physical activity. In almost all cases, none of them were trying to think of a solution to any problem at the time. The provenance seems always to be the unconscious mind. The most usual phrase is that: 'I don't know how I did that. It just came to me.'

When you add this to the fact that *no one* I ever asked said they didn't have any good ideas, then you can see this is an intuitive and normal gift open to all people. It's a renewable and naturally occurring resource. Sometimes these ideas come fully formed. Sometimes, they are partial. The process does respond to practice and to focus. Francis Costello, a California-based marketing consultant, says he doesn't gain ideas but receives 'insights'. These cumulatively build until they form the basis of a whole idea. 'Capacity has to regularly build, though. Like a workout.' He practises Bikram yoga regularly.

'The intensity of the heat creates a different state of mind. One where the insights come much easier.'

Even at a basic practical level, everyone agrees these ideas are important to them. So important in fact, that many don't feel they need research to validate them. They *know intuitively* they are good ideas. Those who use these ideas in large organizations often report coming up with the idea first, then looking for the evidence to support it, so that it could survive other people's critique. Does the seemingly random provenance explain fully why people don't always act on their ideas? 'It's more likely that they don't have the discipline or drive to act on them', says one entrepreneur. 'Remember ideas are easy – it's the relentless execution which is difficult.'

Could it be, that they dismiss the ideas because of the place they happen? That they don't trust their own judgement because of how weird the process appears to be? If so, then we're making some fundamental mistakes in education. There's nothing weird about this. It's universal, natural and has been going on since, well, forever. It's been fundamental to all human progress, way before there were offices, way before people could even read or write.

Education teaches us about ideas but it doesn't teach us where they come from. Most universities, schools and colleges teach knowledge, but not how to study. They're hoping that students will pick up these techniques on the way. Now some might say that without the knowledge of history, how could anyone ever know whether an idea was original. However, if we had to define creativity in the left-brain process we might define it as: 'The history you are ignorant of.' There are no new ideas. It is a supreme conceit often shared among creatives that they've had a new idea. They've simply uncovered a piece of history they didn't know.

So if we set that aside, we can start to look at the benefits of creative provenance for its own sake. Einstein again: 'The most beautiful experience we can have is the mysterious – the fundamental emotion which stands at the cradle of true art and true science.' We heard earlier about the left- and right-brain processes. If we're interested in accessing our potential, we have to think big. To do this, we have to start thinking more about what we are and less about what we do. This allows us to contextualize our situation.

The 'to-do list' versus the 'to-be list'

Everyone is familiar with the to-do list. Sometimes it dominates people's life to such an extent that their lives are organized around 'getting stuff done'.

This is a basic technique for organization, but at the higher levels of problem-solving and creativity we need to go beyond this, which illustrates another problem. People make progress in the early parts of their career by doing things. They do qualifications. They do projects. Then they start to tell others what to do. Normally, the early part of this is process excellence, they get others to 'do things right'. Later, though, they move into a position where they have to 'do the right things'. 'It's the J-word', says Sir Geoffrey Leigh. 'It separates leaders in all walks of life. It's called Judgement.' Leigh is a businessman and philanthropist of many years' standing with wide connections in both politics and business on both sides of the Atlantic. 'Leaders have to stand for something – and it helps if they know what it is!' he says with a chuckle. Leigh says leaders need to be clear about their values because they fill many roles in many eyes. 'Of course, they need to deliver success to everyone, but to the shareholders they need to be trusted, to employees they need to be fair, to colleagues they need to be supportive, to suppliers they need to be reasonable.' The point here is that all these qualities point to what someone *is* rather than does.

An interesting effect is at play here. When you ask people to describe either their leader or parents, they tend to use adjectives like:

- supportive;
- inspirational;
- enthusiastic;
- stubborn;
- calming;
- resourceful;
- loving.

Is it an accident that parents and leaders share similar descriptions? In many instances, they perform similar roles. They guide, they protect, they develop and they nurture. Perhaps this is modesty, but I also think it reflects the prospect that most leaders have no idea who they are or what they're known for. If we extrapolate this, we often hear of companies rebranding themselves. This is all about what the company stands for. But if the people don't know what they stand for, and their leaders don't define it, how can they act in unison? Again, in the words of Reverend Coles, we need to *be*. After all, you can't 'do' creative, you can only be it.

The sense of flow

Alan Lightman is a physicist and a novelist and MIT's first professor with dual appointments in science and the humanities. In *A Sense of the Mysterious*, Lightman recounts one of his first projects as a researcher. He was trying to produce a giant umbrella theory of gravity by writing out the main equations. The more analytical he became, the more the solution evaded him. For months, he tried to find the error in his calculations. He couldn't see a way forward.

He describes his own miraculous moment: '[O]ne morning, I remember that it was a Sunday morning, I woke up about 5 am and couldn't sleep. I felt terribly excited. Something strange was happening in my mind. I was thinking about my research problem, and I was seeing deeply into it. I was seeing it in ways I never had before. The physical sensation was that my head was lifting off my shoulders. I felt weightless. And I had absolutely no sense of my self. It was an experience completely without ego, without any thought about consequences or approval or fame. Furthermore, I had no sense of my body. I didn't know who I was or where I was. I was simply spirit, in a state of pure exhilaration.'

Lightman describes the feeling of the creative moment as like sailing a round-bottomed boat in strong wind: 'Normally, the hull stays down in the water, with the frictional drag greatly limiting the speed of the boat. But in high wind, every once in a while the hull lifts out of the water, and the drag goes instantly to near zero.' He says it feels like a great hand has suddenly grabbed hold and flung you across the surface like a skimming stone. 'Although I had no sense of my ego, I did have a feeling of rightness. I had a strong sensation of seeing deeply into the problem and understanding it and knowing that I was right – a certain kind of inevitability. With these sensations surging through me, I tiptoed out of my bedroom, almost reverently, afraid to disturb whatever strange magic was going on in my head.'

He was oblivious to himself, his body, and everything around him: '[T]he fact is I was completely alone. I don't think any other person in the world would have been able to help me at that moment. And I didn't want any help. I had all of these sensations and revelations going on in my head, and being alone with all that was an essential part of it.' He described this act of letting go as 'a surrender to the mystery of life'. Put simply, he just stopped trying to solve the problem with his left brain.

'I believe that [Einstein] meant a sense of awe, a sense that there are things larger than us, that we do not have all the answers at this moment. A sense that we can stand right at the edge between known and unknown and gaze into that cavern and be exhilarated rather than frightened... I have experienced that beautiful mystery both as a physicist and as a novelist. As a physicist, in the infinite mystery of physical nature. As a novelist, in the infinite mystery of human nature and the power of words to portray some of that mystery.'

The passage above is a good description of how Flow feels from the inside. Dmitri Mendeleev recalled the same moment when trying to work out the order of the elements in his periodic table: 'I saw in a dream a table where all elements fell into place as required. Awakening, I immediately wrote it down on a piece of paper, only in one place did a correction later seem necessary.' Mendeleev's unconscious mind had solved the problem for him. Some believe the resulting breakthrough into Flow is the fruit of the lengthy labour preceding it, others that it is down to incubation. This sentiment is reported not only by my own research, but by many artists through history. Ernest Hemingway had a belief that all creatives should work alone. Agnes Martin, the US abstract painter said: 'The best things in life happen to you when you're alone.' When we look at the individuals later in Chapter 8, we hear this echoed.

The big inhibitors

To some extent then, we can conclude that the enemy of the right-brain process is the left-brain process itself. It's clear from the multiple observation of creative provenance that ideas come when the left brain is distracted by rhythm, habit or routine or under physical strain. It cannot be switched off per se, but it can be distracted.

Part of what Lightman and Einstein were getting at is that the presence of the left-brain processes themselves inhibit those of the right brain. It is not possible just to turn the right-brain process on. It can only come forward when the left brain is distracted. It can be triggered by the left brain being switched off, for example, in states of boredom, near sleep and daydreaming, or with it preoccupied with an automatic, habitual or routine task like having a shower.

Elizabeth Gilbert, the author of *Eat, Pray, Love*, has identified this. In her TED talk *Your Elusive Creative Genius*, she outlines the difference between being a genius and having one. She relates how mystics or shaman would dance until they entered a transcendent state until they had visions or insights. She relates how medieval Moorish crowds would shout 'Allah, Allah, Allah', when these states where achieved. Over time, this became corrupted into the modern Spanish shout of 'Olé!' This shows how repetition can induce a sense of the habitual and routine to induce the state of Flow.

For the creative state to arrive almost involves embracing a paradox – you either get very still or you get very busy into a routine.

Stillness and solitude

Robyn Graham is a young Paris-based artist. She paints either first thing in the morning or last thing at night. 'Every morning, I will have a new thought about the work I was doing the night before, that simply didn't occur to me during the night. Mornings can be the time of day to have an idea for a piece, make a lot of notes or start a rough sketch for a new piece. In that time, I'm very aware of people around me waking and beginning to do things – this can motivate me to think more actively about what it is that I'm making. Because of the repetitive nature of my work it is usually best to paint in the night – I can work for hours without the interruption of meals or other people's routines. I will go into a bit of a trance while I'm painting in the night. A lot of thoughts will occur then too, but these usually go into the piece rather than my notebook. It is very meditative for me and I find if I'm interrupted in these moments, I can sometimes sit for an hour before I am able to start again.'

Graham works on her knees as if in prayer. She will mostly choose to work on the floor because it gives her more freedom than being on a chair or around a table. There's also the practical reason of her work sometimes being so wet and having to dry flat. 'I don't so much feel a connection to faith while working, but there is a slight hushed influence from religion in my practice. During the summers, I've lived with a Muslim family in Tunisia for a couple months. Each time happened to cross over with Ramadan. A lot of what my practice has become, can be compared with what I witnessed and attempted to be a part of, during those summers. Although the days during Ramadan can become a sort of day long preparation of the food that will be consumed in the night, when your day is not broken up by meals and you're trying not to let your thoughts be about yourself or food, a different kind of consciousness becomes easier. It's hard to explain. I try to take that mind-fulness, heightened perception and sensitivity during Ramadan and recreate that every evening in my studio. The resemblance between my actions in the studio from repetitive drawings, kneeling and bowing over my paintings, to not having breaks while painting and those of prayer or fasting is essential to the outcome of my paintings.'

Quiet, or at least routine noise, is crucial to her practice. Cities can provide the perfect white noise for this. 'To perform creatively, you have to be in the right frame of mind. Often knowing that there will be a constant commotion outside, can act as the silence which I find comforting in the night. Quiet is also something ingrained in my personality. I have always been told I am a quiet person. This, along with the reflections people have, while viewing my work has reassured me that the quietness in my person-ality and the silence I work under has found its way into my art. When every-thing is still, I am simply abler to think thoughts through to the end.'

Her ideas come in all sorts of ways: 'I think it's necessary to be open to ideas and experiences, during conversation, being aware of what's hap-pening in the world and questioning everything. Even though I have a shy nature, I wouldn't think of myself as passive. I am more passionate during a debate, than I am during painting. Painting is a tranquil time, in which I can muse over those moments of heated discussion. However, without a truly great and interesting conversation every now and then, I feel my work would fall flat. Sometimes thinking can be the biggest hindrance to creativity, and in that case, I find music is usually the answer. Still, I choose something raw and full of honesty – usually Billie Holiday does the trick.'

The stillness makes her steer away from distractions and stimulants: 'I stay away from caffeine and technology. They both induce anxieties for me and a day that I open my laptop before I sit in front of a painting is not going to be a successful day. I'll try and tidy up a bit when I'm leaving a space, so that the next morning I'm not entering a complete mess. The things I do, before I start working are jump in the shower quickly, before checking my phone, try to consume a lot of fruit for breakfast and make a big cup of herbal tea. If I'm going to work late into the night, I will make sure I've eaten well and take enough water both to drink and to paint with. I'm noticing now, that in many ways, my routine is also slightly similar to preparing for a day long fast.'

Fear

If you get frightened by the blank page or the prospect of having to come up with an idea, then that's completely normal. Elizabeth Gilbert also relates her creative fear. In an interesting passage, she relates her feelings about the prospect that *Eat, Pray, Love* may be her all-time best work. She says she feels terrified that her best work may already be behind her. Fear is one of the potentially negative forces generated by left-brain processes. It compares. It contrasts. It analyses. It is a psychological difference engine. By focusing on the fear, it makes it impossible to attain a right-brain state in order to prove the left brain wrong. It becomes circular.

How to break this cycle? Gilbert says: 'You have to call it out.' She makes the point that she says out loud to the creative process that she's doing her best to record the creative thoughts. She behaves as if the genius is a passing 'Daemon' that is an external concept. By doing so, she distracts her left brain and makes it OK to relax and return to right-brain processes. This is also something that many artists relate to, particularly actors.

Fear and vulnerability – key creative skills

John Peters came to the world's attention in January 1991, when his bruised and battered face flashed onto television screens around the world. He is a former RAF pilot who was shot down during the Gulf War. His aircraft was hit by a surface to air missile, forcing him and his navigator, John Nichol, to eject over enemy territory. The two men were captured by Saddam Hussein's forces and endured seven weeks of torture. After being released, Peters emerged from his experience stronger, more resilient and more confident. He resumed his flying career and retired in 2000 as a squadron leader, using this experience to set up his own management consultancy, providing expertise on leadership, with particular interest on uncertainty, learning, trust and failure. Peters is an experienced speaker of international repute and regularly runs workshops on MBA programmes. He has written two bestselling books and a documentary, *Tornado Down*, which was a BAFTA Award Nominee. Currently, he is writing a new book that focuses on leadership in uncertainty.

Being a prisoner of war was a seminal learning experience. He mentions the story of US Air Force Colonel George Hall, a pilot during the Vietnam War who was shot down and held for seven and a half years as a prisoner of war. He spent those years in prison visualizing playing golf. When he was released, he was invited to the 1973 New Orleans PGA Open. He played to his handicap the first time out and shot a 76! Peters's own experience coincides: 'You escape beyond the solitary through visualization and imagination; it is the mother of invention. The uninterrupted isolation provides time for deep reflective thought and invention.' He now finds that stillness just before sleep. 'The silence of night provides space to think. I'll often be on my way to bed when I get struck with an idea, then two hours later it will be put down and I've got a fully formed idea.'

'The survival instinct concentrates the mind. We all experience fear and vulnerability when we are uncertain.' He feels that CEOs talk to him about this because they share this understanding. 'It's the paradox for leaders: achieve success whilst learning from failures. It is about accepting the most pressing anxiety.' He relates a meeting where a chief executive admitted that he was frightened and then others followed suit. 'He made it OK to admit fear. Once the emotion was shared, he asked, "So what do we do about it?" This problem that the board had been trying to address for three months, they solved in 20 minutes!'

Peters says that RAF flying training provided this mindset. 'It gives you a framework to discover yourself. It's built upon decades of people crashing aircraft. Aviation relentlessly advocates learning from every ounce of experience. Embracing every failure. Each year, 60 per cent of aviation accidents are caused by human error.' Peters says that is what is frustrating about working with other organizations. 'No one is prepared to admit failure. In the RAF, we spent our time studying mistakes that could one day prove fatal. The trick to this is to remove the fear. You have to make it alright to fail. And question assumptions.'

'The accepted view is that I should have suffered post-traumatic stress disorder (PTSD). The opposite is true: the Gulf experience was the making of me; a journey of discovery. Do you know how much confidence it provided?' He realized that everything else afterwards was easy by comparison: 'What's the worst that could happen after you've been threatened with gang rape and beaten incessantly? It occurred to me that this was the most frightened I could ever be. Everything else after would be easy. Failing in business held no fears for me.'

Another gift was the opportunity for deep reflection and time to think. He says that it's vital for the creative process: 'You have to look back and ask what you've learned. Most people are surprised how fast they can learn. It's not about what they've done since the last meeting, it's what they have *learned*. And how quickly and often they repeat this cycle. The key to creativity is curiosity. Become insatiably curious'.

Controlling fear is something you learn to do. Everyone has to learn to do this in their own way. However it's done, it's essential to allowing right-brain processes to flourish. This is because the fear of failure will keep dragging you back into a left-brain process. Steve Jobs once said: 'There is no such thing as failure – failure is just life trying to move us in another direction.' As US writer, educator, artist and designer Debbie Millman observed in *Fail Safe*, most of us 'like to operate within our abilities' – stepping outside of them risks failure.

On her website Brain Pickings, Maria Popova, its editor, picks up issues like this regularly.

She cites Sarah Lewis, Assistant Professor of History of Art and Architecture and African and African American Studies at Harvard University. She holds positions as curator at the Tate Modern and the Museum of Modern Art (MoMA), and is an appointment on President Obama's Arts Policy Committee. Her book *The Rise: Creativity, the Gift of Failure, and the Search for Mastery*, is an exploration of how 'discoveries, innovations, and creative endeavours often, perhaps even only, come from uncommon ground' and why this 'improbable ground of creative endeavour' is an enormous source of advantages on the path to self-actualization and fulfilment. In short, life becomes interesting when worlds collide. She cites some unusually diverse references from Captain Robert Falcon Scott, dancer Paul Taylor and pioneering social reformer Frederick Douglass.

Lewis relates a visit to Columbia University's Women's Archery team. They spend countless hours practising a sport that requires precision. From this sport, Lewis draws a metaphor for the core of human achievement. She watched the female archers suffer for their sport, through determination and the physical demands required. She points out that all mastery requires endurance. Mastery is not the same as success. This is just an event-based victory based on a peak point, a moment in time. Mastery is not merely a commitment to a goal, but to a curved-line, constant pursuit.

Mastery and failure

Lewis argues that failure is central to the concept of mastery. She cites Edison, who said of his countless attempts to create a light bulb: 'I have not failed, I've just found 10,000 ways that won't work.' She relates another, less famous Edison anecdote, when one of his inventions failed. Edison locked himself in his lab with five of his men and did not come out until the puzzle was solved. He spent 64 hours working continuously with no sleep, until he conquered the challenge. Could it be that the obsessive left-brain process has its ultimate conclusion in a transcendent state? The implication is fascinating – that another way of inducing the Alpha State is being so focused on the Beta State. This is almost Flaubertian: 'Anything becomes interesting if you look at it long enough.'

Lewis points out that embedded in the word 'failure' – a word originally synonymous with bankruptcy, is a 'a seeming dead end forced to fit human worth' – is the bias of our limited understanding of its value. She suggests the word failure itself is imperfect. Once it becomes decoupled from fear or self-criticism and we are ready to talk about it. We often call it something else – a learning experience, a reinvention, a turning point, an insight – no longer the dead end binary concept of failure. This is a classic left-brain trait – failure is either black or white. It's binary, simplified and taxonomized but underestimates that learning that leads to mastery, comes directly from failure. Transformation comes from how we choose to think and speak about it in our own narratives. Success is really defined in the Churchillian sense: 'Success is going from one failure to another with no loss of enthusiasm.' Decontextualization may offer an alternative view. The concept of failure is a classic feature of the left-brain process. It does not see the overall process. That, for instance, even getting into the position to fail is itself a success. You don't fail to win a gold medal. You succeeded in getting through the heats to the final.

In my experience of coaching, most people were easily capable of recognizing and condemning themselves for failure. They did not need confirmation from me of this. What they needed was to: 'Labour to keep alive in your breast that little spark of celestial fire, called context' (if I can misquote George Washington).

We are more likely to maintain our drive and enthusiasm when we retain our optimism, belief and purpose. This is why – important as it is to celebrate – we should never confuse one-time success with mastery. The state of mastery is always incomplete. This is a concept embraced by many successful people. As good as they are, all they've become aware of is what still remains yet to be done. As one successful politician put it to me: 'After all these years, I've simply become aware of how little I still know.' For this reason, failure needs to be treated in the same way as success (see Admiral Sir George Zambellas in Chapter 8). If failure generates a list of tasks which are yet to be completed or mastered, then success should do so, too. This also explains why students who equate their success as a reflection of their 'natural ability' are likely to learn less than those who see it as a product of effort. Complacency and comfort leads to a belief that mastery has been attained.

This is also why a 'near miss' can create enough discomfort to go on and win on the next occasion. This is a phenomenon first discovered by Daniel Kahneman and Amos Tversky who, in the 1980s, found people were far more frustrated about missing a flight by 5 minutes than by 30. This could be part of why silver medallists are more likely to win the gold next time around – victory seems possible, yet not as far away as for the bronze medallists, so the near miss is experienced as an encouragement because, well, you're almost there.

Lewis points out that 'a near miss' shifts our view of the landscape. It can turn future goals, into more realistic, more visible events. If we consider temporal distance, as we do spatial, this can change our focus so we plan to attain what lies in our sights. They're masters because they know there isn't an end. Focusing on what still remains to be discovered in your field, is an important feature in any creative endeavour. Most of the experts interviewed in this book consider themselves still to be learning.

Once again, Lewis provides an alternative to a culturally misunderstood word for an important concept. To explain the essence of this kind of surrender, she cites the martial art of aikido, which derives its power from 'strategic non-resistance'. This is embedded into the concept of transcendental meditation – that you should not grasp thoughts but let them pass through and still your mind to be a lake. The nearest we have is the self-absorption in images especially televisual images. The transcendent power of the image has been known for centuries. All societies have had icons and totems. In the mid-19th century, photography made its debut, and Lewis cites social reformer, abolitionist and statesman Frederick Douglass, who believed in the power of visual culture long before science confirmed the visual bias of the brain. Images are another way of kicking the mind into a right-brain state. Sometimes this can be a shocking process.

Douglass used the force of photography in this way. He used pictures of slavery and incarceration to win the argument for emancipation. Pictures don't make rational arguments. They're a 'show' not 'tell'. Douglass described 'the whole soul of man', when 'rightly viewed', as 'a sort of picture gallery, a grand panorama'. What Douglass was getting at, Lewis argues, is the notion of 'aesthetic force'. That pictures and art have an ability to transcend the left brain and win arguments. Good visual images are compelling because they are complete. Nothing else is required. The mechanics of how we see and remember when we are moved is something Douglass was describing, as he saw it, our pictorial process of creating reality.

The power of art

Douglass outraged aesthetics to make a political point. His depiction of a man in chains is ugly and therefore wrong. His visual idea was arresting because it went against the ethics of the time. Some may recall the Benetton adverts of the 1980s that did something similar. Benetton had a reputation for shock advertising that whipped-up controversy and stimulated debate – and helped boost the brand recognition with the 'United Colors of Benetton' slogan.

Now the UNHATE campaign, featuring world leaders kissing Barack Obama, has hit the headlines in a similar way, showing the US president kissing China's Hu Jintao and Venezuelan leader Hugo Chavez on the lips.

Faith in creativity

Jheni Arboine was Artist in Residence at LEWIS in 2015. She often came in to paint in the office and encourage others to take more risks creatively. If there is another more cheerful and calm person on the planet, I've yet to meet them. For her, art and faith come from the same root: 'I first got interested in art as a child. I was farmed out to Aunt Dorothy when my mother and father were both at college. I was given "colouring in" to do, even before I was going to school. Ha! I was taught not to go over the edges, but I loved it.'

Going to church was a big part of her life then, as it is now: 'Church isn't always the most exciting, so I whipped out the colouring books. There's a quiet in that process which was embedded into me which later allowed me to study successfully.' She went on to do a degree in social science which gave her options in local administration. Is there a link between faith and art? 'For me they are one and the same. I share my studio with another person of faith, and when I arrive, my routine is to pray first – just to say thanks.'

For Jheni, the action of painting is also a type of prayer. The provenance of the creativity is the quietness that was installed at an early age. Her environment is also important: 'Constable painted clouds and landscapes. I was brought up in the city so that's what I painted. I use photography to stimulate ideas. I look at the photographs then remove the colours. I love concrete and the grey.' Jheni's work features abstract stripes.

Chelsea College of Arts taught her to process what she experienced and hold it. 'Without this discipline I was just like a butterfly observing things. I didn't really think it through.' There's little doubt that creativity can be improved by training and discipline, but it helps if there is an innate platform. Agnes Martin said that in her mind's eye she would see images and she would just channel these onto the canvas. Jheni studied her work. 'I realized that coming out of sleep is when I was seeing paintings. I'm in that snoozy twilight world.' She relates the time dilation that people experience when in Flow. Jheni also induces this state by humming while painting.

The humming process is interesting in its own right. People hum to calm nerves, feel happier and reduce stress. People hum unconsciously and consciously. Many use humming as a simple and effective way to ease tension and reduce stress. Carole Bourne, writing on her website the healthylivinglounge.com, describes some of the benefits of humming. She says humming grounds and brings you back to your centre. 'It promotes clarity of thinking by refreshing your mind. It has a relaxing and soothing effect on your neck, face, head and shoulder muscles. Humming reduces the number of thoughts that fill your head. When you are humming there is little room for overthinking. Humming slows down your breathing rate significantly.' She says we normally breathe 15–17 times in a minute, but, with humming, that can be brought down to 4–6 a minute which can also help to slow down your heart rate. This can lower blood pressure between 10–20 mmHg.

This calm state of mind is essential to Jheni's creativity and it extends into her working methods and environment: 'I would never use an iPhone when painting. I would have music, but usually always the same disc. I'd leave it on silent so I could speak to my kids, but I check in on my terms, not on its.'

Is there a link between aesthetics and ethics? 'We're always looking at art with sharp criticality. It doesn't matter if people see truth and beauty. We also look at works which are ugly and critique them.' Truth and beauty are subjective.

Is religion ring-fenced in the same way as art? 'Art should be democratic. It should be open to anyone.' She explains that this is not a matter of forcing aesthetic appreciation. 'It's about reducing people's stress.' She continues to explain that art galleries are like public parks. 'People's blood pressure falls when they walk into an art gallery. It's an argument for well-being.' The positive impact of art in the workplace is part of the focus of this book, but in his book, *The Value of Arts for Business*, Giovanni Schiuma argues strongly for a wider-based arts intervention in business.

In what he calls the effect on 'Brainware' he says people's attitude and behavioural traits are dramatically altered by art in the workplace. He lists: 'Confidence; curiosity; emotions and feelings; empathy; flexibility; mental focus; individual energy; instinct; intelligence; mindset; passion; readiness; reflection; self-esteem; empowering; sensitivity; vitality.'

For what he calls the 'software' of an organization the list is even longer: 'Atmosphere; collegiality; commitment; connectivity; cooperative mindset (reciprocity, connectivity, collegiality); culture; energy; identification; intimacy; excitement; interest and engagement; good place to work; involvement; mutuality; reciprocity; routines and practices; supportive, safe, comfortable and idea-rich environment; values; work practices.'

Art is not always a factor in well-being. There are different types of artist. Some art students have serious mental issues – depression, for instance. Jheni adds, 'My mother was a psychiatric sister so she saw a lot of it. She was also a person of faith and that helped her greatly.' She cites an instance when going for a job. 'I'd always been interested in working for Habitat (a store in Croydon where she grew up) but I never saw any black people working there. I came home and told my mother there was no chance because they were racist. My mother said you couldn't judge people in this way because that was just as prejudiced. So I went there and asked about jobs. They gave me an application form and shortly afterwards I had a job there!

'Having creativity and faith has strengthened me and enabled me to cope more. Faith is my in-breath and creativity my out-breath.'

Jheni says that a Greek word *ekphrasis* is what we should be aiming at with art in the workplace – namely, that people become creative when around other works of creativity. Sometimes this could be about the work itself or about the environment the work is in. When people are pressurized at work, they are more susceptible to their environment. She related a time in the office at LEWIS, when she said people had been unsettled by one of the paintings near their desk. She took it down and replaced it with one she'd painted herself. 'Suddenly, people were a lot happier. The picture became a talking point for them and among others. It was almost as if they'd taken ownership of their own space. The effect of art in an office is profound.'

Truth, beauty and aesthetics

To understand more about this, we need to hear Gandhi's views on truth and beauty: 'There are two aspects of things – the outward and the inward. The outward has no meaning except in so far as it helps the inward. All true art is thus an expression of the soul. The outward forms have value only in so far as they are the expression of the inner spirit of man.' Gandhi said that many people call themselves artists, and are recognized as such, but there was 'absolutely no trace of the soul's upward urge and unrest' in their works. 'All true Art must help the soul to realize its inner self. In my own case, I find that I can do entirely without external forms in my soul's realization. I can claim, therefore, that there is truly efficient Art in my life, though you might not see what you call works of Art about me.' He also said that 'productions of man's art have their value only in so far as they help the soul onward towards self-realization. We have somehow accustomed ourselves to the belief that art is independent of the purity of private life. I can say with all the experience at my command that nothing could be more untrue. The art of producing good music from a cultivated voice can be achieved by many, but the art of producing that music from the harmony of a pure life is achieved very rarely.

'I see and find Beauty in Truth or through Truth. All Truths, not merely true ideas, but truthful faces, truthful pictures, or songs, are highly beautiful. People generally fail to see Beauty in Truth, the ordinary man runs away from it and becomes blind to the beauty in it. Whenever men begin to see Beauty in Truth, then true Art will arise.' Gandhi suggested a clear link between aesthetics and ethics. Aesthetics is the critical examination of art, culture and nature. Human conduct is part of culture. Therefore, an ethical action is a beautiful action measured by our values.

Conclusion

You may be asking why we have gone so far as to include Gandhi here. It's because his spirituality parenthesizes so many of the Creative Traits such as being Quiet, Repeating, Releasing, Relaxing and Dreaming. It reflects an attitude that is receptive to art in all its forms. If you want to be creative yourself it's not just an inside-out process. You have to embrace other people's creativity, too. So we can see that, what many of us think is an unusual or strange process is actually quite common. We just don't talk about it or share the process. We go into the shower and we come out with great ideas. But if we do that, then why don't we recognize that it's not the shower, per se, that produces the ideas – it's the conditions of the shower. If we can understand the conditions, then two things can happen. Firstly, we can replicate them and make them happen more frequently and perhaps in the workplace. Secondly, we can create the conditions for others and thus magnify and multiply the creative force. Sorry. Now I'm beginning to sound like Obi-Wan Kenobi.

Generating better ideas

07

By the end of this chapter, you'll have learned how to generate better ideas on your own and then learn how to involve others. You'll find out how to spot the Eight Creative Traits and apply them. You'll also learn important techniques for overcoming objections to creative training. You'll learn principles and practice tips for coaching and how to awaken the right-brain process. Finally, we'll look at examples from the LEWIS Rise Academy and cover how it applies right-brain process thinking in areas such as presentations, the creative cycle and speed reading.

Generating better ideas: it's all about you

So, you've almost made it to the end of the book. For those of you still in your left-brain process, here's the answer to the question on the front cover (you always knew it would be at the back of the book, didn't you?): 'How do you reclaim your personal creativity in a hyper-connected culture?'

Read more

If you want to think originally, then you have to read more. Reading not only improves your long-term concentration, but it also opens you to new ideas and respect for people. Later in this chapter, you'll find a speed reading technique to help you with this and, in the upcoming interviews, Helayne Spivak and Lord Chadlington will provide further insight on the importance of reading.

Get out more

We have to recognize that the space immediately around us deeply affects the way we think about things. Big spaces give bigger thoughts. This seems to be why so many people report getting ideas when on aircraft.

Realize the whole subject is paradoxical

This is perhaps the reason why so many have struggled with it. There are two distinct processes. We analyse things and we do the opposite. It's wrong to call these left- and right-brain activities because both sides contribute. We can, though, call them processes because they are distinct and identifiable, but definitely not located in just one side of the brain. That's why, although many organizations still use brainstorms, ideas often come when we're away from work, on our own or not trying.

Don't allow technology to interrupt

Most people work with their email open. Most have an alert on it. Most people stop and look at incoming email. If we want to think more deeply, we have to stop being interrupted. Check your email regularly but switch it off when you're thinking. Your iPhone is a tool for you to use, not the other way around.

Be present

Teenagers especially exhibit this quality as do some bad-mannered adults. They will be looking at emails and Facebook while you're trying to talk to them. If we're not properly here, then there's no chance that we can harness the moment to be creative because other people can help you develop ideas.

Conventional education may not be the answer

Many are not reaching their potential because they are overloaded by social media, educational and work expectations. The psychological pressure is at epidemic levels.

The next generation is not wrong but different

The post-internet, post-recession generations actually are different. They are paradoxical. They talk less, but communicate more. They're more creative, but less active. They know more, but read less.

Don't mistake the illusion of speed for the reality of it

So many high achievers have done so the hard way. Creativity often walks hand in hand with impatience. We're not good at deferred gratification. We're not used to waiting. Have faith. Sometimes you can't rush things. Slow is smooth and smooth is fast.

Get more sleep and of a better quality

If you really want to use your mind, you have to understand how it works. This means knowing what your brain needs. Sleep is central to it. As Russell Foster says: 'Sleep is the biggest cognitive enhancer that we know.' We also have to know the conditions under which we can sleep best.

It's OK to play

They're not being frivolous, it's just the way they approach life. You can still be a serious creative, if you don't take it seriously.

Learn how to be commercial and creative

As Vanessa Brady says: 'Creative people want to give. If you ask them for 40 hours, you'll get 60. We need to help them to protect themselves.'

Open your eyes and your heart

If we want to be more creative, we have to heighten our visual and sonic senses. We have to listen to music, view great art. We also have to avoid anything that might blunt our senses. On page 182, Lord Chadlington talks about the effect of music.

Be an outsider because there are no insiders

To really get to grips with an issue, we need to see it from outside in as well as inside out. Many of my interviewees reported this: Lord Chadlington described everyone as suffering from Imposter Syndrome. If this is the case, then we can all be outsiders.

Quieten down

Silence has just as much power as stimulation. So many have reported that silence at best or at worst white noise, is an important precondition to the creative state. Stimulation, beyond a point can blunt our senses.

Embrace time and space

It's clear that the brain contributes unconsciously to the creative process and we have to allow time for this natural process. Obviously people are unaware of it, but it happens nonetheless. We must use that, otherwise we end up with ideas that are fresh, but not deep. Total immersion into the subject matter, followed by withdrawal for incubation, is far more likely to deliver ideas.

Creativity isn't just for the 'creative'

Perhaps one of the reasons that creatives are not always perceived as credible, is that they don't have the same standards as others. Do creatives need to adopt all the rigid standards of the commercial rubrics? No, but they can move towards them. Do others need to adopt all the flexible standards of the commercial rubrics? No, but they can move towards them.

When you're doing nothing, you're still doing something

It's not a crime to waste time. Remember Einstein: 'Creativity is the residue of time wasted.' Even when you're sleeping, your brain is working. It's OK to be passive and in the waiting state.

Creative director and teacher

Helayne Spivak is a wired ball of fire. She's intense and focused. Over the course of the years, she has been recognized by *The Wall Street Journal*'s Leaders Campaign, was honoured with the Matrix Award for Women in Communications, was named one of the top 50 Women In Business by *BusinessWeek* magazine and served as a judge at the Cannes Advertising Festival, among other accolades.

Her father was an artist and she knew she wanted to do something creative, so: 'I tried stand-up comedy and acting but, at 24, I worked on my first ad and I realized it was something that I really had to do. As a creative, you take everything with you that you need, no matter where you are.'

She says there will always be a duality to her work: 'Workspaces are for where you get your input, but the output comes elsewhere. Your body needs time to process.' During sleep is when her mind puts everything into its proper box. Like many creatives, she doesn't sleep much but, when she does, her brain organizes everything. But: 'If I wake up and write things down, the ideas are usually rubbish!'

She is strong though, on collaboration. 'I encourage people to talk throughout the creative process. You just can't pull it out of the air. You have to talk to each other. Two people talking is important. You can't just pull creativity out of the air. Too many people are afraid of saying stuff that's stupid.'

One of the big changes is that so many more people are involved in the creative process these days: 'Writers and artists used to work together almost exclusively. These days, planners are making a huge impact with their insights.' And that's not even to mention those who specialize in the customer experience. She believes this needs as much creativity as the other areas, but not all writers and directors understand customer experience design. There's another paradox here because good creativity, experienced as customer design, will always be invisible. When something is creatively successful, it doesn't always get noticed. This is especially true in advertising, where the persuasion is subtle.

She says this is an example of how, over the last 20 years, the creative process has changed to become more joined up therefore less obvious. 'It's become less siloed. Now to do things well, you need to know more about all areas. What the product says is about communications. The product experience can be something else.'

The environment she's in has always been important to her: 'The big spaces allow the ideas to come. The smaller space allows them to develop.'

She points out that women are still under-represented in the creative space as creative directors: 'It's still quite an old-fashioned industry.' Does she think men can write for women? She's diplomatic: 'I was once at a meeting which was to discuss a sanitary product – I think it was a tampon – and the room was full of men discussing it. I just said, look it's up to you, but you might want a woman in the team.' Can they do it? Should they do it? 'No. You probably still wouldn't see a woman writing on a beer ad.'

The essence of her creative process is driven by fear: 'I realized that my energy levels and my fear were directly linked. Sometimes I would really doubt my ability. You can never mistake the edge of the rut for the horizon. You cannot solve your problems with the same thinking that caused them.' Despite the collaboration process, she says you need to have 'alone time', and that often is best early or late in the day. Her creative process is illustrated by her favourite artists like Edward Hopper whose work depicts solitude: 'I'm just drawn to his work.' She says that writers, whether they're lonely or not, 'always return to their cave.'

Does she go into the zone? 'It's somewhere between pain and joy. It's painful because you want to do it well. I hate writing, but I love having written.' Interestingly though, she says she still can't work directly onto a computer. 'It doesn't feel like writing. It feels like typing. I have to do it longhand.' She insists that to be truly creative you need a love for words and pictures: 'You need to have the pictures in your head. Kids in general just don't do this enough. They don't have the patience. Reading books is very similar to respecting people. It takes time.'

The Eight Creative Traits (QED3RPT)

Throughout this book, we've highlighted the Eight Creative Traits. These are the features to look for in creative success. It's unlikely that you will ever be in an environment that has none of these, so in most cases you're not starting with a blank sheet of paper. There will always be some elements of the creative process, if you look closely enough. They may be hidden, but inside even the most desiccated, most driven, most disciplined environments there are creative qualities. When we're trying to change cultures, we need to find and encourage these traits.

Quiet

An excellent text here is Susan Cain's *Quiet: The Power of Introverts in a World That Can't Stop Talking*. She shows how we can gain back control – finding the 'off' switch. It is important for us to get rid of the noise and the clutter so we can experience sounds, smells, touch and the full senses. Creativity often speaks quietly. Silence is therefore to be enjoyed. Creativity also needs concentration. The quiet will stop you being interrupted. The enemies of this are multitasking and juggling. If you are mentally busy, creativity will not come. This is because you cannot concentrate on everything all at once. The body can be busy but the mind needs to be unoccupied. Creativity needs calm.

Engage

You can't do anything without commitment. Creativity needs focus. So do you. Take time to listen. Take time to believe. Have faith. Believe in yourself, even if there's no logic to doing so.

Dream

Creativity needs imagination. Encourage yourself to daydream. Everything around you had to be invented. That meant someone had to dream. Allow yourself time to stop watching the clock. Look at the clouds. What do they remind you of? I know – clouds. Keep trying.

Release

To relax, you have to let go and accept that you can't do everything. But you do need the basics. Sleep is king. Revise Foster's rules for better sleep. There are key relationships between sleep and carbohydrates and sleep and exercise and sleep and mental illness. Understanding the basics can really help. Any of the creative arts can help here – dance and movement, art both in viewing and painting, and creating literally anything.

Relax

Creativity will not be forced. Drive slower. Walk slower. Moving from 'Type A' is difficult, but it might keep you alive. It will not come to the impatient. You may never learn to love the queue or the line, but you can be calm in doing so. Ideas do not arrive by timetable. If you live by the clock, you will not allow creativity to intervene. Waste time. Enjoy being idle. You don't have to be the smartest person in the room. Speak last in meetings. Imagine the future. Focus on autonomy and mastery.

Repeat

To gain any skill, repetition is key. But it doesn't have to be monotonous. You can try different things every day. Creativity should be your daily bread. Food should be a creative exercise. Experiment. Take time over it. Break the routine. Begin the re-education.

Play

Creativity needs you to play. You can't play when you're rushing. Conversation should be playful. Enjoy it. Don't press the same elevator button every day. Take the time to learn new ideas and talk. Walk up to someone and ask them if anyone has told them they're a genius today, laugh like a maniac and run off shouting: 'He made me do it!' pointing at this book.

Teach

This is a vital area. People learn a lot more when they teach. The tutor is often the student – you don't know what you know. Reading is a key part of this if you want to teach. You can't be a prophet in your own land. Sometimes to do this, we need to accelerate the input by reading faster. Always be aware that different ages, genders and cultures learn at different paces and in different ways.

Can you tell if you're too left-brained?

As part of Rise, we also try to audit where people are with their left/right thinking processes. Of course, we don't need a left-brain process or a right-brain process. We need both. But before we become convinced that this is the case, we need more evidence that we are out of balance.

On a scale of 1–10 (10 being most frequent weekly)
How often:

1 Do you daydream?

2 Are you in a quiet place?

3 Do you laugh out loud?

4 Do you take at least 20 minutes exercise?

5 Do you ever think to yourself what a wonderful world?

6 Do you spend time playing a child's game?

7 Do you spend time socializing with a neighbour or co-worker?

8 Do you spend more than 30 minutes over food?

9 Do you get the perfect night's sleep?

10 Have you thought this is what I was put here to do?

11 Do you feel stressed?

12 Do you feel angry or depressed?

13 Do you feel exhausted?

14 Do you feel you want people out of your way?

15 Do you feel like you need a drink, cigarette?

16 Have you reached for a sweet snack to make you feel good?

17 Have you cursed your bad luck?

18 Do you feel you just want to be left alone?

19 Have you felt disliked?

20 Have you felt there are not enough hours in the day?

Total the scores for 1–10, then subtract the total of 11–20.

< –10	You need to take immediate action to slow down and decompress
–10 to –5	You should try to remove some of the more stressful situations and relax more
–5 to 0	Some aspects of your life might be stressful, but they are probably temporary
0 to 5	You're generally OK but could improve some aspects by working at them
5 to 10	You seem on top of your game and enjoying yourself
> 10	You are almost certainly in Flow

This is just intended as a rough guide. There are many more left and right tests online, but it gets people thinking about how they spend their time and what they can do to improve their creativity and well-being.

The 'SQ3R' speed reading technique

I've mentioned the 'SQ3R' speed reading technique throughout the book. This is a method introduced by Francis Robinson from his book *Effective Study*. We teach this technique to enable delegates to absorb more information faster. It's founded on the principle that most people read at the speeds they had when they were adolescents. That speed is usually constant for all type of material – easy, hard, comic or textbook. Critics of this technique have suggested that it deprives the reader of the comfort of having fully read the material. Supporters say it allows a much faster grasp of written material by using 20 per cent of the time to gain 80 per cent of the understanding.

Survey

Stage one is to survey or skim the material. The technique suggests resisting the temptation to read the book and instead just glance through a chapter in order to identify headings, subheadings and other outstanding features. You can quickly look at the first and last sentences of paragraphs. This helps when identifying questions about the contents in the next stage.

Question

In stage two you ask questions about the content of the material such as: What do I expect to learn? Why should I be reading this? What questions do I want answered? The technique suggests converting headings into questions and then looking for answers in the rest of the material. So for this book it might be: Why am I so overloaded? What techniques can I learn to help me? How do I become more creative?

Read

The problem with reading is that it can be very slow. If you ask a friend or colleague to look at your eyes while you're reading, they will be able to tell you the number of times your eyes stop as they're progressing on a line. Most people's eyes will go from side to side across the page then move down. A speed reader's eyes only travel down the page alighting on one line in the centre. To do this requires practice. You need to extend your fixation to take in the whole line on the page. Typographers design text to be used in this way, because they've never set more than 39 characters (1.5 times the alphabet) in that font as their column width. With the background work done in stages one and two above, the reading is much more active in trying to answer the questions raised under stage two. Passive (normal) reading, by contrast, tends not to engage the text as closely. In this stage, you need to read as fast as possible to build your speed. The faster you go, the faster you will go normally.

Recall/Recite

On completing your rapid scan, this is the stage where you match questions with answers. Some of this can be out loud or written to see how much of the material has stuck. It should raise further questions which bring you back into stage two.

Review

This is where you go back over the whole process to evaluate how satisfactory it's been. Are there questions still outstanding? Where would you take the research? What other angles would you like to cover? Do you agree with the propositions made? Are you sure you've covered the gist of the book?

Generating better ideas: it's all about others

Now you know how to make yourself more creative, you might think you're ready to be unleashed on others. They, however, might not be ready for you. So this section deals with how you can overcome objections to creative thinking.

The concept of the 'out breath'

If you're making an argument for creative thinking, you will encounter logic. You need to point out that whenever we're asked to solve a problem, our default is to analyse it. We break it down into component parts and analyse those even more. Right-brain process thinking tries to do the opposite. This creates another problem. Any solution available to us from the right brain is immediately undercut and ironized by the judgemental left brain. As Iain McGilchrist has pointed out: 'The left-brain process is very convincing because it's shaved off everything that doesn't fit with its model. It's entirely consistent, largely because it's made itself so.' The right-brain process is abstract and doesn't have a voice and therefore can't construct logical arguments. That's why we have an entire canon of leadership and self-development texts which concentrate on how to solve problems by focusing directly upon them. Supposing you wanted to perfect your out breath, then you might focus on books that would analyse lung volumes, chest muscles, the airways, oxygen contents, temperature and pressures, etc. But what about concentrating on the exact opposite – the in breath? The left-brain process of analysis always drags us back into focusing directly on the problems and then breaking them down. The left-brain process is thus part of the problem itself. Decontextualizing is the vital gift of the right-brain process. Remember Einstein? 'Creativity is the residue of time wasted.' For example, walking is being rediscovered as a place to think. There are many cases of creative walkers – William Wordsworth, Charles Dickens, Virginia Woolf, George Orwell, Thomas De Quincey, Friedrich Nietzsche and Vladimir Nabokov are just some of the others who have written about it.

The artist attorney

Jason File is one of the most extraordinary people I've ever met. We first met when I was trying to explain a piece of his art to a colleague, who was being particularly left-brained. The work was called *Present Absence* (2013). It comprised a SIM chip mounted on an invisible wire within a bell jar (www.jasonfile.com/works#/present-absence-2013/). The chip appeared to be floating. I explained to my colleague that I found the work inspiring. It was saying that we're connected, but only to other people who are connected. In fact, we have the illusion of connectivity. My colleague was baffled. File came over and sympathized. We got chatting. Turned out he was a high-flying US attorney. He'd just finished as part of the prosecution team in the trial of Slobodan Milošević at the war crimes prosecutions in The Hague.

File holds degrees in fine art from the Chelsea College of Arts, London, and the Royal Academy of Art, the Netherlands (2013), where he currently teaches. He also holds degrees in the humanities, social sciences and law from Yale (1998), Oxford (2000) and Yale Law School (2004) respectively.

'I'd catalogued every brutality and every rape and I'd reached an end', he explained. 'I needed to get out and find a way of expressing myself.'

What File demonstrates is what Gandhi was articulating. Clearly, he was using the process of aesthetic balance to return himself to health and equilibrium. The other aspect of this award-winning artist was that he'd experienced both ends of the left/right continuum. He didn't just excel as an artist and an attorney. He excelled because he was an artist and an attorney. It takes great courage to do this, but File was drawn to it intuitively.

He says that his experience in the legal world taught him that there are many actions or objects existing in institutional, social or political environments that possess rich potential as artistic material, but they are often overlooked or ignored: 'I make art, in part, to highlight some of this potential for diverse audiences, in the hope of revealing hidden aspects of our relationships with institutions and each other.'

He talks about the sort of incompleteness that other professionals report: 'Law just wasn't giving me a complete understanding of the world. I needed to explore the world, and art gives me a conduit. The two may not be at all similar, but they cohabit in my brain quite nicely.' This is quite important. Just because it makes no immediate sense, it doesn't mean you shouldn't do it. Like drinkers, there are two types of problem creatives – those who are too creative and those who are not creative enough.

He agrees and says that the connection is not obvious: 'I do feel like there are moments of inspiration in both areas. Strangely though, I get the best ideas for my legal practice in the art studio and vice versa. They just overlap in some sense.'

He also states that the other major places for ideas are riding a bicycle into work and when falling asleep and waking up.

Does he use a set-procedures or induction routine? 'No. I feel like a lot of the heavy lifting conceptually happens outside the studio.' It seems as if File needs to immerse himself in the process and reflect upon it. Because time is at a premium, he often selects the most profitable creative ideas – which ones are worthy of physical visual expression and which are dead ends: 'For every 20 ideas, I might make only one of them. This process runs for a month or two. I don't ever euthanize ideas. They may just not have reached maturity at this point. I need to find what ideas will stand the test of time.'

File lives between two poles. At one end, a desiccated, unambiguous objective world that offers little engagement. At the other, almost the opposite – a pure metaphor. 'In a criminal trial we need to present the facts in such a way that everyone is certain about the objective truth. In the arts world, it's almost entirely subjective. Law is the ultimate in shared understanding. Art is the opposite. It communicates at the individual level.'

File also produced a work called *Conditions of Performance*. This is a wall of all contractual terms that are currently, knowingly or unknowingly, binding what he does. This is the ultimate mixture of the two – left-brain process precision and right-brain process ambiguity.

Turning his back on law was hard. He says his family thought he was mad, but it made perfect sense to him. 'I felt like it was met with unspoken criticism. They thought I was having a midlife crisis. Like going into art was a character flaw', he says. Life without art, he suggests, would've been like having 'an empty performance space'.

It's clear that courage and determination are key variables when accessing potential. Whether it's the courage to pursue a different career in life or the courage to separate from the crowd. It also takes courage to embrace solitude.

Be ready for scepticism

You will always be up against this when trying to bring forward new ideas and techniques. You should expect it. Never underestimate the Stockholm syndrome which the left-brain process can engender. This is also known as capture-bonding, which is a psychological phenomenon where hostages express empathy, sympathy and positive feelings toward their captors, sometimes to the point of defending and identifying with them. The left-brain process has many allies! In my own experience, as a coach to senior politicians, celebrities and business achievers, I've noticed this manifest in two different ways. Sometimes I'm referred to people I cannot help. This is because, in order to access potential, you have to make people aware of the right-brain processes and how they can work. In rare cases, some people are so convinced of the logic of the left brain that they identify all forms of alternative as a threat. The net result is scepticism about any idea other than those they are already familiar with. Sometimes they just won't let go of their left-brain process.

We're not machines

It would be so much easier if creative access was as simple as opening a throttle or throwing a switch. If we want to maximize creative output, we must accept that this is not a linear process and that humans are not machines. This is where we return to a concept espoused in Tony Schwartz's *The Way We're Working Isn't Working*. Here, he talks about people being able to access greater energy by allowing themselves to 'pulse', to take breaks between work, as a way of allowing greater long-term energy management. Schwartz makes the point that humans oscillate: 'The human body is hardwired to pulse. To operate at our best, we need to renew our energy at 90-minute intervals – not just physically, but also mentally and emotionally. When we build this rhythm into our lives, it changes everything.'

Look inside out

We can build on this principle by asking 'what would happen if we applied this to the creative process?' Concentrating on creative output solely as a way of maximizing it might be wrong. We could look at creative output from the outside. We must move to the counter-intuitive. If we want to improve creative ability, maybe we need to move to the opposite of stimulation which is silence and stillness? If Einstein is right, then in order to boost creativity, we may need to improve the quality of solitude or the way in which we 'waste' time. Creativity is profoundly human. We know that we can best enjoy something when we've been deprived of it. 'Hunger is the best pickle', as Benjamin Franklin put it. If this is true, then abstaining from the creative process may be a way of promoting it.

Finance is like fire

Finance is a good servant, but an evil master. 'Sometimes creatives feel they are fighting without a narrative, against the money men', says Joanna, a California-based creative director. 'They just don't get that creativity is not linear. It comes when it comes.' This speaks to the problem of harnessing creativity for profit. Most creatives work in Flow. They are so absorbed by their process, that they lose sight of time, resource and commercial viability. 'Sometimes you can be working for days on a problem, then it all comes to you a week later. Why don't they get this?' This illustrates a common problem. You can summarize by saying that everyone wants to add value – it's just that finance people need to deliver it in the short-term. Creative people tend to be more in Flow than finance people and sometimes lose sight of the short-term imperatives. In my experience, it's not the creatives that need to adjust their mindset.

The rules change higher up

What works at one stage in a career may not work at the next. In leadership terms, people often get to management level by process excellence (a left-brain skill). Essentially, this is doing things *right*. Leadership from this stage on is different. It involves a moral dimension. Essentially, it's about doing the *right* things (a right-brain process skill). This is a classic example of the left-to-right switch. Understanding this is essential in a leadership culture. Take financial problem-solving, for instance. At one level, this involves focusing on the problem, analysing it, researching it and investigating it. Essentially, these are left-brained skills. There comes a point when analysing a problem can no longer be achieved by reduction. Then we need to ask the question: 'Why are we even doing this? What would happen if we didn't?' This is the moment when black boxing and taking it to the higher level happens. How one system relates to another is divergent thinking. Essentially, this is a right-brain process skill. There's a paradox here that says the harder we try, the worse we get. This is against all received wisdom.

Training principles

It's not enough to think you'll engender a creative culture through a one-off training event or workshop. It needs courage to bring about a major shift in culture. To do this the programme needs to:

Be systematic

To engineer change you need to be thorough, organized and focused on the outcomes. You need to measure as much of the output as possible. You also need to show how the training has changed the prospects of the individuals concerned. Remember that training is also an opportunity to observe performance.

Be long-term

You won't change a culture overnight. It's more likely to be a long-term process. Be sure though that you set an expectation on what change looks like and when it's likely to happen. Be sure that you see the wider impact of your investment. You do need to try and measure short-term impact, but be careful not to oversell immediate benefits. Training is a poor word for what we're doing here. We're releasing potential. People usually appreciate this and talk about it. So strike out training and write in 'word-of-mouth marketing'.

Be consistent

To see progress, you need to be able to compare session with session, and to gather feedback which can help improve your training. Be clear about the standards you're trying to achieve and what is acceptable. People usually like to be assessed and given feedback and this is in no way inconsistent with fun. This can especially be the case when peer group critique is used (see George Blacklock in the case study on pages 57–61).

Gain accreditation

If you're bringing about change, it's not enough for it to be internally validated. It means more when an independent third party is involved. This can be any recognized standards organization, but it's worth taking the time and expense to do this. You want certificates from recognized authorities.

Involve senior people and not just trainers

Cultural change must come from the top. There's no point having one rule that says seniority can do what they like, provided that everyone else changes the culture. The people at the top need to be the values, not only to set the example, but to show that they support and appreciate them. The best way to ensure this is to involve them in the training.

Remove people from their usual context

If you want to open people's minds, you do have to take them away from their normal workplace. This provides perspective and the opportunity for them to bond with others. It can be difficult taking people away from family and partners but, if planned, it's doable and allows people to focus all their energies on the learning.

Take people out of their comfort zone

Trust is the key here. You can get people to try new things if you take them a step at a time. Learning new skills (really of any kind) can be a precursor to releasing someone's potential. Sometimes this can be quite as simple as travelling to a new location, meeting fresh people and taking on new group tasks with new people.

Be physical and practical in terms of activity

The best type of training gets out of the classroom and gets people moving around and improvising. The growth in corporate cooking classes is a good example of the way some firms tackle the process. Sometimes this activity can be brought into the office, for instance, with an artist in residence that physically uses an office for painting. Again, with the right organization this can involve team members. It's surprising what potential you can release when you put a paint-brush in someone's hand.

Be realistic

You will not be universally praised by anyone for training people. Finance people will not love you, nor will HR, because you will not cure staff churn by training – you may even accelerate it. But there are two alternatives here. You can retain poorly trained staff for ever. Or you can run the risk that some will repay the training investment by leaving. If they do, however, they will take your training with them and you must trust that they will pay testament to it (if it's any good!).

So, what else do you need to know?

Leading in the field of creative education is all about coaching rather than lecturing. Perhaps the best book in this field that I've come across is Jenny Rogers's book *Coaching Skills: A Handbook*. This book is packed with wisdom and it's all the more relevant because Jenny spent decades working at one of the biggest creative organizations in the world – the BBC.

She says the harder you try to solve a creative problem, the less likely you are to find a good solution. 'I'm not a believer in "brain-storming". You just have to let the ideas come', she says. She's not even sure that 'creativity' is a 'skill' that can be coached in the trad-itional sense: 'I often hear clients put themselves down by saying that they are "not creative" and by that they mean they will never write a play. You can be interested in "creativity" by enjoying art or cinema without thinking you've "failed".' What she thinks is more important is to cultivate habits of open-mindedness. She has noticed that many people can get into flawed thinking patterns and need to learn how to look all around a problem before concluding that it can't be solved. She believes De Bono's 6 Thinking Hats is a good example of how to do this and that Myers–Briggs Type Indicators (a personality test) can also help. Rogers adds that often the mistakes creative people make are the same as those which everyone else makes: 'Giving up too soon, failing to seek a wide enough range of opinion, not trusting their instinct or trusting it too much. It all depends on levels of psychological maturity.'

She sees a lot of people in executive team meetings stuck to their devices, openly texting or doing their emails: 'Even walking along any street can be hazardous these days with people bumping into you because they're transfixed by their phones!' This is not only dangerous, but negates the breaks offered by walking. But it's funny as well and that's a key part of what she believes is correct style for creative coaching. She says it's important for people to have fun with what they do. You can do this on your own, but shared laughter is a good indicator of people having fun.

She also places importance on the location. People like to work in places they perceive as creative. For this reason, London is a top destination for international careers. London has easy access to cinema, theatre and museums. Creativity should be coached in all organizations: 'It has the power to free people up, create fresh perspectives and everyone should harness it.' Rogers adds that having some creative DNA in organizations helps, because they tend to hire people just like the people they already have. So, if there are a lot of 'creative' people, you will get more of the same. It's important to think about where you base people.

She says that there is a debt from coaching to psychotherapy but the two are mutually exclusive. Some of the techniques she points to are where the coach says: 'I'm at the limit of my skills as a coach.' Rogers stresses the importance of personal responsibility in coaching. This is all around believing that you have a choice over your life that you choose, your behaviour, your feelings, your thoughts and your reactions. This is essential. You cannot take responsibility for making someone else creative – it has to be your choice.

She believes that avoiding the principle of choice always involves a pay-off. 'If I claim my organization is causing me hideous stress by overworking me, my pay-off is that I am a victim and I will attract sympathy, attention, and possibly financial compensation as well.' It's vital for creative people to accept the principle of choice and this does not involve blame, of either yourself or others.

Rogers outlines a number of useful questions for creative coaching:

1 What problem are you trying to solve?

2 Why does it need to be done now?

3 Who owns this?

4 How important is the creative element (from 1–10)?

5 What have you already tried?

6 What does success look like?

7 What are the options for action here?

8 How do the options match the requirements?

9 What's the first step?

10 When will that happen?

She also makes the point that most people already know what the solutions to their creative problems are. You just have to tease them out, but their feelings get in the way. She says the most powerful questions for coaching people are short:

- How does that feel?
- Tell me more?
- Why do you say that?
- What do you want to happen?

Then summarize and summarize again:

- Have I got that right?
- Is that what you're saying?
- Is that a good summary?

Creative coaching has to be done carefully and it helps to rehearse and role-play.

Now you can see that it's one thing to activate your own right-brain process. It's another to induce it in others. Coaching is a real art form and it's worth taking advice and guidance from those who coach for a living.

Taking others into the zone

Culture is always set from the top. You might say that you've known departments or groups that have had their own separate culture and of course this can be true. It's the parentheses of behaviour that's set from the top – the range of activities that are tolerated. In Daniel Pink's book *A Whole New Mind*, he explores the concepts of autonomy and cites examples of organizations where the culture has been engineered to create a wider parenthesis. Sometimes this can happen around one charismatic individual, but seldom does an individual have this much impact without exhibiting signs of autocracy. Once the culture is created it can be self-policing.

Pink cites cases where companies have scrapped holiday allowances completely. It seems that 80 per cent of staff take as much holiday as they feel they need and no more. Roughly 20 per cent abuse the system. He points out though, that the productivity and engagement gained by raising performance in the 80 per cent, is worth the hassle of dealing with the 20 per cent. In many instances, he says the negative behaviour is policed out by the culture. Although Pink's cases are interesting and compelling there's a bigger problem here and it relates to capital structure.

Many large organizations have remote capital. These people or organizations have expectations based purely on financial grounds. Consequently, these organizations are measured on short-term metrics like total shareholder returns. Often these are applied rigorously and relentlessly in the short term. This may work for a short while, but anywhere this has been done to extremes, the result has often been disaster.

This is the left-brain process writ large – compare, contrast, ana-lyse – measure everything. Ordinary relationships don't survive under this duress, so why do relationships at work? The answer lies in un-willing compulsion. You don't have to be in a relationship with someone. You do need to have a job. The conditions of compulsion are anathema to developing Flow. Of course, anyone can do a job, but to really tap into people's Flow, the conditions need to be created – what Pink calls Purpose, Mastery and Autonomy. But how to create such conditions? These are engendered by culture, which can't be cre-ated overnight. One of the problems that militates against this is em-ployee tenure. According to the US Federal Bureau of Labor Statistics the average worker stays in post 4.5 years. For the workforce's youngest employees, it's probably half that. If Millennials spend less than three years in post, they can expect to have 15–20 jobs over their career. This undermines the case for investment in training and skills in traditional eyes.

A 2012 survey by Net Impact found that 88 per cent of workers considered 'positive culture' important to their dream job. Extreme labour flexibility is a perfectly normal reaction to what Millennials see as increased insecurity. What is the point of staying in a post if the loyalty is not reflected? As technology has eroded more jobs, the stigma associated with leaving a job early has diminished. So far from being the representation of capricious whim, it looks more like learned survival behaviour. Some might envy their footloose freedom, but it comes with a downside – their financial insecurity is worse than any other generation in the past half-century. So while baby boomers started working with an eye on gaining sta-bility, raising a family, and 'settling down', that is beyond many young workers. The house is probably unaffordable and the stu-dent debt too high. Instead, as shown by Net Impact's survey, they're more concerned than their predecessors with finding happi-ness and fulfilment in their work lives. To do that, they need to roam in search of this.

One might even call them the 'Flow generation'. So how best to manage them?

Jeanne Meister writing for *Forbes* magazine in January 2016 had this advice:

Offer workplace flexibility

Flexible hours and generous telework policies are even more important to younger workers than salary. They need the chance to adjust their schedules when the situation calls for it. Yet managers (from a different generation invariably) do not rate this as one of the most important factors.

Listen to your employees

Generation Y workers want to be heard and taken seriously. Because you climbed the ladder and went through hell, that's no reason for them to. Personal development is one of the main reasons workers job hop in the first place.

Communicate the company's mission and values

Unsurprisingly, colleagues want to work at a company whose values match theirs. The same Net Impact survey found 58 per cent of respondents said they would take a 15 per cent pay cut in order to work for an organization 'with values like my own'.

Values need to be communicated during the recruiting process. If applicants know what they're signing up for, the ones who would leave due to value differences will self-select.

Perhaps one of the hardest issues to address, is with recruiters who often sift out what they perceive as job hoppers. This new normal behaviour, though, from Millennials, can have an upside. Those in search of new skills and a better way of working are showing ambition and dissatisfaction with the status quo. If you're a challenger brand, then you can build a culture on these restless people, provided they are prepared to build the new Jerusalem rather than just dream about it. This generation has one overwhelming advantage to the baby boomers – they're seeking fulfilment. This means they are open to new ideas and new approaches. This inclination to innovation is vital in building a creative culture.

An excellent post on millennialmarketing.com argued that 'Gen Y' is defined by creativity. It named several marketing campaigns that harness Gen Y's creativity. It even suggested that Gen Y had been wrongly named – that it should be called 'Gen C' for 'Creative' – because creativity and self-expression were core Millennial values. A survey of women in their twenties when selecting three values that best describe them from a list of 20, picked 'Creativity' as the value chosen most often. It also postulated that Gen Y sees social media less as a social platform and more as self-expression.

One thing is clear – Millennials are visually sophisticated and will not revisit sites that load slowly or that are badly designed. They choose products based on design. They will not apply for jobs to companies with poor online presence or limited social channels. A favourite Gen Y art sharing site, Deviant Art, is one of the most trafficked sites on the web and skews heavily to 18–34-year-olds. Millennials are interested in creative pastimes like fashion, cooking and the arts. Apparently, 65 per cent of 18–24-year-olds consider cooking a 'pleasurable hobby'.

They are also more likely to want to tap into their personal creativity potential. We might think of the ability to tap into our potential as being an efficiency boost or a way to keep ourselves personally healthy, but its presence in this generation cannot be ignored.

The Rise Academy at LEWIS

Rise was launched in April of 2014, based in San Diego, California – a location known for 276 days of sunshine per annum. It's easy to hold outdoor classes and exercises there. To engage and excite the company's six hundred staff across the globe, we ran a 'name the Academy' competition. An executive from the Paris office won the competition with 'Rise' – an emotive word which is understood in all languages and which suggests progression and energy. The outdoor nature of San Diego is conducive to physical activity, to refresh the brain. We decided the Academy should run for two weeks so that people are taken out of their usual work and home routines and are therefore liberated to think and 'do' differently.

How it works

Ten to twelve delegates from every region are invited to attend. This is a deliberately small number so the experience is intense. Often the delegates have not met or worked with their Academy colleagues beforehand. The curriculum training is designed to help the delegates, working in two teams, tackle two projects: a business project and an art project. To help them learn to work quickly and effectively together, at the start of the Academy an interactive workshop on people's preferred work behaviours is run. This helps the delegates understand each other, so they bond as a team and achieve the desired team goal. The art project is to stimulate thinking in pictures and colours. With inspiration drawn from exploring San Diego's Balboa Park, the delegates enter a professional art studio, with an artist as tutor, to be greeted by two huge blank canvases on the walls and copious amounts of paint. The size of the white blank space and the shortness of time (eight hours across three mornings) is daunting. Each team must agree how they want to fill the canvas and what their story will be. Every delegate wants to express their ideas as an individual, but they have to work as a team.

The transformation process

The challenge is both emotional and practical. Usually, no one has painted since childhood. To do so as an adult, the delegates need to 'have a go'. Mistakes can be made and they can be painted over or, perhaps, realization dawns that nothing is a mistake. It is art. Once the canvases are finished, the sense of achievement and pride is huge and the delegates 'own' their painting. They invested themselves in the work and it became personal. Part of the exercise is for each team to openly talk about their painting, how they arrived at the finished result, and what they learned about themselves, their abilities, and their teammates along the way.

Back to the real world

At the same time, business projects are set with 'live' business conundrums that the company faces and is dealing with. As the projects are valuable to the company, not simply a theoretical exercise, and the delegates' recommendations could be actioned, the teams set about tackling the briefs with vigour. The delegates must use the power of their right brains to recommend alternative solutions to the norm.

Juxtaposition

The skills and temperaments needed to tackle the business project and the art project have proved to be quite different so the team dynamics change for each project. The delegates must learn in real time, and under a degree of pressure: who has what skills, what potential, and how best these should be applied; how to negotiate with each other; when and how to lead; and when and how to follow.

Doing nothing is not doing 'nothing'

People learn a lot between the lines at Rise: from simply talking together over an intense period of time; from sharing life experiences, working practices and learning about other cultures. People, delegates and tutors start the Academy as awkward strangers and leave as lifelong friends. The commonly shared experience of liberating their right brains creates a strong bond. There are tears on departure at the end of every Academy. Long after attending the Academy, groups have monthly calls, visit each other, and chat over WhatsApp. As more and more graduate Academy networks are formed, so our global business functions more seamlessly as our people across the world are truly connected by more than just work.

Many of the Academy tutors are from within the organization. The tutor becomes the student. Tutors learn how to engage people better with more interactive sessions involving role-play, mini projects and tasks, and (educational) games. Candidate feedback after each Academy enables the tutors to hone their training for maximum gain. Their communication becomes sharper.

Exposure to seniority

During the second week of the Academy, each delegate has a chance to talk one-on-one with our Academy leader. Personal realization and growth at the Academy is discussed privately and honestly, as well as the personal and professional ambitions of the delegate. The Academy experience opens people's minds and horizons. These individual talks have led to people relocating to another country, expanding their domestic remit to a regional or global remit, joining another team with a completely different specialism. A number of Academy graduates take up art in their leisure time. They join art classes and painting workshops to continue to express themselves visually and to help them relax. Most Rise graduates run art team-building socials when they return to the office. In recent office moves, Rise graduates have inspired their colleagues to paint and decorate the walls. In many cases, the offices double as art galleries. These feature local student art which is sold (without commission) to clients, students and other partners.

Bringing creativity into a presentation

Rise teaches that there's no such thing as reality. There is only what seems to be. It's no use pointing out that you have experience and knowledge, unless it appears to be so to the receiver. It's a 'show, not tell'. Never is this truer than with public speaking.

As part of the Personal Branding module delegates learn how to appear spontaneous and speak without notes. By all means, have a PowerPoint running in the background, but remember, it's the magician's assistant, not the magician. In a formal theatre, you can place markers on a stage then associate each of them with a part of your story. Then you just walk the route on the stage and repeat what comes to mind at each waypoint.

Another way, is the 'Taxi Driver Technique'. This involves thinking of a journey you repeat frequently, such as arriving home at night. Recall the things you see in order as you arrive, eg front gate, path, door, doormat, hall, living room, etc, then associate an image with each of these items to help you memorize each part of your narrative.

The more bizarre the images, the better. These techniques can be learnt quickly and easily. Some forward-thinking politicians are already using them and are hailed as geniuses, but they're simple to learn. A key element is always to remember the visuals – the bigger, the brighter, the better. The vast majority of what people will recall about your presentation is visual – whisper it – they're not actually always listening to what you're saying.

The Rise Four I's Creative Cycle

In order to better understand how creativity happens, it helps if we use our visual right-brain process. We know there are distinct phases, by the way people describe creative provenance. Many say the ideas occur after some form of immersion in the material and the problem. These can be enhanced and made more efficient through practice and discipline. Often what people call idea generation is just a small part of a much wider process. Given that we tend to focus more on the inspiration – and this is largely unconscious – by far the most important part is the problem definition and information gathering. Research is usually seen as the least attractive stage. We'd all rather just get onto brainstorming.

We created this visual representation by working closely with the Rise delegates and observing how the process operated in reality. This is useful because it guides the allocation of resources to the various stages and encourages greater application of time at key stages. By doing this, you will make the creative cycle easier, faster and more productive.

Induction

By far and away the most important part of the Four I's process is Induction. This should be about 40 per cent of the total process. This is the briefing, problem analysis and research phase. It involves conversation with people affected by the problem, gathering comments and views. This is the phase of where we look at all the points of view.

We need here to look at the widest level? What would happen if we don't solve this problem? What would happen if this issue had never been noticed?

Incubation

Another major part of the Four I's process is Incubation. This is literally where we must do nothing and leave it to the unconscious mind. So how does the brain process information without us being aware? 'We don't know. But we know the net is closed during the day, but the brain when it's relaxed allows that net to expand', says neuroscientist Russell Foster. We can rely upon this. Most of the research points to how the brain organizes information, especially when asleep. That's why we often have a 24-hour test. Sleep on an idea and see whether it still looks as good in the morning. Is there an optimal time for this? It seems to depend on whether people are able to intensively relax. Shirley Conran, wife of the designer Terence, described this process in her book *Superwoman*. When stressed, she would retreat to her bedroom for a day or more and withdraw. The more intense our relaxation, the more likely it is that we will develop alternative perspective. Doing nothing in the face of a problem requires discipline and resistance to criticism. Nobody will ultimately remember how long it took to solve the problem. It is more efficient to go slowly and be more thorough. We should also remember that sometimes we have to present our solutions to seniority. They are often short of time and will need to be convinced that all full consideration has been given to all factors. In this phase, we can consider the information and knowledge we have gathered actively, but we should try to avoid jumping to premature conclusions. We should allocate around 30 per cent of our time and resources to this part of the process.

Inspiration

This bit is often what people really think about as the ideas phase, but it can't happen properly without the previous two phases. This should be about 20 per cent of the process. Half of this should be spent alone and half discussing it with others. It's clear that there are many different types of creative provenance. These split mainly into:

- **Peer provenance** – where the ideas come from discussion. This could include being anywhere from a bar to a brainstorm at work.

- **Personal provenance** – where the ideas come on your own. The conditions for this to happen could include:

  - showering;
  - bathing;
  - driving;
  - working out in the gym;
  - running;
  - walking;
  - on an aircraft or train.

We should grow to trust our instincts when we know we've had 'the' idea. Often our passion and confidence for an idea can be a key indicator. It's important to recognize, though, that it will be subject to the left-brain processes we've seen in the 'Job Interview' in Chapter 4. We will initially be scanned critically and we need to get them on our side. We need to use empathy to see their point of view and cooperation to establish rapport.

Ignition

This is the wider team part of the process. We need to be able to validate the idea and test it to see whether it's an acceptable solution. This should be about 10 per cent of the process. Then the solution should be taken into the Induction phase to look at the points of view to see whether the solution can be refined. Here we can present a number of alternatives and use the 'what if?' technique. The more of a leap our idea is, the more we need to use this. We can get better at this by using some of the coaching techniques discussed below. When we approach people with an idea, we should be careful to ask an opinion on the problem and to ask what solutions there already are. Finding out what has already been tried and failed is also useful. If we can understand why something failed, then we can use our 'what if?' technique.

Figure 7.1 The Rise Four I's Creative Cycle

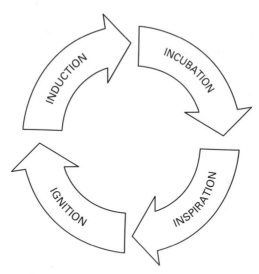

SOURCE LEWIS Rise Academy.

Conclusion

The environment that we work in has become faster and more demanding. If we want to retain our health and creativity we have to reorganize to make that happen. This means firstly changing the way we work as individuals so we have the space and time we need. We also need to learn new techniques, like SQ3R, to accelerate the way we absorb information. It also means we need to change the way we work with others to create a new environment where others can be coached. The Rise Academy is a useful template for this. We can and should teach creativity both before and after people start at work. Next, we hear directly from the leaders themselves.

How leaders apply creativity

08

We heard from some of these people earlier. If we want to understand how creativity can be used in all its forms, we need to hear how it's used by successful people from all walks of life. What's common to all of them is how much fun they seem to be having. This is reflected in their endeavours and consequently in how skilled they have become. There seems to be a virtuous circle here. First, they choose their approach, which is usually playful, positive, upbeat and constructive. This is reflected by people around them and starts to change the environment. The atmosphere around them changes. It's enjoyable, it's playful and small mistakes are easily forgotten. This makes it easier for more people to spend more time in that culture. Consequently, due to the rule that competence always follows preference, they get better at what they do. Excellence in all things is not a single act, it's a habit. Hence the group, however small, gets better results and people notice it. Creativity is at the heart of everything they are and everything they do. Whether in problem-solving or fresh thinking, it's their embrace of the Creative Traits that makes them so successful. They are all immensely productive, but they still have time. They concentrate on doing fewer things, better.

A business success that doesn't understand business

It's a beautiful 2016 spring morning in Hampshire. A MAMIL (Middle Aged Man in Lycra) has just arrived in a Range Rover. He's unstrapping a mountain bike from the rack. We're about to conduct a two-hour interview, but with a twist. We're going to be travelling through large amounts of mud on two wheels.

Sinclair Beecham is an argument going somewhere to happen. Garrulous, superintelligent, forthright, successful, energetic and deeply analytical, he co-founded and built one of the most successful food retailers ever. I honestly don't think he's ever knowingly agreed with anyone.

Of course, there were sandwich shops before Pret a Manger, but he and his partner Julian Metcalfe made them healthier, more consistent and more accessible. Now one in three Londoners eat lunch at Pret. The business is a phenomenon.

It's not difficult to realize why he's sought after by business people. For many people Beecham is an icon of business success. Everyone wants to ask him about business and how they can be successful, so what he says to me while going down a hill is surprising: 'I don't understand business people.' An uphill section intervenes, which means I can't do anything except try and keep up with him.

'Have you any idea how bizarre that sounds?' I say, catching my breath.

'Well, they're all so short-term. They concentrate on profits when they should just focus on what makes customers happy', he adds. 'Once you know this, you can get better and more efficient at delivering it. But if you don't know that, you can waste huge amounts of time and money.' This sounds simple enough.

'My best ideas come when I am not working. When my brain is not trying to solve other problems or organize things. So the ideas tend to come when I am in bed, on my bike or in the shower.'

The going gets tough. By now we're carrying our bikes at shoulder height and wading through mud: 'What problem-solving skills I do have, developed when I learnt to trust my instincts. For years I had used my analytical brain to solve problems and usually overthought things and reached the wrong conclusion. Finally, in my early thirties,

I realized my instincts were better than my analysis and learnt to trust my judgement. That was a turning point for me.' We stop and take a break.

'Most businesses are operationally led, and the operations teams tend to be running systems rather than creating them. I think the skill of running a system is very different from developing new ideas. Most businesses focus more on delivery than creativity.'

The birds are singing. There are daffodils at our feet and the sun is flickering through a canopy of trees. 'Solitude is important for free thinking', he says. The birds seem to agree.

Fighter

John Caudwell is a very successful businessman. He is forthright in his views and speaks honestly and directly about business problems.

He had a tough childhood growing up in the Potteries in Staffordshire: 'The toughness of my early life taught me how to fight for what I wanted.' Did he learn this skill? 'Overall, it's just luck. I think of this when I'm working with Caudwell Children. Sometimes, it's just the luck of the draw.' He's devoted a great deal of his time to his own charity Caudwell Children and created a new centre for studying autism at Keele University.

But despite his success, he remains no stranger to misfortune. Seventeen people in his family were struck down with Lyme disease. Typically, he's tackled this with his usual directness, forming an organization to campaign for greater awareness – www.caudwell-lyme.net. He's determined to exert political pressure to make people aware of how widespread the condition is: 'The medical establishment needs to understand much more than they do, but they don't accept how serious it is and they lack the budget to do anything about it.'

He says that solving complex business problems involves a great deal of creativity. This was the thinking behind an unusual move over a decade ago. He decided to ban email from his company Phones4U. He noticed that many of his shop managers were spending too much of their time dealing with email. He says the problem was easy in retrospect: 'A lot of customer service is damaged by email. It's just so much easier for people to cancel an order or tell someone an order won't arrive by email. It's a communication media for cowards.'

The results were spectacular in terms of renewed profitability and followed by many other companies. Where does he get ideas like this? 'When I'm on the toilet in the morning. Sometimes I go in with a piece of paper and a pen. It's boring but quality time. The business I sold in 2006 was created as a concept in the toilet. I did business plans in the loo. The ideas come as numbers or in a picture or in any format. I also get ideas in other places, such as being in a board meeting when I'm racking my brains and trying really hard.'

So for Caudwell it seems an unusual process, to be both conscious and unconscious, solitary and in company. The underlying quality this man has, though, is the sheer drive and determination to make whatever he sets his mind to happen on a big scale.

The outsider's insider

Peter Gummer (Baron Chadlington) has been successful at just about everything he's done. He built the UK's largest PR company in seven years flat. Then he sold it and went on to do it again with a public group, Huntsworth. He was a close adviser to the former prime minister David Cameron and chairs his local constituency association. He now runs a strategic consultancy advising governments, large organizations and colleagues in the industry.

When he comes up with ideas, they are usually because he has completely immersed himself in the subject. It's an intellectual process, which leads inevitably to the creative solution. Again, we hear that the two extremes are working together.

The tendency to go into ever greater detail at university is a huge mistake. He initially didn't want to go to Cambridge. His father sat him down and said that it would teach him to think.

'Mathematical logic, psychology and philosophy. I came out of Cambridge able to think. It allowed me to become so engrossed in a subject.'

'I've become better at that over the years. Sometimes the barriers to the great ideas are more about who takes the glory. I don't need to do that any more so it's easier for the ideas to get adopted. Young people face a number of barriers. One is concentration. Many young people can't do that for any length of time. Because so much of what they do is website- and screen-driven so the concentration span is shortening because they get fed up. The previous generation really got involved in the adventure of learning. This is very different to screen-based learning.'

You can research something very precisely these days and find out just that alone. Lord Chadlington says there's no penumbral learning: 'They learn narrowly. When I went to look up something, I went to the encyclopaedia and looked up the word euthanasia then I would notice other words beginning with E and I'd learn other things.'

The passive sense of listening and studying has been the foundation of his later success. Ask young people under 25 how many books they've read. The number will be small. Reading and learning to read is the most important thing you can do to differentiate yourself.

Lord Chadlington was at university when JFK was president. 'He was a great reader. He used speed reading but I never did. I loved the process too much to speed it up.' Not only does he like reading, but he also likes hard-copy books and likes the way the book feels. His house, he says, is full of hundreds of books.

'People have lost their sense of awe. Big open spaces give that to people.' He says he often sits in the local church, not because of religion but because of the silence. 'Young people are overloaded. It's in large part the fault of the parent. If they send them to the school that has the best academic results and send their pupils to the best universities, they have their priorities wrong.'

He sent his son to Eton and he had a series of bad reports. He asked him about this: 'What are you thinking about right now?' And his son said: 'How long is this going to go on for?' Lord Chadlington continues: 'You can't tell your children how much you're spending and what a waste. What matters is whether they come out understanding, sensitive and balanced people. It's about getting our humanity back. The duality of this sensitivity and intellect is what I'm really interested in.'

Every year he has two separate weeks away from his family, on his own just to think: 'Nobody can disturb me. It's a cleansing of the brain and body. I listen to a lot of music. I find it to be incipient spirituality. I listen to Bach all the time. The Bach Cello Suites are hard work. Nobody is used to listening to music which is hard work.'

He says spirituality is important because it leads towards a particular attitude towards ethics and a sensitivity towards people. There's a direct link between the aesthetics of music and the ethics of public life.

'So much of life blunts the senses. There's nothing wrong with pop music or pornography or booze, except that it blunts the senses. Creativity comes from sensitivity. Crude unthinking insensitive people can't be creative.'

He remembers hearing Mozart's 39th Symphony for the first time: 'It stunned me, it was the most beautiful thing I'd ever heard. That was one of the most memorable moments of my life. It was completely life-changing for me. Not about getting a degree. It was about learning.'

'You can't be spiritual by luck. It involves discipline and effort.' He tries to read a poem every night before going to sleep.

How much time does he spend playing? 'I've had the "imposter syndrome" all my life. It's all been a hoot! But we all have this. We're all play-acting to some extent. The higher up you go, the more you feel it. You've got to keep your feet firmly on the ground. That's where your home life and spirituality helps.'

He sees himself as an outsider, which is unusual for a real insider. But at least I now understand why.

An unlikely CEO

Fred Cook is CEO of communications firm GolinHarris. His book *Improvise: Unconventional Career Advice from an Unlikely CEO*, tells his story. Fred and Al Golin, built GolinHarris into one of the top 10 largest PR firms in the world. Fred is not a typical CEO. He barely graduated from college, never took a business course, had no corporate connections, didn't own a suit and rode a motorcycle. Along the way, he picked up skills in people management, problem-solving, and had a successful career. He argues that the ability to improvise is a critical skill that sets young professionals apart from the pack and helps them get ahead of the competition.

Cook's book is evidence of the quality of the man. Many CEOs write books about their industry as a way of hitting back. But he wrote his in typically generous style for those starting out in the industry. There is, though, an obvious issue – generally young people are reading fewer books. He said his publisher told him he couldn't have picked a worse audience, because 'they just don't buy books'. But it has allowed him to create a platform at colleges around the world, in the United States, Russia, China and the UK.

How important does he think creativity is? Is it nice to have or is it a fundamental strategic priority for business in general? 'It's become a fundamental strategic priority.' Cook is a man after my own heart. He believes in training. He is the first CEO ever to work at his day job as well as the director of the centre of public relations at USC (University of Southern California): 'Creativity is particularly critical for PR firms, but it applies to everyone, particularly in this era that we're operating in. I think that there's so much information that unless you do in a way that's gonna attract people and make them want to talk about it and share it, you're just going to be irrelevant. They're bombarded by so many messages that they're tuning out the vast majority of them.'

Cook also sees problems with the online news groups like Mashable and BuzzFeed not meeting their expectations and starting to lay people off. He says they're being subjected to the same problems that print saw – that so much of the news is being aggregated and distributed by social media networks.

If people want stories to be heard, the methods for storytelling have to become a lot more diverse. You can tell a story with a photograph, animation, a YouTube video. 'There's a lot of different ways to tell a story in a more personal and a more dramatic way and these must rely more on the more human aspects as opposed to the more statistical aspects of it.'

He cites client experience with the Rotary Club International, which is working on curing polio: 'We're looking at the end of polio, and people don't really care about it any more. People think it's been cured so giving them lots of facts and figures about that isn't really very effective. But when you talk about these workers who are going out on the hinterlands of Pakistan who are risking their lives to vaccinate little children – it becomes a much more compelling story. We were even talking about having one of these workers taking a virtual reality camera with them so you could experience what it's like to go into a remote village in Pakistan and ask the parents if you can vaccinate their children or give them the vaccine orally. To be able to be in that moment would be a really amazing story that we can now tell with this technology that we wouldn't have been able to do even a year ago.'

He says he owes his creativity and career to being an outsider: 'I think that's probably the main point in my book. I use several examples. But in my own life, I never really had the credentials to be a CEO or even to work in this industry. I barely graduated from college, I never studied business, I didn't have any background in journalism. But I had a lot of experience. I'd had all these different jobs all over the world doing all these crazy things and in my opinion the creativity comes from that – you're not born creative.' Cook says creativity is really the function of connecting the experiences and the ideas you have in your head with new and different ways: 'If you believe that, then the more ideas you have, the more experiences you have, the more creative you can be.' He says this is different to the interns he sees coming – with experiences very similar to one another. 'If creativity is based on diversity of life experiences, I don't think the younger generation now is having as many of those life experiences.'

Cook also says that he's naturally always been full of ideas: 'They come at me at different times. Sometimes they come at me when I'm sleeping, sometimes when I'm in the office.' Cook runs a lot, almost every day. 'That's a very fertile time for me. I usually do it in the morning.' He says ideas are a sort of 'currency'. He adds that: 'It was always the thing I was best at. Even if I'm not really familiar with a topic, I can learn about it really quickly. I can think of things that can apply to that and creative ways to talk about it or explain it.' He says he gets a lot of ideas on his own: 'The ones that I come up with in a group are more focused on a specific topic. They're more directed.'

Somehow he's managed to keep pace by organizing his day better. Although he's busier now than ever before, he thrives on and relishes the challenge. A lot of this is staying calm and focused: 'I do find you need some calmness of mind or your thoughts become so erratic and so quick that you're not constructive. So I don't drink any caffeine anymore. I do try at some point during the day, usually in the morning, to meditate for a few minutes to get a sort of basis of calmness. I find that sometimes in the morning your ideas are fresh and your mind is clear but by the time you get to the afternoon you've been bombarded all day long. It's then difficult to concentrate on writing something that's very thoughtful or creating something. I find that by 3 pm I have to focus on things that are more mundane and tactical because my brain just isn't operating as well as it was earlier in the day.'

A key feature of Cook's style is playfulness. He points to an idea he helped create: 'We do this thing called an "unternship" programme. It was based on my book, and one of the women that runs our Dallas office called me one day and said, "I read your book and would never have hired you to work here. That's a problem." We need to be a little more open-minded about the kinds of people we're hiring. So she created a programme call the untern. The difference between an untern and an intern is that for the first three months, we pay them never to come to the office. We pay for them to go out into the world and experience things they've never done before. We hired our first untern two years ago and for three months he lived with an Amish family and hiked to the bottom of the Grand Canyon. He went to an Indian sweat lodge, he went to a retreat where you don't speak, he climbed a mountain in Hawaii. And we paid him to do all this stuff. And he came back and worked in our Dallas office. He still works for us.'

Is there a relationship between a sense of humour and creativity? 'Unless you create an atmosphere where people feel comfortable sharing their ideas then you'll never get much creativity. I have a lot of ideas and many of them really bad ideas and people kid me about that. So, I'm always willing to be the brunt of a joke in order to get people relaxed and in the mood to share ideas and participate.'

This in itself requires the courage to laugh at oneself. 'You have to be bold and willing to put yourself out there in a way that is easily rejected. Creative people are easily rejected all the time. Every good idea has been received with the answer "No" 50 times. So there is a certain courage associated with being creative. And I think you can't teach people to be brave but you can show them how to do it. And you can give them examples of bravery and you can get them to identify with that and not feel so afraid.'

If he could go back and talk to his younger self, what advice would he give? 'I would tell my younger self to relax. That's what I say to college kids who are all stressed out about everything. I say relax, you're young. It's not all going to be perfect. But be brave and try new things and it'll probably all just work out fine.'

'You can't polish a turd'

Jackie Cooper is the global creative chair at communications market leader, Edelman. She is a PR veteran with over 30 years' experience in brand marketing, creative conception and personality strategy. Cooper is a member of the Superbrands Council and acts as board adviser for Jamie Oliver Holdings and Wings of Hope, a UK-based education charity which funds schooling in India and Africa.

There's something wonderful about Jackie Cooper. She didn't go to university. She had no breaks. She left education early, but she still built a company, sold it, made a fortune and ended up in global leadership position.

She was educated 'in a fog' at a secondary school in West London during a great comprehensive education experiment: 'The only thing we guinea pigs learned was how to fight. Our year was always getting beaten up by the year above. The whole experience taught me to run screaming from any academic building. Even now I feel this way. In those days, if you didn't fit in, that was it. If you had oxygen in your thought, that didn't matter, because you didn't fit in. I didn't fit in.'

I know exactly how she feels and had a similar experience. Nowadays, both of our own daughters could not have had a more different experience: 'They've been taught a love of learning and greater diversity', as she puts it.

This is just as well because the generation coming through will have, maybe, 10 careers over their lifetime. The ability to creatively reinvent yourself is vital as an enabler.

Her school experience taught her to rebel during the punk rock years. I, too, shared her experience. A season ticket to profanity can, indeed, be a means of propulsion. At least it helps you move away from the things you don't want.

She's also a fan of Ken Robinson: 'Seeing his video was liberating. It made me realize that it wasn't just me. He's giving hope to people whose minds function in different roles.' She subsequently got to meet and work with him professionally and she was thrilled: 'Sometimes it's not good to meet your heroes, but in this case I wasn't disappointed.'

She says she just didn't realize what career options there were: 'I came to the ladder very late and I must say they are not necessarily a good thing, because sometimes the best move in life is to go sideways. You don't have to be ladder-focused – you can go sideways quite happily and still have an interesting life. There are all different types of education and many roads to achieve success.'

Now she's the global chair of creativity in a successful company connected to the rich and famous – is she an insider? 'Inside what? It doesn't feel like that. The outside always looks a lot more sorted than the inside. We're just getting started.'

She doesn't see herself as a master of her art because there's always more to do: 'It's never the status quo.' She's just not a settler. She's perpetually dissatisfied. She always wants more: 'I'm never going to turn down an opportunity.' This, perhaps, defines her creative approach more than anything. She sees opportunity everywhere: 'I hate complacency. We have to keep asking, what are we going to do that's new?'

How does she cope with the pace? 'The new communciations world is fast, disposable, critical, and yet it's still principled. But this generation does not know how to be still. This is a massive problem because the relationships they have are driven by the internet. Parenting is going to be more challenging. There will be so much more influence from beyond the family.'

Peace and quiet is important for her. She works four days a week: 'I don't want to be lonely, but I do need to be quiet.' Some days she won't speak to anyone else for the majority of the day: 'It's a very important part of the creative process. I don't think people understand how important it is.' This is something she feels should really be taught: 'Make your life good and you can make your job good.' She recognizes that she can be erratic: 'There are some days when I know it just won't happen. I must have choice of when to work.'

Well-being is important to her because she gets her best ideas in the bath: 'My family knows when I'm in the bath I'm not to be disturbed. But I can also get good ideas from talking to people. I follow my Dad's advice which is to meet everybody at least once.' Of course, she remains very driven but, 'I'm disciplined. When I'm with my family, I switch my phone off. Sometimes, people are scared of not being in touch.'

She feels strongly that capital structure effects the creativity? 'Yes. That's why I sold my company to Edelman. It's no picnic, but the craft comes before everything else. The days of the advertising agencies being the brand custodian for the client are gone. Communications firms wanted a seat at the table and now we have several. Earning the story is important. We're crafting stories that people want to share. We've earned our way in.'

I can't think of anyone that's earned it more.

Expelled for reading too much

Paul Holmes is publisher and CEO of The Holmes Group and has been writing on the creative industries for over 20 years. He launched the Creativity in Public Relations Awards, which grew to become the largest in the United States.

In 25 years of commenting on the creative industries, Paul Holmes has seen huge development and change: 'Creativity is something we should take as a serious strategic issue', he says. 'Creativity is really just problem-solving. It's the ability to find an elegant solution to a challenge.' He says the creative industries have a tendency to define creativity narrowly. 'In the PR and certainly in the ad industry historically it's been more about the bells and whistles and balloons rather than problem-solving.'

He doesn't like the term 'creative' – because it creates a false dichotomy: 'I think everyone is, or should be trying to be, creative. However, I do think that cultivating an outsider perspective is helpful to creativity. I think both seeing yourself and functioning independently autonomously outside of a structure is helpful.'

He says to take opportunities you also need resilience: 'Almost everything that I've done over the last 25 years has followed the same pattern. I make a big decision, the decision blows up somehow in my face, then I find myself in a situation that's better than it would have been if the decision hadn't blown up.'

He describes what happened when he was expelled from school: 'The reason I was asked to leave my high school is that I stopped showing up. This is the geekiest expulsion story you'll ever hear in your life. I would go into school in a morning, take roll-call, and then I'd sneak into town and spend the entire day in the local town library. I would read anything I could get my hands on. Literally anything from Plato's *Republic* to Alistair MacLean's *Ice Station Zebra*. Trash and literature and non-fiction, just everything. Sometimes I would read a book in a half a day. Then they found out. It didn't really fit their definition of what I was supposed to be doing.' So he was kicked out and joined a local newspaper. He then discovered that was what he'd always wanted to do, until he got into an argument, then he quit that job and fell into a much better job almost immediately. He ended up in New York City with a magazine that went out of business four months after he arrived. He then started his own company: 'Either I'm extremely lucky or I respond well to adversity. I actually like it when things go wrong. It's the unpredictability. It focuses me like nothing else. I like having an antagonist. I like when there is a major obstacle or challenge thrown down. That's exciting.'

One thing he learned from school was that argument was at the heart of creativity: 'I did have a history teacher who enjoyed my rather creative approach, historical interpretation – he showed me how to present the facts to fit any argument. The creative process is argumentative, even if it's just with yourself. I don't necessarily know what I think until I've had an argument about it.'

The notion of creativity as argument is a compelling one because arguing is not always encouraged among creatives: 'This is why I don't associate the sciences with creativity because there is only one right answer and it's at the back of the book.'

This is a particularly strong premise when you see the way broadcasts – one-way messaging via adverts – has been replaced with two-way messaging via social media. In a one-way channel, messaging can be visual, sonic, simple and repetitive. It can be drilled into people. In an environment where it's two-way, then the creativity has to be more argumentative and it has to anticipate counterarguments. Therefore, that naturally would favour people who are competent in the 'full duplex' environment, where people are talking to each other at the same time. So the argument would run then, that creativity using communications agencies is far more effective in a two-way environment than the simple broadcast asynchronous delivery of a message from advertising.

Holmes says this requires a greater empathy and 'a genuine curiosity about other people, and how they live their lives. And it probably requires higher emotional intelligence. That's the kind of creativity that I'm talking about'. And this sophisticated argument needs to be presented visually. Holmes says this comes down to moving images, in every sense of the word: 'They need to have an emotional rather than rational impact. In the way that good books do.' Books have been at the core of all Holmes's success: 'I'm never not reading a book. The reason I prefer baths to showers is it's really hard to read your Kindle in the shower. If I have a two-stop subway ride I'll read a book; if I'm waiting for someone who's five minutes late for an appointment, I'll read a book. I read almost constantly and usually I have something trivial and something thought-provoking going at the same time.'

Although he has no direct evidence of this, he suspects that books aren't consumed with the voracity he had as a youth. Social media, though, is not all bad: 'It has helped find connections for people who have none. You only need to look at what's going on in the United States right now with the rights of the transgendered. Ten years ago most of those people were either living in very small isolated communities assuming that everybody who wasn't part of that community either despised or ignored them. Now they understand the level of support that they have. I think it's brought people together who have isolating problems or conditions.'

He's emphatic about the need for argument: 'I worry that we have too many consensus seekers in our business. I understand why that's the case because a lot of it is finding ways to build bridges between opposing viewpoints and competing interests. But we need more people who are prepared to kick in doors rather than knocking politely on them and waiting for an answer.'

Just your average cat-breeding, stargazing, portrait-painting, military reservist politician

I first met Penny Mordaunt after a couple of glasses of Champagne. I'm sorry to say I didn't believe a word she said. The following morning, though, I did my research and found two things were true. Everything she said and that I was a complete ass.

This Catherine Deneuve lookalike is actually a member of Parliament and was Minister of State for the Armed Forces. She was the first woman ever to hold this position. She was responsible for all UK military force generation. She's also the only female Royal Naval Reservist in the House of Commons. She's also a fellow of the Royal Society of Arts, a member of the British Astronomical Association, and a patron of the Victoria Cross Trust. In 2014, she dived off a 10-metre board, live on Saturday night national TV, to raise money for a local charity.

Everything she's done has been larger than life and very successful. To pay her way through sixth-form college, she took the job of a magician's assistant. She also has a successful career in business and communications. She was communications director for Kensington and Chelsea Council. In 2006, she became director of Diabetes UK, the largest patient organization in Europe. She's worked with UK Prime Minister John Major and on US President George W Bush's campaigns. In 2014, she became only the second woman to propose the loyal address in reply to The Queen's Speech from the throne and made reference to her Royal Naval career.

Her maternal grandmother was an artist: 'A big turning point was when she came to live with us.' She remembers learning from her about how to do things better: 'I would set up my paints at night, so I could be up early to paint the sky.'

Courage, she says, is at the core of everything and this is something that's common to her art and her politics: 'You're setting yourself up to be judged, so it takes courage.' She doesn't show her art, because she doesn't want to 'wear her heart on her sleeve'. She's taken commissions for other people's portraits.

Apart from courage, painting is similar to politics in that you need a good understanding of someone else's point of view: 'You have to be able to look at something in a different way. How do I think creatively to stop this problem?'

She paints extremely fast – a portrait can be done in nine hours, but she doesn't always know when to stop. Sensitivity is important: 'Empathy is probably the greatest skill in politics. You've got to understand how people feel.' You have to be able to cope with the job and not lose this skill. It takes resilience.

Complete focus

Sir Martin Sorrell is the chief executive of WPP, the world's largest employer of creative people and biggest advertising conglomerate by revenue. Through a combination of dealmaking, relentless work, near-constant travel and tireless promotion of the company, Sorrell has given WPP a stock market valuation of more than £20 billion. The numbers go on to be staggering. In March 2016, it announced preliminary results of record profits of over £2 billion. It operates in 112 countries and employs 190,000 people. It now includes some of the best known names in marketing, advertising and public relations, including Young & Rubicam, Ogilvy & Mather, J Walter Thompson and Burson-Marsteller.

If you think the world's largest advertising and communications group would be in an expensive and glamorous location, surrounded by staff, think again. The office is simple, functional, modest, practical and business-oriented. So is this a metaphor? It is perhaps, closer to the truth about him than most people would believe. Sorrell's reputation is the stuff of legend, but not the stuff of fact. Perhaps everyone wants the reality of enormous wealth creation to be about something extraordinary. But it isn't. Just because you deal in extraordinary numbers, it doesn't mean you behave in an extraordinary way. Yes, you do need to be bright, but above all, you need to be determined. And these are qualities that everyone can have if they choose. Success then is not an act but a habit, and Sorrell's habits are worth mentioning.

First of all is the speed at which he operates. In the years I've known him he's always taken pride in responding to email personally and quickly. 'People think large companies are slow, but you'd be surprised how fast they can move. They have a lot of resources', he says.

Although he deals with enormous complexity in codifying the structure of deals, the essential business principle is mutuality. Don't let anyone kid you about this process. You cannot be successful in the long-term without the principle of 'I win, you win'. The nature of the businessman as a predator is, frankly, a ridiculous one. Yes, you can negotiate deals, but if these are so bad, the other person loses everything – that's not good business.

When you strip away the myths then, what do you have? Firstly, a man that reads widely, travels extensively and thinks deeply. When you ask him for an opinion, therefore, he's really thought about it. We're talking about the state of the world economy and what has happened since 2008: 'The world is growing more slowly since Lehmans; it's become much more conservative. The premium is not put on long-term thinking any more. The average tenure of a CEO now is 6–7 years, so he or she is very focused. They're thinking more like a prime minister or president.' He says this has become like a disease because most business leaders are managers rather than owners: 'You have zero-based budgets at one end and activist share-holders at the other. These are very difficult times. CEOs are now very focused on the short-term. I can't see any change ahead in that approach.'

He says that long-term thinking is required for long-term success and at present no one is thinking that way. This, then, is perhaps the biggest bellwether of what's likely to happen in the next five years. He points out that round the world there's very little growth: 'Buy-backs and dividends exceeded retained earnings for the first time in Q1 of 2015 for the S&P 500, and throughout 2015 they exceed retained earnings. So if the S&P 500 was a company it would've shrunk. That means companies think shareholders have a better idea of what to do with their money than we do. Has that anything to do with technology or attention span? No. It has more to do with the fact that the 2008/9 recession was vicious and made companies very conservative.'

One clear theme in success for Sorrell is control: 'The only companies that can take a long-term view are the ones I call the protective companies that have effective control structures. The two companies with the best long-term prospects are Murdoch-controlled Fox and News Corp and Roberts-controlled Comcast because they're dynastic and they have complete control. Some think that's a weakness. I think it's a great strength.'

This, for Sorrell, is one of the great insights, because the separation of ownership and control undermines many a success story: 'Management must have control so they act like owners and not managers. For instance, Jeff Bezos has control of Amazon – he doesn't need to make money in the short-term. We've become too short-cycle. Every morning you get things which can blow you off course. You must always come back to the strategy.' This is something he says politicians are bad at, thinking too short-term. It's like a disease.

Control is an interesting issue because of what he says of his own creative process. At this stage he proffers the brilliant little book, *A Technique for Producing Ideas*, by James W Young: 'The best creatives are the ones that believe the magic dust is made more effective by analysing data sets. There's something about the mind in a relaxed state when it's not thinking at all. You put all this stuff into your brain and then you can let it work. It happens to me a lot, particularly when I'm in the shower or on a plane. Suddenly, you get what you think is an inspired idea or see a way through and it happens.' He uses this especially for problems which are difficult to solve. Easier problems are dealt with consciously, but the tricky ones need to be incubated.

Does he think creatives understand the importance of data? 'Some do, some don't. I think they refuse to believe that mathematical process or numbers can help them. Or maybe they're worried that it will replace them.' Here, he talks about Dynamic Creative Optimization, where creative work is pulled down mechanically according to a person's consumption habits. They don't want to think that what they do can be replaced by something mechanical. They don't like the idea that some form of intuitive genius can be replaced.'

How important is sleep in this process? 'The more sleep you have, the better you are, but I don't dream solutions.' He tries to measure the type of sleep with apps, but they don't measure the quality. Apart from rest, it's also important to him to drive the use of his mind. He agrees that attention spans are shortening and people are reading fewer books: 'They're less good at mental arithmetic as well. If it's true that your brain is like a computer and the more you use it, the better it gets, then the converse is also true. The more you do, the better at it you become. The more a Google search is run, the more accurate it becomes.' This is certainly true in his case.

Is there a link between ambition and imagination? 'Our industry has gotten tougher. There's more a belief that you should flit from flower to flower, from company to company. There's a view that longevity is a bad thing, which is ironic because the most successful companies are ones that do long-term branding. It's not less competitive but it's less dynamic because the big battalions have become more powerful.'

We talk about heroes for a while and the names of Lord Sieff, Lord Weinstock and Sir Jules Thorn come up, but is there anyone else he sees today that he admires? 'Vincent Bolloré (Havas) is by far our most dangerous competitor. He's built a dynastic structure with sons and has control of the business and he will stand the test of time.'

Does he agree that the left- and right-brain processes need to be used together? 'There used to be a question of strategy versus execution, but you have to do both. Whether we're teaching this is a moot point: universities tend to be too theoretical and not practical enough. I don't think we have enough people willing to become entrepreneurs.'

This is not just about earning money – it's about a fascination with business, with people and the world around. In that respect, Sorrell is one of the most complete creative leaders I've seen.

The power of logic and emotion in leading the Royal Navy

Creativity in the military space is punishing if you get it wrong. One of the best examples of the combined left- and right-brain process skills is Admiral Sir George Michael Zambellas, the former head of the

Royal Navy. Faith is central to his mission. This is not a religious belief, but it may as well be. 'We learn at an early stage in the Navy, that the first time you set foot on the bridge as an officer, you set the tone for the day. This means being relaxed, confident and forgiving small mistakes.' He says it's important to be fun to work with, because people perform at their best when they are relaxed and confident and don't fear making mistakes. 'In a 12-hour working day, I'm enjoying myself about 75 per cent of my time. If I wasn't fun to work with, I would consider that a fundamental failure of my leadership.'

Sometimes it's easier to see this as an outsider, maybe this is why so many outsiders have risen to lead. Zambellas himself was born to Greek parents and brought up in southern Africa: 'I agree with this. I started with a short service commission. I didn't know this is what I wanted to do. Being an outsider and having no expectations helped me hugely.' He studied aeronautical and astronautical engineering at the University of Southampton and became a helicopter pilot.

When Zambellas started in his position, he was told there was no money and no public support for the Navy. So, he says, he couldn't change anything. So he chose to reinvigorate the 'belief' in the service: 'I just wanted my team to get its mojo back.' He says the first period, when he was trying to reinvigorate the ideas and values of the organization, was a lonely uphill task.

Zambellas understood his organization instinctively and what ideas it would respond to: 'A combination of irreducible belief allied to brain power is phenomenally strong. Some of my colleagues have had to face an unremitting barrage of belief and merciless accuracy in the detail. This was a creative use of management information and sheer bloody belief in the rightness of our cause. The combination of extreme logic and belief can release tremendous power within organizations as well as individuals.'

He says he identified two key allies – someone to handle the communications and an engineering expert – who both had the sort of relationship with him where they could critique. 'It was important to me that they could call me an idiot if they felt I was getting it wrong, but we collectively believed in what we were trying to do, so the trust was there.'

This, he says, was also the source of many of his ideas. 'I'd just get up in front of my guys and come up with ideas for the plan. I was just in flow and the ideas would pour out. In many cases, with a few tweaks that's exactly what we did.' Sometimes though he says he would just wake up with the ideas already formed in his head.

How does he deal with cynics? 'Relentless logic allied to sheer weight of personality.' One of the first things he did, was to break down the hierarchy. Zambellas says the leader sets the tone for this. 'It's vital to talk to all of the people. Status is irrelevant because they are all capable of sharing your belief, no matter where they are in the organization.' This, he says, is one of the key tests of how unified an organization is, top to bottom. The Navy is a prime example of unified mission and values. It *is* something.

This is the message that he took to the politicians, reminding them what the Royal Navy is and again proving his case with relentless logic and passionate commitment. This is a great example of what you can do when you understand both engineering and the role of belief. Zambellas learned his political craft very early, from being a private secretary to two chiefs of defence. He saw the Iraq War close up. He could then visualize the whole process from the bottom up. 'That helped me to see the reality of governmental finances. If I'd crashed into that later on, I would not have been able to reinvent my approach, but I had years of preparing for it.'

'When you're trying to lead young people, you've got to emphasize how important failure is. Young people fail a lot. That's because they're not fully formed. They may be imbalanced. They might be too tetchy. They might be too artsy. Ultimately, though, that's why they're so successful. Creative success is about failure. We have to be proud of our failures so we can found success on them.'

Zambellas says he can reach out to technically minded people who feel they have shortcomings because that's exactly what he was like. One of the contradictions is how this highly decorated officer, Admiral Sir George Michael Zambellas, GCB, DSC, ADC, DL, FRAeS, makes himself so accessible to new ideas. 'I just need to make them aware that I'm just an ex-apprentice who can do his own wiring and fix his own car.' He just seems to have layered the strong beliefs onto a foundation of solid engineering expertise to engineer emotion.

He says he will often go back over his creative mistakes with his own people in public so they can see the weaknesses that he has: 'It's a very powerful tool for motivating people. They can see the only thing that separates us all is our position. It's not our ability. We can all make mistakes.' It's an unconventional approach, but then just about all successful military creative thinkers have been. 'The only thing that really makes my blood run cold is conformity. I think people can reconcile being themselves and still being devoted to a cause.'

What's interesting about this approach is that a modern navy has diversity as well as discipline. Homogeneity would be a weakness in problem-solving. Zambellas's approach is probably years ahead of its time and American in its philosophy. *E pluribus unum* (out of the many comes one) rather than a phalanx of hearts of oak. A lot of what the Navy does is a passive task – waiting. Sometimes it's difficult for people to realize that you can't just deploy a force immediately. It takes time to coordinate things. Zambellas is a former amphibious commander and can see how complicated modern warfare can be.

His creative challenge is deadly serious. He needs to imagine and plan for what the demands on his service are going to be, but he won't find out how successful it's been, until it needs to be used: 'The real test of our creativity comes not in peace, but in war.' Will he be writing a book of his own? 'No. Generals that write books just make themselves look like fools. I'm too loyal and committed to my colleagues to ever think about doing that.'

Conclusion

We do creativity a grave disservice by not recognizing all the different types of people who consider themselves to be creative. All problem-solvers can and should develop their creative skills. Good leadership will constantly evolve systems and this requires the contribution of all members of the team. The narrower we define creativity, the less people believe it's their remit. It's a responsibility that all of us should have, not only because it requires all members of a team to engage, but also because it's a waste of resource if they do not. Furthermore, a creative element of work that is enjoyable and sustaining is vital to the development and well-being of the organization as a whole. All of the people interviewed here bear witness to this.

Confession

So in *Too Fast to Think* we looked at how the rapid increase in social media has driven the overload and made us busier. We have more information to process in our lives than ever before, so we have to filter it. Sometimes, this means we get a more negative view of the world and the net result is cynicism which erodes creativity. The overload also means we don't spend enough time cultivating key Creative Traits such as Quietness, Relaxing, Releasing and Dreaming. We learned in Chapter 2 that we're not reading as many books as before and our attention spans are narrowing. Education is evolving, but not fast enough to cope with this change. Psychological stress is growing among the young, as they communicate more but converse less. They enter the world of work, frequently in personal debt, and have yet more pressure piled upon them. The workplace is trying to adapt as well, but is all too frequently driven by left-brain process, short-term thinking. This creates an illusion of progress but a frustrating reality. We then looked at what the brain needs to thrive and how it copes with the overload, deploying the left-brain process as a self-defence mechanism. This can make us rush to judgement in business situations like interviews and meetings, instead of seeing the bigger picture. Above all, if we want our brains and bodies to be healthy and creative, we need sleep. This is so important as to warrant an entire chapter of its own. We also saw that some are using sleep as a direct tool for creativity, programming themselves before they go to sleep. We then looked at the mysterious area of creative provenance – where people are and what they're doing when the ideas come. We saw that, although we think these places are unusual, they are in fact very common. We can also see that more time spent in the incubation phase can yield better results. If only we can find the time – and this is the key. Given time, you will find your creativity and balance. But even if you have achieved balance, how long will that last before you become overloaded again. Because creativity speaks with such a quiet voice, we don't always hear it. Especially when many of us actually like going fast.

Why does anyone write such a book? Well, you've probably guessed it. I didn't just write this book for you. I felt compelled to do it. I just had to. It was written in just six weeks and everyone said it couldn't be done. My right-brain process would not allow anything else. (You'll be reassured to hear that my left-brain process has just contributed and told me that's why the book is rubbish. Nice.)

For much of my professional life, my creativity has been delivered despite an overload of information and a lack of sleep. In truth, it still is. Many years ago I wrote a book called *The Unemployables*. It was about high achievers from all backgrounds – what we now recognize as the pursuit of 'mastery'. *The Unemployables* foreshadowed the growth of LEWIS globally. It reads like a prologue to what actually happened in a way that *Too Fast to Think* may well do in years to come.

It's wrong to call people like us workaholics because we don't recognize what we do as work. We're involved in the perpetual process of mastery. We're obsessed by what we don't know. We're not that interested in money either. The word I love the most is initiative – it's like enterprise but without the commercial edge. Sure, money comes in handy, but I've never knowingly done anything just because it made money. I did it because I wanted to do something better, provide a better service, provide a better vision, to provide more colour in a grey world. What is the point of arriving on the summit after all that effort, just to selfishly reflect on the view. Right-thinking people offer a hand up so others can share the experience. It's definitely not about money. I hate the cynicism that surrounds capital endeavour. Some people are obsessed by money, but most of us, at the very core of it, see the money just as a by-product of happy teams and happy cultures. We know we can get by without it – after all, we did in the beginning.

To stand on your own – creatively or not – needs courage. If you're going to have ideas, by definition you will stand out from the crowd. The next generation will find this easier than the previous. As we've heard, 'creative' is the one word it universally identifies with, but I'm anxious that the price they pay for it is not as great. You cannot be successful if you have a reasonable amount of courage. 'Reasonable' sounds like such a friendly word, but I've never found excellence anywhere I've found the word 'reasonable'. You can tell when you're in the presence of passion, because you stop measuring. Try telling your partner that you have a reasonable amount of love for them. See how that works out for you. Don't be reasonable. Be passionate. That's what you were put here to do. Deep down, you know this is no dress rehearsal. Don't benchmark yourself by others. They may look normal, but normal people are just the ones you don't really know. Underneath, we all have passions, and the greatest tragedy of all is that we let them be diluted and eroded by the pace of our lives.

So here's my confession. I, too, find myself moving too fast to think. And I'm still trying to find the balance. And that's why I wanted to find out more. Not just for you, but for me as well. You knew it all along, didn't you? All preachers are clothed in piety and every church needs sinners.

It's just before dawn on Wednesday 18 May 2016. An overcast London is shaking off the night and night is creeping shyly away across St John's Gardens, Westminster, where I live. My mind is a tropical fish tank of weird-looking vivid ideas floating dreamily around. I'm sitting in front of a bright screen (emanating blue light!) in a darkened room listening to the rumble of the first exploratory London buses sniffing the day. It's delightfully cool, quiet and peaceful. My iPhone is switched off and I'm here in the moment. I'm focused on the writing but can hear the roller coaster song of blackbirds swapping notes on the new day. The poetry of twilight is evaporating as the practicalities of the day emerge. The City is beginning to stretch, yawn and take itself off to work. I'm at peace and in Flow. I'm ready for what's next.

Thanks for listening.

Chris

A final note on your creative potential

Four gods were talking about the best place to hide the secrets of Man's potential.

The first said: 'We should bury it in the deepest hole.'
The others said that man would find it there.
The second said: 'We should sink it to the bottom of the deepest ocean.'
The others said that man would find it there, too.
The third suggested: 'It should be placed atop the highest mountain.'
The others said that man would find it there as well.

Listening to all this, the fourth and wisest said: 'I have the perfect place to hide the secret of man's potential. Let's hide it in the mind of Man himself. He'll never think of looking for it there.'

INDEX

Note: **bold** page numbers indicate figures; *italic* numbers indicate tables.

Access Youth Academy, San Diego 54
advertisements 13
aesthetic balance 159–60
aesthetic force 141
'always on' environment
    balance, achieving 74
    data overload 65
    disinhibition 66–70
    Fear of Missing Out (FOMO) 73
    greeting people 78–79
    Hurry Sickness 70–74, **72, 73**
    meetings 77–78
    office layouts 79–80
    Type A personality
        behaviour 74–77
    work, changes in 63–65, **64**
Anderson, Jeffrey 96, 97
anonymity on social media 66, 69
Arboine, Jheni 142–44
architecture
    creativity in 5–6
    Marina Bay Sands Hotel,
        Singapore 5–6
art
    and faith 142–44
    power of 141–42
    in science 56–61
    and truth and beauty 144–45
Asia, creativity in 5–6
audit of left/right processes 155–56
availability bias 27

bathroom phone usage 14–15
BBC 21
beauty and truth 144–45
beauty standards, unrealistic 32
Beecham, Sinclair 180–81
belief, religious 40, 142–44
Benshetrit, Dror 124–25
biology and art 56–61
bipolar disorder 107

Blacklock, George 39, 57–61
blue light exposure 120–22
body clock 122–23
Bourne, Carol 143
Brady, Vanessa 33–36, 43, 45, 149
brain physiology
    audit of left/right processes 155–56
    collaboration between two
        halves 86–87
    corpus callosum 85, 86
    creative/analytical processes 89
    detachment, capability for 90
    and digital habits 29
    dominance of one side 88
    education in 107
    empathy 84–85
    first impressions and left/right
        processes 98–101
    Flow 104–07
    input from other people 84
    interviews 98–101
    left-brain processes 88–89, 93, 96,
        105, 107, 134
    left/right side in history and
        culture 97–98
    mental health and
        creativity 102–04
    neocortex 117–19
    nutritional needs 84, 95–96
    overload, impact on structure
        of 90–92
    plasticity of, continuing 91–92
    prefrontal cortex 116
    processes 87–89
    right-brain process 87, 93–97
    right/left brain theory 86
    simplification in
        communication 101–02
    and sleep 116
Breus, Michael J 120–21, 122
burnout, danger of 29

business and creativity 33–36, 43–44,
        51, 60–61, 149, 150
busy-ness
    case study 10–12
    and having ideas 129
    and leadership 10–12
    obsession with 4
    and productivity 10

Cain, Susan 153
capital structure of organisations 168
capture-bonding 160–61
Caudwell, John 181–82
ceiling height and thinking style 80
change as key debate 2
childhood hardship 111–12
choice, principle of 167
church attendance 40
coaching in creativity 165–68
coffee, consumption of 13
Coles, Alasdair 38–40, 66
collaboration 151–52
colour of interior walls 79–80
commercial business and
        creativity 33–36, 43–44, 51,
        60–61, 149, 150
communications
    continuous, expectation of 27–28
    of mission and values 170
    scale of overload 12–14
    simplification in 101–02
communications technology
    brain physiology 29
    changes in 9–10
    as disrupting creativity 1–2
    impact on millennial adults 16–19
competition and confidence 41–43
confidence and competition 41–43
Conran, Shirley 176
continuous communication,
        expectation of 27–28
Cook, Fred 184–88
Cooper, Cary 80–82
Cooper, Jackie 188–90
corpus callosum 86
Costello, Francis 129–30
Crawford, Matthew 46–47
creativity
    abstaining from as
        stimulating 161–62
    in all industries 3

alternative approach 76
architecture 5–6
art, use in science 56–61
Asia 5–6
bad news focus 25
barriers to 58–61
Beecham, Sinclair 180–81
and business 33–36, 43–44, 51,
        60–61, 149, 150
Caudwell, John 181–82
coaching in 165–68
collaboration 151–52
communications as
        disrupting 1–2
Cook, Fred 184–88
Cooper, Jackie 188–90
criticism and 66–67
culture, organisational 168–71
defining 128
Europe 5
and faith 40, 142–44
and finance 162
Four I's Creative Cycle
        175–77, **178**
Generation Y 171
genetic factors 102–04
Gummer, Peter 182–84
healing environment 54–55
Holmes, Paul 190–93
importance of 2–3, 4–5
location, importance of 166
and mental health 102–04
millennial adults, impact of social
        media on 16–19
Mordaunt, Penny 193–94
overcoming objections to creative
        thinking 158–63
present, being 59
in presentations 174–75
quiet, role of in 2, 4, 81
reading, lack of 28–29
separation of time 34–35
Sorrell, Martin 194–97
teaching 59–60
Tony Palmer on 16–17
training programme for 163–65
trauma in early life 111–12
United States 5, 6
Zambellas, George
        Michael 197–200
see also Eight Creative Traits; ideas

criticism and creativity 66–67
Csíkszentmihályi, Mihály 104–05
culture, organisational 168–71
cyberbullying 69

De Haan, Peter 49–51
de Rojas, Jacqueline 76–77
Dewey, John 106
Dillon, Rod 56
disinhibition
    anonymity 66, 69
    cyberbullying 69
    game, online life as 68
    illegal behaviour 69–70
    imagining characteristics of
        others 68
    job security 69
    misrepresentation of self 67
    ownership of posts, lack of 67
    on social media 66
    speaking out 68
Douglas, Ron 122
Douglass, Frederick 141
dreams 119, 153

Eagleman, David 84
education
    aims of 46–47
    balance as lacking 41
    brain structures and functions 107
    competition and confidence 41–43
    creativity and business 43–44
    differences to work culture 47–51
    employers, relationship
        with 44–45
    financial crisis 2009 44, 45
    ideas generation 149
    increased university education 41
    manual labour 46–47
    newspaper industry
        comparison 48–49
    Portsmouth College 52–53
    pressure on children 38
    professions, private school
        domination of 42
    as siloed and
        institutionalized 43–44
    system problems 43–45
    teaching creativity 59–60
    technical 46–47
    timetables 52–53

training programme for
    creativity 163–65
underemployment of graduates 38
university entrance as end point
    for 38
work experience 44–45
see also universities
ego of the creative 58
Eight Creative Traits 6
    dream 153
    engage 153
    play 154
    quiet 153
    relax 154
    release 153–54
    repeat 154
    teach 154
Elliott, Keith 19–20, 21, 22
email
    bathroom phone usage 14–15
    frequency of checking 14
    misunderstandings, clearing up 34
    scale of overload 12–14
    turning off 148
emotional impact of Hurry
    Sickness 73
empathy 84–85, 99
employers, education's relationship
    with 44–45
endurance and mastery 139
energy, personal, managing
    106–07, 161
engagement 153
ethics and success 106
Europe, creativity in 5
extremists 22–23

failure
    fear of 137–38
    and mastery 139–41
    and near-misses 140–41
faith 40, 142–44
fear 61, 136–39, 152
Fear of Missing Out (FOMO) 73
File, Jason 159–60
filtering of irrelevant news 22
finance 162
first impressions and left/right brain
    processes 98–101
flexibility/insecurity of labour 169
flexible hours 170

Flow
    barriers to 58–59
    conditions for 105, 169
    emotions in 104
    energy, personal, managing 106–07
    and finance 162
    happiness 105
    inside experience of 132–33
    left-brain processes 105, 107
food combining 95–96
Foster, Russell 94, 110–12, 117, 122
Four I's Creative Cycle
        175–77, **178**
Frampton, Steve 52–53, 110
Friedman, Meyer 74

game, online life as 68
Gandhi, Mohandas, Mahatma 144–45
Generation Y and creativity 171
genetic factors and creativity 102–04
Gilbert, Elizabeth 134, 136
Gioia, Dana
graduates
    financial crisis 2009 44, 45
    underemployment of 38
    unemployment of 44, 45
greeting people 78–79
Gummer, Peter 182–84

Hand Clasp Test 88
happiness 105
Hay, William 95–96
healing environment, creativity
        in 54–56
Holmes, Paul 190–93
hospitals, creativity in 54–56
Huffington, Arianna 112
humming 143
Hurry Sickness
    balance, achieving 74
    challenge dimensions **73**, 73–74
    defined 71
    emotional impact of 73
    example 70
    impact of 71
    manifestations of 71–74, **72, 73**
    physical impact of 72
    rational problems from 73
    spiritual problems from 73
hypnosis 99

ideas
    art, power of 141–42
    and busy-ness 129
    collaboration 151–52
    commercial and creative 149, 150
    distracting left-brain processes 134
    education 149
    failure 137–38
    fear 136–39
    Flow 132–33
    Four I's Creative Cycle 175–77, **178**
    images 141
    immersion then withdrawal 150
    opening the senses 150
    outsider, being an 150
    overcoming objections to creative
            thinking 158–63
    places people have ideas
            128–29, 130
    play 149
    present, being 148
    provenance of 129–30
    quiet 150
    reading, increasing 147–48,
            156–57
    scepticism 160–61
    sleep 149
    space 148
    speed, illusion of 149
    SQ3R speed reading
            technique 156–57
    stillness and solitude 134–36
    technology, turning off 148
    to-be lists vs to-do lists 131–32
    truth and beauty 144–45
    two processes involved 148
    waiting 151
    see also creativity
Ignition 177
illegal behaviour 69–70
images 141
Incubation 176
Induction 175–76
infographics, rise of 20–21
information overload
    brain physiology, impact on 90–92
    continuous communication,
            expectation of 27–28
    disconnection 107
    Hurry Sickness 70–74, **72, 73**

impact on millennial adults 14–19
less understanding of the world 22
news, changes in 22–25
news reporting and reading, impact
on 19–21
problem of 4–5
scale of 12–14
women, effect on 29–36
world, improvements in 26–27
insecurity/flexibility of
labour 69, 169
insomnia 112–13
Inspiration 176–77
internet, rise of 2
interpersonal skills, undergraduates as
lacking 39
interruptions
impact of 9
work and social life 10
interviews 98–101
invaders 1

job security 69, 169
Jobs, Steve 138

Kalman, Maira 106
Knight, India 112
Knowledge, the, impact on brain
structure 91–92
Kurzweil, Ray 117–20

labour market
financial crisis 2009 44, 45
flexibility/insecurity 169
layout of offices 79–80
leadership 76–77
Beecham, Sinclair 180–81
and busy-ness 10–12
Caudwell, John 181–82
Cook, Fred 184–88
Cooper, Jackie 188–90
ethics and success 106
and followers 76
greeting people 78–79
Gummer, Peter 182–84
Holmes, Paul 190–93
left-brain to right-brain
move 162–63
meetings 77–78
Mordaunt, Penny 193–94

parents, comparison with 131–32
and sleep 115–16
Sorrell, Martin 194–97
and tolerance 77
values 131
Zambellas, George
Michael 197–200
learning cycle 105
LED lights 121
left-brain processes 88–89, 93, 96,
105, 107, 134
audit of left-right
processes 155–56
left/right brain thinking 3, 86
left/right side in history and
culture 97–98
Leigh, Geoffrey 131
Lewis, Sarah 138–41
liberators 1
light
blue light exposure 120–22
body clock 122–23
LED lights 121
Lightman, Alan 132–33
listening to employees 170
location, importance of 166
logic, overcoming 158

Maguire, Eleanor 91–92
management by walking
around 78–79
manual labour 46–47
Marina Bay Sands Hotel,
Singapore 5–6
Marshall, John 121
mastery
and endurance 139
and failure 139–41
as incomplete 140
and near-misses 140–41
McGilchrist, Iain 85–86, 107,
128, 158
media
filtering of irrelevant news 22
impact of overload on 19–21
see also information overload
meetings 77–78
Mehegan, David 28
Meister, Jeanne 169–70
Mendeleev, Dmitri 133

mental health
   bipolar disorder 107
   and creativity 102–04
   sleep 115
   universities, problems in 38–40
metaphor 60, 61, 118–19
Meyers-Levy, Joan 80
Milgram, Stanley 90
Millman, Debbie 138
misrepresentation of self 67
mobile phones
   bathroom phone usage 14–15
   messaging apps, use of 15
Mordaunt, Penny 193–94
music before surgery 55

neocortex 117–19
news
   bad news focus 25
   changes in 22–25
   filtering of irrelevant news 22
   frivolity/serious 24–25
   less understanding of the world 22
   pictures 24
   radicals and extremists 22–23
   reporting and reading, impact of
        overload on 19–21
   speed/truth, inverse relationship
        between 23–24, 24
   unwillingness to offend 23
   see also information overload
newspaper industry, education
        comparison 48–49
Nielsen, Jared 97–98

office layouts 79–80
open-mindedness 166
out breath 158
outsider, being an 150
overload see information overload

Palmer, Tony 15–17, 66
pattern recognition 119
Peters, John 137–38
photography 141
physical impact of Hurry Sickness 72
pictures 19, 24, 141
Pink, Daniel 168
Pinker, Steven 26–27
place, importance of 166

play 149, 154
political system, private school
        domination of 42
Popova, Maira 138
population, improvements in 26
Portsmouth College 52–53, 110
poverty, improvements in 26
present, being 59, 148
presentations, creativity in 174–75
private school domination of politics
        and professions 42
process 76
productivity
   and busy-ness 10
   case study 10–12
professions, private school
        domination of 42
pulse 106, 161

QED3RPT see Eight Creative Traits
quiet 2, 4, 81, 134–36, 150, 153

radicals and extremists 22–23
Rady Children's Hospital, San
        Diego 54–56
rational problems from Hurry
        Sickness 73
reading
   changing habits of 19–21
   creativity and lack of 28–29
   increasing 147–48, 156–57
   for pleasure, lack of as problem 66
   SQ3R speed reading
        technique 156–57
   and young people 19
relaxation 154
release 153–54
religious faith 40, 142–44
repetition 154
Riedl, René 123
right-brain process 87, 93–97
   audit of left/right
        processes 155–56
right/left brain theory 86
right/left side in history and
        culture 97–98
Rise Academy, LEWIS
   art project 172
   beginnings of 171
   business project 172–73

delegates and activities 172
Four I's Creative Cycle 175–77,
        178
impact on delegates 173, 174
juxtaposition 173
presentations, creativity in 174–75
seniority, exposure to 174
transformation process 172
Robinson, Ken 37–38, 41
Rogers, Jenny 165–68
Rosenman, Ray 74
Rothenburg, Albert 103–04

Sadler, Blair 54–55
Sample, Ian 102
San Diego
        Access Youth Academy 54
        Rady Children's Hospital 54–56
scepticism 160–61
Schiuma, Giovanni 143–44
Schwartz, Tony 106, 107, 128, 161
science, use of art in 56–61
senses, opening 150
silence *see* quiet
simplification in communication 101–02
Singer, Frederick 48
sleep
        attitudes against 112
        brain physiology 116
        disruption 72
        dreams 119
        employers 116–17
        ideas generation 149
        importance of 109–10
        insomnia 112–13
        and leadership 115–16
        learning, impact on 115
        mental disorders 115
        poor, impact of 110, 114, 125
        prefrontal cortex 116
        reasons for 113–14
        and technology 120–22
        times **72**
        tips for 115
        working while sleeping 124–25
social media
        anonymity 66, 69
        as anti-social 33–34
        beauty standards, unrealistic 32
        criticism and creativity 66–67

disinhibition 66
as a game 68
imagining characteristics of
        others 68
impact on millennial adults 16–19
lack of talking as problem 66
mainstream, younger users concern
        about 15
misrepresentation of self 67
ownership of posts, lack of 67
scale of overload 13
women, use of by 29–31
solitude 134–36, 152
Sorrell, Martin 194–97
speed, illusion of 149
speed reading technique 156–57
speed/truth, inverse relationship
        between 23–24, **24**
spiritual deficit 73
spiritual problems from Hurry
        Sickness 73
Spivak, Halayne 65–66, 151–52
SQ3R speed reading
        technique 156–57
Stefánsson, Kári 102, 103
stillness 134–36
Stockholm syndrome 160–61
stress
        Hurry Sickness 70–74
        and social media use 32
        technostress 123
Sword, Rosemary 71

talking, lack of as problem 66
taxi-drivers, impact of the Knowledge
        on brain structure 91–92
Taylor, Jill Bolte 89
teaching
        as Creative Trait 154
        of creativity 59–60
technical education 46–47
technology
        as disrupting creativity 1–2
        and sleep 120–22
        turning off 148
        and well-being 123
technophobes 1–2
technostress 123
telephonobia 20
telework policies 170

time, separation of 34–35
timetables, college 52–53
to-be lists vs to-do lists 131–32
toxic disinhibition
    anonymity 66, 69
    cyberbullying 69
    game, online life as 68
    illegal behaviour 69–70
    imagining characteristics of others 68
    job security 69
    misrepresentation of self 67
    ownership of posts, lack of 67
    on social media 66
    speaking out 68
traditionalists 1–2
training programme for
        creativity 163–65
trauma in early life 111–12
truth and beauty 144–45
truth/speed, inverse relationship
        between 23–24, **24**
Tutu, Desmond 39
Type A personality behaviour 74–77

underemployment of graduates 38
United States, creativity in 5, 6
universities
    differences to work culture 47–51
    employers, relationship
        with 44–45
    entrance as end point for
        education 38
    interpersonal skills, undergraduates
        as lacking 39
    mental health problems in 38–40
    work experience 44–45
    see also education

values 12
    and leadership 131
violent deaths, reduction in 26

walking 158
well-being and technology 123
'what if' technique 177
women, information overload, effect
        on 29–36
Woollett, Katherine 91–92
work
    culture of, education's
        differences to 47–51
    data overload at 65
    environment, changes in 63–65
    experience of 44–45
working lives, changes in 9–10
world, improvements in 26–27

Zambellas, George Michael 197–200
Zimbardo, Philip 71
Zimmer, Carl 86–87
zone, the
    barriers to 58–59
    conditions for 105, 169
    emotions in 104
    energy, personal,
        managing 106–07
    happiness 105
    left-brain processes 105, 107